16.50

SELECTED PHILOSOPHICAL PAPERS OF ROBERT BOYLE

Strasbourg Cathedral Clock

SELECTED PHILOSOPHICAL PAPERS OF ROBERT BOYLE

edited with an
introduction by
M. A. STEWART

Hackett Publishing Company
Indianapolis / Cambridge

Printed in the United States of America
99 98 97 96 95 94 93 92 91   1 2 3 4 5 6 7 8 9 10

Cover illustration: Portrait of Robert Boyle by William
Faithorne, courtesy the Ashmolean Museum, Oxford.

For further information, please address

Hackett Publishing Company, Inc.
P.O. Box 44937
Indianapolis, IN 46244-0937

Library of Congress Cataloging-in-Publication Data

Boyle, Robert, 1627–1691.
　　[Selections.　1991]
　　Selected philosophical papers of Robert Boyle/edited with an
introduction by M. A. Stewart.
　　　　　p.　　　cm.
　　Includes bibliographical references and index.
　　ISBN 0-87220-123-6: ISBN 0-87220-122-8 (pbk.)
　　1. Philosophy.　I. Stewart, M.A. (Michael Alexander), 1937–
II. Title.
B1201.B431　1991
192—dc20　　　　　　　　　　　　　　　　　　　91-25480
　　　　　　　　　　　　　　　　　　　　　　　　　　CIP

The paper used in this publication meets the minimum requirements
of American National Standard for Information Sciences–Permanence
of Paper for Printed Library Materials. ANSI Z39.48-1984.

∞

CONTENTS

Frontispiece   *Strasbourg Cathedral Clock*

This clock, occupying the whole of a transept wall, was built in 1570–74. At ground level the main features were, in the centre, a 3-foot astronomical globe with a 24-hour movement, and behind it a 10-foot rotating calendar and clock recording years and months, days and nights, equinoxes and festivals; above this presided the titular deity for the day of the week. Two fixed side-panels recorded the eclipses. At first-floor level the central astrolabe plotted the position of the planets in the zodiac and marked the hours; minutes and quarters were shown by the dial at the front of the balustrade. The dial above the astrolabe depicted the current phase of the moon. At the third level, rotating jacks struck the quarter-hours and Death the hours. The whole structure was elaborately sculpted and painted with religious, allegorical and secular motifs. The tower on the left housed the weights and was surmounted by a mechanical cockerel, which sprang into life after each carillon but was damaged by lightning early in the seventeenth century. The clock was derelict by the late eighteenth century and was redesigned and rebuilt in 1838–42.

PREFACE

This volume has been prepared for the use of those who are working in the history of philosophy and of the philosophy of science, and those who are interested in the interaction of philosophical, scientific and religious ideas in the period of the Scientific Revolution. Theory and experiment are, in Boyle's work, mutually dependent, and to try to preserve the experimental context I have reproduced, wherever feasible, whole papers rather than brief excerpts. Some materials had eventually to be excluded for reasons of space. But a substantial part of Boyle's *Disquisition about Final Causes*, significant for his criticism of Descartes, can be found in D. C. Goodman's *Science and Religious Belief 1600–1900* (Bristol, 1973); and the important 'Advertisements' to *The Mechanical Origin or Production of Divers Particular Qualities* can be found in Marie Boas Hall's *Robert Boyle on Natural Philosophy* (Bloomington, Ind., 1965).

The present collection was first published by Manchester University Press in 1979. To avoid needless new expense and to preserve what is now an established pagination, the introduction, texts and notes have been retained intact from the original printing; but for complete accuracy, the reader should note that in two places corrections entered in the text were not acknowledged in the textual notes, and should mark four further places where the text now stands to be improved. On page 11, line 32, 'ingenuously' is an editorial correction of 'ingeniously'; on page 13, note *c*, 'confessions' is a correction of 'confession'. Two of the new emendations to be made are identified in the 'additional note' at the foot of page 246, and I can now add that both errors were detected, and compensations made, by the contemporary Latin translators of the originals.

As regards the remaining corrections, I report on page xxiii the preservation of two leaves of the manuscript of *A Discourse of Things above Reason*, among the Royal Society's collection of Boyle Papers. Their discovery in 1979 came just in time to confirm Boyle's authorship of this anonymous and disputed work, but further research revealed that there are at least five surviving leaves, scattered at three locations and corrected in Boyle's hand. They relate to pages 214–15, 219–20, 230 and 241 of the present edition. I have reported in detail on these and other manuscript matters in 'The Authenticity of Robert Boyle's Anonymous Writings on Reason', *Bodleian Library Record* 10 (1981), showing that the dialogue underwent extensive early revision, including some apparently arbitrary shuffling of parts between the speakers. Even in these few passages it is sometimes an open question whether Boyle genuinely revised his text for publication or simply overlooked his copyist's or compositor's errors; but in two places on page 214 it is possible to see how the manuscript text was misread or miscorrected and needs to be restored. At line 12, 'men' is a misreading of a poorly written 'we'. At line 19, instead of '*de compositione continui*', the draft reads 'whilst you were speaking of the Compositio Continui'. Restoration of the words 'whilst you were speaking' serves to remove the worst instance of what I had criticized as Boyle's tendency to introduce 'the same illustrative examples more than once with the same sense of novelty'.

Only one page of manuscript was transcribed for this volume (page 119). It has been reproduced without imposing normal printing conventions, since there is no reason to think Boyle wrote it for publication. There was no shortage of printed materials to fill the remaining space, and at the time of my original compilation two manuscripts which were being considered for inclusion were withdrawn because they appeared to require textual surgery and annotation disproportionate to their overall novelty or importance. But serious researchers cannot avoid quarrying in the manuscripts, despite their chronic disorder and poor decipherability, and they have now been served with the provision of a useful finding list under the direction of Dr Michael Hunter. A competent transcription of the main unpublished manuscripts remains a desideratum, if only to reduce the amount of nonsense that is written about them.

Those works which were prepared for publication in Boyle's lifetime are here presented in modernized form, but with closer attention to intended sentence structures and to the wording of Boyle's lifetime editions than has been customary in previous posthumous editions. As I have noted, the lifetime editions are not impeccable; but where manuscripts are lacking, they are the best guide to Boyle's intended wording that we have. Thomas Birch usually gets the dubious credit for the six-volume Collected Works, put out by a consortium of London booksellers in 1772, which is now frequently promoted as the canonical edition. But Birch, who took no serious pains to establish an accurate text for his own 1744 collection on which it is based, was six years under the ground by the time the booksellers clubbed together for this most corrupt of all Boyle editions. Of the numerous deviations in wording between the 1772 and lifetime editions, almost all are to the detriment of the sense. But the lifetime editions, though more credible in their wording, were still poorly prepared both for and by the printer. Different volumes reflect very different practices in paragraphing and typographic convention; and rather too often, even by the standards of the time, the punctuation yields countersensible alignments of clauses.

Those who wish to understand Boyle's obsolete chemical terminology will find the combined resources of the *Oxford English Dictionary* and M. P. Crosland's *Historical Studies in the Language of Chemistry* (London, 1962) adequate for most purposes. For other background on personalities and movements in the history of science, the reader is referred to E. J. Dijksterhuis, *The Mechanization of the World Picture* (Oxford, 1961) and J. R. Partington, *History of Chemistry* (London, 1961 onwards). On Boyle's own chemistry in context, see Marie Boas, *Robert Boyle and Seventeenth-Century Chemistry* (Cambridge, 1958; repr. New York, 1968); and on his physics, the magisterial recent study by Steven Shapin and Simon Schaffer, *Leviathan and the Air-Pump: Hobbes, Boyle, and the Experimental Life* (Princeton, 1985). Charles Webster's *The Great Instauration* (London, 1975) is a more reliable guide to the political and intellectual milieu in which Boyle worked than J. R. Jacob's *Robert Boyle and the English Revolution* (New York, 1977), which sometimes sits too loosely to the texts. Two useful perspectives on the metaphysical debates of the period are provided by Norma E. Emerton's *The Scientific Reinterpretation of Form* (Ithaca, 1984) and Barbara J. Shapiro's *Probability and Certainty in Seventeenth-Century England* (Princeton, 1983).

Among recent journal literature I would especially recommend J. J. MacIntosh's study of Boyle's 'Cartesian' psychology in 'Perception and Imagination in Descartes, Boyle and Hooke' (*Canadian Journal of Philosophy* 13 (1983)) and Timothy Shanahan's study of Boyle's natural theology in 'God and Nature in Robert Boyle' (*Journal of the History of Philosophy* 26 (1988)). Shanahan is not the first to question J. E. McGuire's work which I cite on p. xxii. See also J. R. Milton's important discussion of Boyle in *The Influence of the Nominalist Movement on the Scientific Thought of Bacon, Boyle and Locke* (Ph.D. thesis, Imperial College, London, 1982), chapter 4.

Those of us who have come to Boyle through the history of philosophy have tended to emphasize his role as precursor of Locke. Locke gave some ground for this interpretation, by his lifelong friendship with Boyle, the famous tribute in his 'Epistle to the Reader', his penchant for Boylean examples when illustrating the corpuscularian philosophy, and his adaptation of chemical models to describe the operations of the mind in compounding, decompounding (that is, compounding from compounds), and associating its ideas. Peter Alexander's *Ideas, Qualities and Corpuscles* (Cambridge, 1985) comes closest to integrating their epistemologies and psychologies into a single system of thought. My own view now is that the integration is to be resisted. Despite the personal friendship, Locke and Boyle did not move actively in the same circles. Boyle was no plenist, and took final causes seriously; but for all that, he was more of a Cartesian than Locke throughout his life, or else he was indifferent to those matters, such as innateness, on which Locke disagreed forcibly with Descartes. Boyle's introduction of impenetrability, in anticipation of Locke's solidity, as one of the essential attributes of matter, occurs but once – in *The Origin of Forms and Qualities* (p. 18 below, repeated in summary on p. 50) – and without any sense that this is a point of principle; elsewhere, he is indifferent on the question. Where Locke reduces qualities to powers, Boyle reduces powers to qualities. He uses the term 'secondary qualities' – 'if I may so call them' – only once (p. 32), and 'primary qualities' never; but instead adopts an important distinction, rarely recognized by Locke, between the primary moods or affections of matter and its mechanical affections, the latter but not the former being dependent on there being a plurality of corpuscles in the world. This distinction is identified in the index, as also the distinction which Boyle normally draws between corpuscles and particles, and all I can do here is leave the reader to follow up the references.

I have pursued some of these matters more fully in a number of contributions to *The Locke Newsletter*, nos. 10 (1979), 11 (1980), 12 (1981) and 18 (1987).

Canberra
April 1991

INTRODUCTION

1. BOYLE'S LIFE AND WORK

Robert Boyle was born on 25 January 1627 at Lismore in Munster.[1]
Boyle's father, Richard Boyle, a native of Canterbury, had in 1588
given up an impecuniary apprenticeship, first at law and then as a
government clerk, to seek his fortune in Ireland; there, despite early
scandals and setbacks, he obtained extensive estates, secured various
offices culminating in the Earldom of Cork and appointment as Lord
Treasurer of Ireland, and came to exercise wide influence and
patronage until the outbreak of the Civil War and the Irish
Rebellion. By a second marriage the Earl of Cork had fifteen
children, of whom Robert Boyle was the fourteenth. His father's
estates supplied Boyle with an ample income throughout his life,
except during the dislocation of the Civil War, and he used the
advantages of his birth to promote sundry scientific, religious and
charitable causes.

Apart from three years at Eton, Boyle was educated by private
tutors, of whom the most significant was the last, Isaac Marcombes,
a French Calvinist settled at Geneva, with whom he toured and
studied in France and Italy and at Geneva, from 1639 until after the
death of the Earl of Cork in 1643. Early in 1645, Boyle took
possession of a family manor at Stalbridge in Dorset; this was his
home, apart from periods away mainly on family business, till
around the end of 1655, when he moved to Oxford to join forces with
some of the leading scientists of the day. A plaque now marks the
site of his Oxford apartments, on the High Street adjoining
University College, where excavation a few years ago uncovered
what is thought to have been some of his laboratory glassware. He
worked with others for the foundation of the Royal Society in the
early years of the Restoration. He left Oxford in 1668, by then an
honorary Doctor of Medicine of the University, and thereafter
settled in London, at the home of his sister Katherine, Lady

Ranelagh, until they both died within a few days of each other in December 1691.

An early grounding in French and Latin had been supplemented at Eton by studies in mathematics and history. Under the tutelage of Marcombes, Boyle added theology and philosophy. His strongest early interest in philosophy was in Stoicism, but from reading Diogenes Laertius he gained some acquaintance with Epicurean atomism and other ancient movements; his early writing shows some familiarity with Aristotle, more in Latin translation than in Greek, and some acquaintance also with the Platonic tradition, though not particularly with the works of Plato himself. At the same time Boyle was learning about the new developments in continental science. He was in Florence with Marcombes when Galileo died and learnt Italian to be able to master Galileo's writings. He was a keen observer of nature and read extensively in the works of explorers and navigators, building up a store of first-hand and second-hand information from which he drew in later work. Although the practical utility of studies such as surveying and fortification appealed to him in his youth, writing in later life about 'the Usefulness of Mathematics' he regretted the time he had spent on these at the expense of pure mathematics.

Very soon after the completion of his formal education and his settlement at Stalbridge, Boyle started writing in earnest about ethics and religion. A work of *Ethical Elements* or *Aretology* in several books and divisions survives in manuscript in three drafts (Royal Society MSS 192, 195), one of them substantially complete, together with a volume on vices and virtues (MS 196). These drafts show wide evidence of classical reading, and indeed an almost excessive use of Latin tags, but their ultimate direction is theological, offering true 'felicity' as a *post mortem* state of union with the divine. Other ethical and theological writings predominate in a list of his manuscripts 'begun or written' drawn up by Boyle in January 1650, but it was many years before any of these pieces was published.[2] Of those that eventually were, *Occasional Reflections upon Several Subjects* (publ. 1665) was plundered by Swift for *Gulliver's Travels* as well as satirized in his *Meditation upon a Broomstick*; and *The Martyrdom of Theodora and Didymus* (publ. 1687), a sentimental historical romance, was adapted by Thomas Morell for an oratorio text for Handel.

This speculative and imaginative side to Boyle's character was matched by a practical and humanitarian side. The circle of his family acquaintances in London[3] and the necessities of life as an estate manager in Dorset combined to stimulate his passion for useful knowledge. In his early correspondence are references to self-taught studies in 'natural philosophy, the mechanics and husbandry', the establishment of a laboratory, and the destruction in transit of more than one furnace. While no doubt drawn to chemistry by its value to medicine and husbandry, he was also intrigued by its ambitions to transmute metals, a project with potential humanitarian applications. These practical interests developed into theoretical ones, and Boyle was an important figure in the movement to turn chemistry from an occult science into a study which combined well-grounded theory with responsible experiment and observation. His theory reflected the new 'mechanical' tradition of continental science and philosophy typified by Descartes and Gassendi,[4] while his 'historical' method of cumulative experiment and observation owed much to the native influence of Bacon.

In Boyle's earliest writing, and in later publications which date from the early years, his scientific and theological interests are relatively self-contained. But as his thought matured, these interests partially converged, and there is no clear line at which the science of nature ends and the theology of nature begins. The philosophical interest of his writings, in the modern sense of *philosophical*, spans both areas, but lies more in the first than the second. The new 'mechanical' or 'corpuscular' theory of matter, though similar in content to the ancient atomic theory of Epicurus and Lucretius, was argued afresh in the seventeenth century, on grounds partly *a priori*, partly experimental, according to the emphasis of individual authors. Though Boyle used it initially as a weapon against the alchemical tradition in chemistry, he saw it equally as a weapon against the Aristotelianism prevalent in 'the Schools'. For what it was worth he accepted Aristotelian logic, and respected Aristotle as a natural historian, but rejected the interposition of metaphysics in natural science. This interposition had come about through the gradual reification by the scholastic philosophers of 'matter' and 'form' (originally introduced as relatively harmless abstractions by Aristotle, in *Physics I* and elsewhere, to solve a *conceptual* problem in countering presocratic arguments against the possibility of change). Boyle and his contemporaries accepted the reification of matter, but redefined it, and sought in the operation of matter alone for an explanation of many things which had formerly been attributed to form, notably the cohesion of bodies, the nature of perception, and the determination of species.[5]

An important feature of the new theory of matter was the associated doctrine of qualities. The distinction between what came to be called *primary* and *secondary* qualities, which was later promoted by Locke and travestied and assailed by Berkeley, is familiar to most students of philosophy, and it has its antecedents in Galileo, Descartes and Boyle. Most subsequent debate has taken something like Locke's *lists* of the two kinds of qualities and argued over whether there is any experiential basis for the distinction. It is now coming to be realized that the criterion for the distinction should, and historically did, precede the lists. Indeed the language of 'primary' and 'secondary' (or 'first' and 'second') qualities, just as much as the language of 'matter' and 'form' (and 'substance' and 'essence'), is part of the scholastic inheritance that was redefined in the corpuscular theory of matter. Primary qualities – originally hot, cold, wet, dry – were initially qualities associated in pairs with the four *elements*, and secondary qualities were their *causal derivatives*. When the theory of elements gave way to the corpuscular theory, the primary qualities became the uniform qualities of all the *parts* of matter, and the secondary qualities were still their causal derivatives. The new primary qualities appear to be deduced *a priori*, at least until Boyle; but the tentative use of experimental evidence to show that the remaining qualities can be derived from the mechanical action of matter in motion goes back among modern writers at least to Galileo's *Il Saggiatore*. The precise nature of the reduction of secondary to primary qualities is a matter of current dispute, because of some confusion in the original sources, between primary qualities and the *powers* that derive from them, and also between the powers and their *activation*, and some resulting indecision as to whether the perceiver has a necessary role in the *existence* of sensible secondary qualities.[6] The epistemological questions as to how far, and in what sense, given the distinction between primary and secondary qualities, we perceive the world as it really is (or indeed how far we perceive the world that really is at all) are subordinated in Boyle to the ontological question of whether 'real qualities' in the scholastic sense – that is, as reified forms – can be eliminated from the theory. There is some significance in Boyle's choice of the term *qualities* for the reducible features that bodies derive from their corpuscular structure and interaction with other bodies, but *mode* or *modification* for the primary features of the parts of matter in terms of which the reducible features are explained. For matter variously 'modified' is but matter still. It is not two things – matter *and* its modification – in the way that the scholastic matter and form had sometimes been made to look.

Besides throwing important light on the nature and origins of the distinction between primary and secondary qualities, Boyle's work in promoting the corpuscular theory of matter includes at least three other significant contributions to the history of ideas. First, it led him, particularly in *The Origin of Forms and Qualities*, to important reflections on the nature of species, the determination of classes, and the basis of classification, which are the direct ancestor of Locke's discussion of nominal as against real essence, and avoid some of the psychological complication in Locke's account. Secondly, it led him into theorizing about scientific methodology – into questions about the status of hypotheses, the role of experiment, and the criteria of a good hypothesis – about which he wrote more fully than most of his contemporaries, his views clearly crystallizing side by side with his efforts in actually promoting the corpuscularian hypothesis against its rivals; his writing as a methodologist is at least as important as his (often inconclusive) experimental work in explaining Boyle's success as an advocate of the new philosophy.[7] Thirdly, it led him into taking a leading part in the revival of natural theology, a movement which, despite the assaults of Hume and others a century later, continued to receive powerful support until well into the nineteenth century.

Part of Boyle's influence here was posthumous. The same concern for the faith that led him to subsidize the publication of Gaelic Bibles caused him to provide in his will for an annual series of sermons which has lasted into the present century. Some of these became famous and influential in their own right, notably Richard Bentley's 1692 sermons on *The Folly and Unreasonableness of Atheism*, Samuel Clarke's 1704 sermons on *A Demonstration of the Being and Attributes of God*, and William Derham's *Physico-Theology* of 1711–12. But in his own lifetime Boyle wrote extensively on the relation of science to theology – partly, certainly, to counter the public impression created by Thomas Hobbes and his circle, that atomism tended to atheism: it is significant that Hobbes was never quoted by Boyle as an ally, but was always quoted in contexts where he could be opposed. The mechanical world-view which led Boyle constantly to compare the macrocosm, or individual parts of organisms, with the great cathedral clock at Strasbourg (which in the history of the Design argument is the precursor of Paley's watch) has led many later thinkers into fatalism or atheism. In trying to understand why the image of clockwork led Boyle so naturally in the direction of a designer, instead of to the view that we are mere cogs in a machine, it is important to realize both that he accepted wholeheartedly the Cartesian separation of mind and matter, and that any clock, and particularly the complex Strasbourg clock, was at that time the greatest work of ingenuity contrived by man: it symbolized the highest known intelligence and exemplified in the most elaborate detail the adaptation of means to ends. A modern proponent of the Design argument, alive to other implications in the concept of clockwork, might look for a computer-age or space-age model with less overtly mechanical associations.

Some of Boyle's most famous scientific work, which can be found in standard histories of science, has been passed over here – notably his work on temperature, hydrostatics, and air and gases, the last of which issued in the preliminary formulation of what has subsequently become well known in the English-speaking world as Boyle's Law. This is of no direct philosophical interest, except in so far as it led Hobbes into ill-advised public controversy on matters he did not understand.[8] But it may be worth remarking in conclusion that this work, primarily in pure science, which dates from the time of Boyle's settlement in Oxford, was all published relatively promptly. On the other hand, Boyle delayed for years, and then staggered over long intervals, his cycle of papers on the nature and justification of the corpuscularian hypothesis, particularly in so far as it relied on chemical experiment. Whether this was because the project gave him much more difficulty, or because he was dissatisfied with his success, or because one interest simply displaced another, we cannot really tell; but it is certain, from further references in his published works and from the state of his manuscripts, that the programme was never completed.

2. THE PAPERS IN THIS EDITION

The Origin of Forms and Qualities

The Origin of Forms and Qualities According to the Corpuscular Philosophy (all Boyle's secondary titling in the book adopts the word-order '*Qualities and Forms*') was first published in Oxford in 1666, and went into a second edition the next year. It consists of a number of papers written in the 1650's purporting to develop the theoretical and experimental bases of the corpuscularian philosophy briefly enunciated in *A Physico-Chemical Essay ... touching ... Saltpetre*. The latter work, to which Boyle sometimes makes reference, did not in fact appear until 1661, and by the time *The Origin of Forms and Qualities* was published five years later Boyle had already presented brief expositions of the corpuscularian philosophy in several other works.

In the first edition, which was printed without adequate supervision or instruction, one essay was omitted and others disarranged; in the second edition, the additional essay was still misplaced, and there is some uncertainty as to which divisions are coordinate with which others. On grounds both of style and of content, it is best seen as made up of two main *sets* of writings, incompletely fused: (*a*) a collection of 'Considerations and Experiments', dealing with Forms as well as Qualities, divided into theoretical and experimental ('historical') halves, each made up of numbered divisions; (*b*) a separate treatise, containing both theoretical and experimental discussion, written in a more discursive style in two parts, one on Substantial Forms, the other on Subordinate Forms, both possibly intended to be subsumed under the early, later cancelled, title 'Of the Origin of Forms'. It is the first half of (*a*) and the first half of (*b*) that form the two principal papers in this edition. The essay on Subordinate Forms, though not without merit, is very long, and since it consists only of an extension of the corpuscularian theory to counter an extension of the scholastic doctrine of substantial form, it was thought unnecessary to include it here.

Some subdivisions have confused the commentators. In 'The Theorical Part' the 'Excursion' introduced after the third Particular *ends* with the start of the fourth Particular. This is clear both from the sense and from the printer's break in the first edition. But the second edition omitted this break, so that Birch had the 'Excursion' run on, inappropriately, to the end of 'The Theorical Part'. Two other divisions of 'The Theorical Part', Particulars VII and VIII, have exaggerated headings in the original editions, and for this edition these have been transferred from their centre-page prominence to the beginning of their sections. In the experimental appendices to 'Of the Origin of Forms', the section headed 'Doubts and experiments touching the curious figures of salts' is an excursus within the supplementary paper on the 'Production and Reproduction of Forms'. It *ends* at the printer's break which, in both first and second editions, follows the fourth of the 'considerations' by which Boyle was 'inclined to the conjecture about the shapes of salts'.

'The Theorical Part' contains an outline of the full corpuscularian hypothesis about the general nature of matter (which adds the atomists' notion of impenetrability to the Cartesian characteristics of extension and divisibility), the deduction of its determinable 'primary moods', and the reducibility of secondary qualities, together with an extension of the account to illustrate the nature of species and of substantial change (the change of one substance into another). 'Of the Origin of Forms' goes more fully over this latter ground, denying any agency to 'substantial forms' except in so far as they are redefined as the mechanical texture of particular bodies. In the traditional doctrine of form and matter, scholastic theory distinguished 'substantial' from 'accidental' form, the substantial form being the single species-determining factor in any natural kind. Boyle's polemic is concerned with demonstrating both that a species may be defined by a *combination* of factors, and that in the sciences this cuts across any supposed division between natural and synthetic kinds.

'Pyrophilus', the nominal dedicatee both of this work and of those immediately following, was Boyle's nephew Richard Jones, later Earl of Ranelagh, who was born in 1641 and tutored in his youth by John Milton and Henry Oldenburg. Even before the completion of his studies he had been appointed an Irish M.P., and nominated to be one of the first Fellows of the Royal Society, from whose lists he was subsequently removed. Biographers have tended to regard him as a political careerist and a scoundrel. Spasmodic addresses to

'Pyrophilus' survive in Boyle's works over many years; in an obscure dialogue about transmutation published in 1678, the name seems to be a pseudonym for Boyle himself.

An Introduction to the History of Particular Qualities

This important paper is the opening piece in a miscellany of otherwise minor *Tracts*, issued at Oxford in 1671. It appeared in only one edition. The publication of the miscellany, against Boyle's better judgement, was due to the pestering of his publisher, and in chapter III of this paper there are unresolved discrepancies clearly surviving from the manuscript stage.

The project of a History of Particular Qualities was one of Boyle's lifetime ambitions, announced in the Proemial Discourse to *The Origin of Forms and Qualities*. But after his early treatises on Fluidity and Firmness (1661) and Colours (1663) – and on Cold (1665) if one discounts its rather different format – the programme rather petered out, and in 1675 Boyle was to collect together most of the publishable papers remaining and issue them in a single volume. The projected Introduction included in the present edition opens with a backward reference to *The Origin of Forms and Qualities* but does not suppose a knowledge of any other writings.

Chapter I clarifies Boyle's use of the term *quality* (for the scientific properties of different kinds of substances, not for attributes in general), and chapter IV aims to show that the corpuscular structure which accounts for the sameness of certain qualities in different substances can still consistently account for their diversity in other qualities. But the piece is more concerned with extending the concept of matter beyond that expounded in *The Origin of Forms and Qualities*, than in saying anything new about 'particular qualities'. It also shows Boyle trying to formulate criteria for establishing the methodological superiority of the corpuscularian principles. The largely *a priori* character of the concept of matter developed here, and indeed the existence of an Introduction without the Histories, suggests that, at the time of writing, Boyle's theory was still some way ahead of his practice. When a few years later he published *The Mechanical Origin or Production of Divers Particular Qualities* (1675), his prefatory 'Advertisements' to that work paid rather more attention to the status of the corpuscularian hypothesis and its experimental basis. That text can be consulted for comparison in M. B. Hall, *Robert Boyle on Natural Philosophy*, pp. 232 ff.

MS Notes on a Good and an Excellent Hypothesis

This is a manuscript list of heads, probably for a projected and much-heralded dialogue of which only the opening speeches and a few miscellaneous notes survive; either the work was lost in one of the periodic catastrophes that befell Boyle's manuscripts, or it never progressed very far. The page is reproduced by permission of the Royal Society from Vol. XXXV of the Boyle Papers. Two other versions of the same notes (one in lamentable verse) are reproduced in M. B. Hall, *Robert Boyle on Natural Philosophy*, pp. 134–5.

Of the Imperfection of the Chemists' Doctrine of Qualities

This tract appeared in 1675, bound in with *The Mechanical Origin or Production of Divers Particular Qualities*, prepared in London for an Oxford publisher, and reissued without change in 1676. On most subjects other than the purely experimental, Boyle planned both a narrative work and a work in dialogue form, though the plan was not often completed. *Of the Imperfection of the Chemists' Doctrine of Qualities* is a relatively well-structured work, which does succinctly some of the things that the dialogue *The Sceptical Chemist* (1661) did at tortuous length. One reason for its greater succinctness is a better appreciation on Boyle's part of the distinction between methodological and experimental questions. The work is best considered, for its negative assessment of chemical and scholastic orthodoxy, alongside the matching positive assessment of the corpuscularian hypothesis in the next selection, since it was in the context of this dispute that Boyle tried to formulate the criteria for evaluating hypotheses.

About the Excellency and Grounds of the Mechanical Hypothesis

This work, which went into only one edition (London, 1674), was published, probably for tactical reasons, as an appendage to *The Excellency of Theology Compared with Natural Philosophy*, but it is nowadays one of the most quoted of Boyle's writings on the corpuscularian hypothesis. It is the only important paper on the subject which he wrote independently of the cycle addressed to 'Pyrophilus', so is likely to be a fairly mature work, and marks a shift of emphasis from his other methodological writings. Whereas elsewhere he was apt to imply, if not to say, that other systems were in competition with his own, here he allows explicitly for the possibility that they might be subsumed under it, so giving new sense to the suggestion of earlier writings that corpuscularian principles are more 'catholic and universal' than any others.

The essay shows slight confusion of purpose by the end. The Recapitulation is a cross between a summary of the virtues of the corpuscularian hypothesis and a summary of the hypothesis itself. (An account of the actual hypothesis was only included in the body of the text as *illustrative* of its capacity to generate a maximum number of results from a minimum base.) But the main heads of the essay proper can usefully be compared with those of the MS Notes previously quoted, of which it provides some verbal echoes. On Boyle's own showing, the corpuscularian hypothesis appears to meet the requirements of a good hypothesis, but it is not clear that in itself it meets the last requirement of an excellent one.

An Essay, Containing a Requisite Digression

This was the fourth essay in a collection, *Some Considerations Touching the Usefulness of Experimental Natural Philosophy*. The first edition, published in Oxford in 1663, was issued without Boyle's name on the title page, and a copy, now apparently lost, was presented by him anonymously to the library of the Royal Society. However in several extant copies the authorship is indicated by the publisher on another leaf, and is given away by the address to 'Pyrophilus' that runs through the essays. A second edition, dated Oxford, 1664, survives in two versions. J. F. Fulton in *A Bibliography of the Hon. Robert Boyle*, 2nd ed., distinguishes these as *Issue A* and *Issue B* (but wrongly says that the two Bodleian copies are both of Issue B), and gives grounds for thinking that Issue B was a later resetting, for combination with a second volume of *Considerations* that came out in 1671. Indeed Issue B is not just a resetting of Issue A, but a very careless resetting in the case of this particular essay, and its misprints were adopted fairly consistently by Birch. For present purposes, Issue A is treated as the only serious second edition and variants in Issue B are not recorded.

Boyle had by 1663 already published two substantial works in theology and biblical criticism. But this short essay, which contains his first of many expositions of the Design argument as a natural corollary to scientific study, and one of his most succinct expositions anywhere, was written at an earlier age, originally for a different dedicatee. Boyle aims in this paper to resist the atheist tendency in certain atomist writings, and one mark of its youthfulness is his references to the 'atomists' as apparently the only important proponents of mechanical explanation; he draws no clear distinction between atomists and Cartesians, though a reference to some non-'Epicureans', who 'can conceive a clear and distinct notion of a spirit', is no doubt an allusion to Descartes. There is nothing youthful, however, about his businesslike illustration of the way that mechanical explanation avoids the animism of common speech.

The source of the Lucretius verse translation, if it is not Boyle's own, has not been traced. All the translations here printed in footnotes were originally grouped at the end.

A Free Enquiry into the Vulgarly Received Notion of Nature

Boyle's very long treatise on Nature appeared in a single edition, in London, January 1686. He wrote it nearly twenty years earlier ('some lustres ago'), i.e. late in his Oxford period, but, 'the youth to whom I dictated it having been inveigled to steal away, unknown to me or his parents, into the Indies (whence we never heard of him since)', it took him sixteen years to knock it into shape and three and a half more to get it published. The selection in this edition consists of all of Section II, and omits from Section IV only the concluding pages, which Boyle himself authorized the reader to 'skip' if he did not 'relish the knowledge of the opinions and rites of the ancient Jews and heathens'.

The ostensible target of the book is the now archaic notion of nature as an active agent, and much of Boyle's polemic is biblical or theological in character. But the work also contains some of the best examples of his capacity for conceptual analysis, and it is this which is represented in the extracts included here. This capacity goes along with some interesting exercises in ontological reduction (the reduction of 'notional' entities to the operation of matter in motion), which led him to a view of natural law and natural causation which pre-echoes Berkeley. With hindsight it is possible to detect premonitions of the same view in some of his other works. For fuller discussion, see J. E. McGuire, 'Boyle's Conception of Nature', *Journal of the History of Ideas* 33 (1972).

Some Physico-Theological Considerations

Boyle's paper on the Resurrection originally appeared under his own name, as the second half of a volume which also included *Some Considerations about the Reconcilableness of Reason and Religion*, which since the time of its publication has been understood to be Boyle's also. It appeared in London in a single edition in 1675. Fulton regards it as one of Boyle's more whimsical pieces, and many commentators ignore it. But apart from being a fair example of the way in which Boyle sought to accommodate reason and revelation (hence the circumstances of its publication), it contains one of the more extensive discussions of the concept of identity prior to Locke. Boyle's interest is exclusively in issues of bodily identity. The determination of bodily ownership by attachment to the soul, and the continuing identifiability of separated souls, are things that he took for granted as posing no conceptual problems, despite his recurrent criticism of Descartes elsewhere for leaving the body-soul link unexplained. He also appears in this paper to be indifferent to the conceptual importance of resolving whether 'the true notion of body consists ... alone in its extension, or in that and impenetrability together'.

A Discourse of Things Above Reason

This work was published in a single edition in London in 1681, coupled with *Some Advices about Judging of Things said to Transcend Reason*, and ascribed to 'a Fellow of the Royal Society'. C. C. J. Webb (*Bodleian Library Record* 4 (1953)) wrongly questioned Boyle's authorship, which is attested by Locke and other contemporaries, and confirmed by cross-comparison with the style and content of cognate writings. At least two leaves of the original draft survive in Vol. XXXVIII of the Royal Society Boyle Papers, with corrections in Boyle's own hand.

The *Discourse* is not a particularly finished work. Apart from occasionally excessive clumsinesses of style, it introduces the same illustrative examples more than once with the same sense of novelty, as though they should have been alternative rather than successive stages in the draft. But as Boyle unaccountably thought he had some aptitude in the *genre*, one specimen of his dialogue style should be in any collection, and in this case the dialogue presentation is philosophically more substantial than the corresponding narrative essay (*Reflections upon a Theological Distinction*, published in 1690 as a supplement to *The Christian Virtuoso*).

While one may hope that the style is not typical of the kind of intellectual soirée that prompted John Locke to go away and plan work on his *Essay Concerning Human Understanding*, the subject of discussion certainly could be, and the views expressed in Boyle's dialogue are worth comparing with those on the limits of human understanding, the operation of reason, and the distinct provinces of reason and faith, in Book IV of Locke's *Essay*. Boyle, for example, has a classification comparable to Locke's intuitive, demonstrative and sensitive knowledge (the last limited to the extent of our experience), but unlike Locke he thinks intuitive knowledge to be innate. This is no doubt due to his reading of Descartes, a reading however which was not close enough for him to realize that Descartes's 'clear and distinct ideas' were not mental images, so that Descartes *denied* (e.g. in *Meditation VI*) that we can imagine a chiliagon in the course of *asserting* that, as he thought, we have a clear and distinct understanding of it. Boyle's views are also studied extensively by Locke's adversary John Norris, in chapter III of *An Account of Reason and Faith* (1697).

3. EDITORIAL PRACTICE

The textual editor's aim should ideally be to engineer the production, so far as he can, so that the reader reads the author without being aware of an intermediary. An uncritical reproduction of the editions from Boyle's lifetime would no more meet this criterion than would a reproduction of Birch, for the reader must perforce stumble from time to time upon sense-destroying conventions attributable to the ignorance of scribe or compositor. The alternatives are the two extremes of a corrected seventeenth-century text or a fully modernized one. Some of the papers exist in only a single printed edition from Boyle's lifetime, and none in more than two. There is therefore not a great deal of material on which to build a critical edition with any confidence. But modernization by definition involves taking what some scholars will regard as liberties with the text. Some of these have been deliberately marked in this edition, in deference to their sensibilities, but only after I have been assured that the reader who is not interested in these editorial interventions can quickly train himself to ignore them.

(1) *The substantive text.* The original editions, in conjunction with their published *errata*, do not often yield intrinsically suspect collocations of words, as distinct from casual misprints. I have taken the wording of the printed originals as an adequate basis for a modernized text, except in a handful of places where I have indicated editorial changes by recording the original reading in the end-notes. It is possible that greater familiarity with seventeenth-century idiom or science would have led me to propose more changes, but I do not believe it could have led me to propose fewer.

There is a borderline area, where the original editions contain erroneous quotations from or erroneous references to identifiable passages in other authors. If the only way to restore sense to a passage is to assume and correct a misprint, I have done this. In other cases where Boyle's quotation is free or inaccurate, I have felt obliged to leave it, since Boyle's contemporaries accepted different standards of accuracy from ours; but where it does not do violence to Boyle's sense, I have tried to bring the punctuation within quotations into line with the intentions of the original author.

I have felt less inhibited about wrong or incomplete references. While there is no reason to suppose that wrong references in Boyle are misprints, there is no reason either to suppose that he meant them to be wrong, and where I have detected wrong references I have corrected them, usually without comment. For the sake of uniformity across the volume, I have expanded Boyle's more compressed footnote references and adopted certain standard forms. These standardized references are Boylean in general character (e.g. I have retained the traditional way of referring by book ('lib.') and chapter ('cap.') to Aristotle's writings), but they have been amplified where possible to make for easier identification in library catalogues. In an authentic text one might have included both Boylean and modern references, one on the page and the other in an appendix. In the case of quoted books which occur in more than one edition, it is rarely possible to identify which edition Boyle himself was using. Undocumented quotations have defied identification.

Barring undetected errors, these are the only deviations of wording that I have allowed myself from the printed first editions of Boyle's works. Second-edition variants, where they have been detected, are recorded in the end-notes. I preferred to follow the first edition of *The Origin of Forms and Qualities* and *An Essay Containing a Requisite Digression* because I doubt if various minor second-edition variations are genuine corrections; but nowhere does anything significant hang upon the choice of editions.

All lettered notes at the foot of the text are Boyle's own, allowing for the standardization of references already mentioned; there is no attempt to distinguish those which were originally printed as marginalia or as parenthetic notes in the text. Editorial numbered notes are deferred to the end of the book, and are exclusively concerned with minor matters of reading. Readers who are not interested in these should ignore the superscript numerals in the text.

(2) *Accidentals.* It is normal practice in a modernized text to drop the italicization of proper names and the initial capitals on substantives, to adopt modern spelling, and to recast the punctuation. It is mere sentimentality to hold in general, as some textual editors do, that capital letters had a significance for earlier readers that will somehow be recovered by printing them for present-day readers; but in some Boyle editions capitals were sometimes used as an alternative to italics for emphasis, and the editor has to consider whether to retain at least some convention for emphasis if the author wished it.

I have modernized the spelling where modern English has still the same words that Boyle used, but I have left in all genuinely obsolete words where the only way to modernize would have been to replace the words. So I print the obsolete *theorical* and not *theoretical*, since these are distinct words with slightly different etymologies; I print *opacous* instead of *opaque*, since although their ultimate etymology is the same their proximate origins are different; and I retain the negative prefix *un-* in certain compounds where it has now been displaced by *in-*. I have not however retained conventions which were due solely to accidents of pronunciation, like *'tis*, or *for brevity sake*. There have been borderline cases where an arbitrary decision had to be taken.

My greatest departures are in punctuation, since the significance of different kinds of pointing has changed considerably since Boyle's day. I have not therefore tried to take Boyle's punctuation as a base and then merely tinker with it, since that seemed the least likely way to achieve reasonable consistency of practice. I have repointed from scratch, conscious of the need to give a clear lead as to the general structure of Boyle's convoluted periods, and to make his prose *flow* as naturally for a twentieth-century reader as the archaisms in vocabulary and syntax will permit. Even by seventeenth-century standards, Boyle was a poor stylist, too much given to weak cadences. I have tried to assess the function of every clause in relation to its adjoining clauses and to punctuate suitably. I have neither wilfully changed, nor slavishly followed, Boyle's distribution of full stops. So I have occasionally combined sentences which in Boyle's printed text were separated, particularly where subordinate clauses had become stranded from their main clauses; I have also occasionally separated self-contained sentences which in Boyle were divided by less than a full stop, where I am sure it will help the reader's concentration. There are precedents for these practices in some of the contemporary Latin versions that had Boyle's authority; and it is no part of my criticism of Birch that *he* adopted eighteenth-century punctuation for an eighteenth-century edition. Any reader who believes I have misjudged the clause or sentence divisions is at liberty to adjust his text, and he would have to do the same if he read the original editions. I cannot hope to satisfy on this those to whom any editorial adjustment is anathema; but I believe that any reader who accepts the principle of a modernized text and compares this edition with the published originals will satisfy himself that it would have been misplaced pedantry to annotate these particular deviations.

Finally, there are three areas where an editor's powers of intervention may be disputed, and where therefore all such interventions in this edition have been carefully but unobtrusively flagged by a special convention.

(*a*) *Parentheses.* There is a presumption that brackets, more than almost any other kind of punctuation, are deliberate and have a distinctive purpose, and these have normally been retained from the early editions – though in a few cases their function is debatable, and in a few other cases brackets could as well have been included, in consistency with Boyle's general practice, as omitted. Brackets are also a useful resource for anyone who is trying to mark out the complex structure of a long latinate period, and serve a function nowadays which was sometimes performed for Boyle by one use of semi-colons. Since Boyle does not use dashes, another resource open to us for the same purpose, I have felt free to use dashes to mark editorial parentheses, reserving brackets for Boyle's own, since the reader could justifiably complain if he did not know which were which. The positioning of Boyle's brackets has occasionally been adjusted to the demands of sense or syntax.

(*b*) *Paragraphing*. Most of the paragraphing in the early editions is sensible, if not always ideal, but occasionally it is confusing or unhelpful. Again, comparison with the Latin versions over which Boyle had some supervision suggests that the original divisions were not sacrosanct. The fault lies usually in too little division in the English editions; but occasionally there is an out-of-character proliferation of divisions, and some of Boyle's paragraph breaks come in mid-sentence. A superscript $+$ at the end of a paragraph in this edition indicates that the original was continuous; a vertical | in the course of a paragraph marks an original paragraph break. Otherwise I follow the first editions.

(*c*) *Italics and quotation marks*. Boyle did not normally use quotation marks, but he wrote a great many things which might involve a modern writer in their use. I have reserved quotation marks for actual or purported quotations from given sources, and for the occasional use of scare-quotes in actual or virtual *oratio obliqua*, of a kind perfectly familiar to any modern reader. The modern convention of using distinctive quotation marks for the *mention* of single words or expressions as terms of a language was unknown to older writers, but Boyle frequently used italics for the same purpose. I have accordingly followed his own convention here, even though it has meant retaining italics, as Boyle did, for more than one function, since it does not create any serious ambiguity.

Other functions for which italics have been retained are, selectively, for stress (restoring many of the italics that Birch removed), and for titles and foreign expressions. The purely conventional use of italics for names and for persistently recurrent key-terms and naturalized technical terms has been discarded. In standardizing the practice of italics for titles and foreign words, and in very occasionally adjusting the boundaries of italicized phrases, I have not thought it necessary to indicate where I have deviated from the original editions. In all other cases editorial italics (which are in any case confined only to establishing uniformity in practices which are already widespread in the text) are marked by a superscript $°$. These are (i) the occasional use of italics to mark stresses Boyle had sometimes marked instead by initial capitals, in words (like auxiliary verbs) which conventionally never have them; (ii) their use to pick out key terms or phrases from items in series, where Boyle's text did not always complete the process it began; (iii) a few formerly unmarked cases of word-mention or semi-quotation. Once again a comparison with the Latin versions shows that this is a kind of editing that was acceptable in Boyle's day. Indeed all the editorial italics in this edition of *The Excellency and Grounds* are anticipated in the Latin version. It is not a crime to introduce such consistency and mark it; it is only a crime to do it and keep quiet about it. In conformity with the editorial principle enunciated at the start of this section, I had to decide which would get more in the reader's way – marked consistency or unmarked inconsistency. I took the flattering view that the modern reader expects higher standards of textual preparation than did Boyle's contemporaries, and the unflattering one that he will find enough unavoidable anomalies in Boyle's style not to wish to be faced with avoidable ones as well.

4. SUMMARY OF TEXTUAL CONVENTIONS

⁺ indicates that there was no paragraph division in Boyle's text at this point.

| indicates that there was a paragraph division in Boyle's text at this point.

° indicates that the italics are not original.

Superscript letters refer to Boyle's own annotations printed on the page.

Superscript numerals refer to editorial end-notes relating to the textual reading.

NOTES

[1] All biographers of Boyle are indebted to the *Life* published by Thos. Birch, on the basis of materials assembled by Henry Miles, F.R.S., in 1744. Some correction (especially of dates) and addition of detail is now provided by R. E. W. Maddison, *The Life of the Hon. Robert Boyle, F.R.S.* (London, 1969). On his early life the principal source is still Boyle's own autobiographical *Account of Philaretus during his Minority*, written *c*. 1648 and reproduced in variant versions by Birch and Maddison.

[2] This list, in Vol. XXXVI of the Royal Society Boyle Papers, is reproduced by Maddison, *op. cit.*, p. 64. The titles in the list are rough and ready and more of these works survive, in print or manuscript, than Maddison allows. 'Of the Interpretation

of Scripture' is the original of *Some Considerations touching the Style of the H. Scriptures*, published in 1661 but 'written divers years since to a friend'. 'Of Atoms' can be assumed to be the early essay 'Of the Atomicall Philosophy' which survives in Vol. XXVI of the Boyle Papers, marked 'These Papers are without fayle to be burn't'. R. S. Westfall copied the first two leaves of the MS on Atoms in 'Unpublished Boyle Papers Relating to Scientific Method: II' (*Annals of Science* 12 (1956)), overlooking that the next twelve leaves are also intact, merely out of order; and he started a romantic fiction, taken over by R. H. Kargon (*Atomism in England from Hariot to Newton* (Oxford, 1966), pp. 95–6), that Boyle wanted to burn the papers because he was nervous of being accused of atheism. But the same instruction to burn – which was a late instruction to his executors, not an early instruction to himself – applied equally to some of Boyle's youthful theological writing and personal correspondence (cf. Maddison, *op. cit.*, pp. 179–80).

³ See C. Webster, *The Great Instauration* (London, 1975), pp. 57–67. Webster argues convincingly for the separate identity of two groups formerly supposed to be identical: (i) a (perhaps family-based) 'Invisible College' which figures in some letters and MSS of Boyle from the years 1646–7, whose membership and organization are not fully known, and (ii) a broader group whose point of contact was the educational idealist and scientific intelligencer Samuel Hartlib, with whom Boyle only became acquainted in 1647. The old idea, inherited from Birch, that either of these groups had any connection with a scientific meeting at Gresham College, London, whose members later formed the nucleus of the Royal Society, is now discredited.

⁴ Descartes and Gassendi differed over the existence of atoms and vacua. Boyle initially wrote as an atomist (cf. note 2 above), but later opted out of this particular dispute, though for other purposes he accepted the existence of vacua and, without altogether appreciating its significance, accepted impenetrability as a defining characteristic of matter, thereby differentiating it from space. Descartes and Gassendi were convenient allies to name, because both, like Boyle, believed that mechanistic explanation in natural science was compatible with an orthodox theism. For an influential recent discussion of certain analogies between the thought of Descartes and of Boyle, see L. Laudan, 'The Clock Metaphor and Probabilism', *Annals of Science* 22 (1966). Among English authors, Boyle acknowledged some debt to earlier writers on magnetism, and to Kenelm Digby's *Two Treatises* (1644), but he was already set in his thoughts by the time of Walter Charleton's *Physiologia* of 1654.

⁵ For a more detailed explanation of the way that this new conceptual system took over the function of the old, see H. R. Harré, *Matter and Method* (London, 1964). In an old but still important critical essay, 'The Experimental Philosophy of Robert Boyle' (*Philosophical Review* 41 (1932)), P. P. Wiener contended that Boyle and his contemporaries overreacted against Aristotelianism, in so far as they did not understand the scope for genuinely logical and metaphysical enquiries any better than their opponents understood the scope for genuinely physical ones.

⁶ Boyle's fullest, but I do not believe fully consistent, treatment of these matters is in the 'Excursion' and Particulars V-VI of 'The Theorical Part' of *The Origin of Forms and Qualities*. For a cross-section of recent discussion of the issues, see E. M. Curley, 'Locke, Boyle and the Distinction between Primary and Secondary Qualities', *Philosophical Review* 81 (1972); P. Alexander, 'Boyle and Locke on Primary and Secondary Qualities', *Ratio* 16 (1974) (also further papers by Alexander in *Philosophical Review* 83 (1974) and *Proceedings of the Aristotelian Society* 77 (1976/7)); F. J.

O'Toole, 'Qualities and Powers in the Corpuscular Philosophy of Robert Boyle', *Journal of the History of Philosophy* 12 (1974); J. L. Mackie, *Problems from Locke* (Oxford, 1976), and reviews of Mackie's book in the main professional journals; D. Palmer, 'Boyle's Corpuscular Hypothesis and Locke's Primary-Secondary Quality Distinction', *Philosophical Studies* 29 (1976); M. B. Bolton, 'The Origins of Locke's Doctrine of Primary and Secondary Qualities', *Philosophical Quarterly* 26 (1976).

[7] For further discussion of this, see Westfall's paper cited in note 2. Westfall has already published (with minor deviations) the MS paper included in this volume.

[8] Boyle had some less public contact with quite a number of figures familiar in the history of philosophy. He had intelligence of the late work of Gassendi through Samuel Hartlib. He had a fruitless exchange on scientific matters with Spinoza, through Henry Oldenburg as intermediary (see A. R. and M. B. Hall, 'Philosophy and Natural Philosophy: Boyle and Spinoza', in *Mélanges Alexandre Koyré, II* (Paris, 1964)). He had more direct contact with Leibniz, who visited him and knew and admired *The Origin of Forms and Qualities* and some of the theological works (see L. E. Loemker, 'Boyle and Leibniz', *Journal of the History of Ideas* 16 (1955)). Boyle's professional acquaintance with Locke over a period of years is well documented, and most of the other prominent English philosophers of the later seventeenth century were also Fellows of the Royal Society.

THE ORIGIN OF FORMS AND
QUALITIES ACCORDING TO THE
CORPUSCULAR PHILOSOPHY

THE PROEMIAL DISCOURSE TO THE READER[1]

As it is the part of a mineralist both to *discover* new mines, and to *work* those that are already discovered, by separating and melting the ores to reduce them into perfect metals,[2] so I esteem that it becomes a naturalist not only to *devise* hypotheses and experiments, but to examine and *improve* those that are already found out. Upon this consideration (among other motives) I was invited to make the following attempt, whose productions coming to be exposed to other eyes than those for which they were first written, it will be requisite to give the public some account of the occasion, the scope, and some circumstances. And this I shall do the more fully, because the reasons I am to render of my way of writing in reference to the Peripatetic philosophy must contain intimations which perhaps will not be useless to some sorts of readers (especially gentlemen), and, by being applied to most of those other parts of my writings that relate to the School philosophy, may do them good service, and save both my readers and me some trouble of repetitions.

Having four or five years ago published a little physico-chemical tract about the differing parts and redintegration of nitre, I found, as well by other signs as by the early solicitations of the stationer for a new edition, that I had no cause to complain of the reception that had been given it; but I observed, too, that the discourse, consisting chiefly of reflections that were occasionally made upon the phenomena of a single experiment, was more available to confirm those in the Corpuscularian philosophy that had already somewhat enquired into it, than to acquaint those with the principles and notions of it who were utter strangers to it, and, as to many readers, was fitter to excite a curiosity for that philosophy than to give an introduction thereunto. Upon this occasion it came into my mind that, about the time when I writ that *Essay about Saltpetre* (which was divers years before it was published), I had also some thoughts of a

History of Qualities; and that, having in loose sheets set down divers observations and experiments proper for such a design, I had also drawn up a discourse, which was so contrived that, though some parts of it were written in such a manner as that they may serve for expository notes upon some particular passages of the *Essay*, yet those parts with the rest might serve for a *general preface* to the History of Qualities, in case I should ever have conveniency as well as inclination to make the prosecuting of it my business: and in the meantime might present that *Pyrophilus* to whom I writ some kind of introduction to the principles of the Mechanical philosophy, by expounding to him, as far as my thoughts and experiments would enable me to do, in few words, what according to the Corpuscularian notions may be thought of the nature and origin of qualities and forms, the knowledge of which either makes or supposes the most fundamental and useful part of natural philosophy. And to invite me to make use of these considerations and trials about qualities and forms, it opportunely happened that, though I could not find many of the notes written about particular qualities (my loose papers having been, during the late confusions, much scattered by the many removes I had then occasion to make), yet when last winter, being urged to publish my *History of Cold* (which soon after came forth), I rummaged among my loose papers, I found that the several notes of mine that he had met with under various heads, but yet all concerning the origin of forms and qualities, together with the Preface addressed to Pyrophilus (though written at distant times and places), had two or three years before, by the care of an industrious person with whom I left them, been fairly copied out together (which circumstance I mention, that the reader may not wonder to find the following book not written uniformly in one continued tenor), excepting some experiments which, having been of my own making, it was not difficult for me to perfect, either out of my notes and memory, or (where I doubted their sufficiency) by repeated trials. So that if the·urgency wherewith divers ingenious men pressed the publication of my new experiments about cold, and my unwillingness to protract it till the frosty season, that was fittest to examine and prove them, were all passed, had not prevailed with me to let those Observations be made public the last winter, they might have been accompanied with the present essay of *The Origin of Qualities and Forms*, which may be premised to what I have written touching any of the particular qualities, since it contains experiments and considerations fit to be preliminary to them all.

But though I was by this means diverted from putting out the following treatise at the same time with the *History of Cold*, yet I was without much difficulty prevailed with not to alter my intentions of suffering it to come abroad, because divers of my historical accounts of some particular qualities are to be reprinted, which may receive much light and confirmation by the things delivered in this present treatise about qualities and forms in general. To which inducement was added the persuasion of some ingenious persons, who are pleased to confess their having received more information and satisfaction in these papers than I durst pretend to give them: though indeed the subject is so noble and important, and does so much want the being illustrated by some distinct and experimental discourse, that, *not only* if I did not suspect my friends of partiality, I should hope that it may gratify many readers and instruct more than a few; but, such as it is, I do not altogether despair that it will prove neither unacceptable nor useless. And indeed the doctrines of forms and qualities, and generation and corruption, and alteration, are wont to be treated of by scholastical philosophers in so obscure, so perplexed, and so unsatisfactory a way, and their discourses upon these subjects do consist so much more of logical and metaphysical notions and niceties than of physical observations and reasonings, that it is very difficult for any reader of but an ordinary capacity to understand what they mean, and no less difficult for any intelligent and unprejudiced reader to acquiesce in what they teach – which is oftentimes so precarious, and so contradictious to itself, that most readers (without always excepting such as are learned and ingenious), frighted by the darkness and difficulties wherewith these subjects have been surrounded, do not so much as look after or read over these general and controverted matters about which the Schools make so much noise, but, despairing to find any satisfaction in the study of them, betake themselves immediately to that part of physics that treats of particular bodies: so that to these it will not be unacceptable to have any intelligible notions offered them of those things which, as they are wont to be proposed, are not wont to be understood; though yet the subjects themselves, if I mistake not, may be justly reckoned not only amongst the noblest and most important, but (in case they be duly proposed) among the usefullest and most delightful speculations that belong to physics.

I consider, too, that among those that are inclined to that philosophy, which I find I have been much imitated in calling *Corpuscularian*, there are many ingenious persons, especially among the nobility and gentry, who, having been first drawn to like this new way of philosophy by the sight of some experiments, which for their novelty or prettiness they were much pleased with, or for their strangeness they admired, have afterwards delighted themselves to make or see variety of experiments, without having ever had the opportunity to be instructed in the rudiments or fundamental notions of that philosophy whose pleasing or amazing productions have enamoured them of it. And as our Pyrophilus, for whom these notes were drawn up, did in some regards belong to this sort of virtuosi, so it is not impossible but that such readers as he was then will not be sorry to meet with a treatise wherein, though my chief and proper business be the giving some account of the nature and origin of forms and qualities, yet, by reason of the connexion and dependence betwixt these and divers of the other principal things that belong to the general part of physics, I have been obliged to touch upon so many other important points that this tract may, in some sort, exhibit a scheme of, or serve for an introduction into the elements of, the Corpuscularian philosophy.

And as those readers that have had the curiosity to peruse what is commonly taught in the Schools about forms, and generation and corruption, and those other things we have been mentioning, and have (as is usual among ingenious readers) quitted the study of those unsatisfactory intricacies with disgust, will not be displeased to find in our notes such explications of those things as render them at least intelligible, so it will not perhaps prove unacceptable to such readers to find those matters, which the Schools had interwoven with Aristotle's doctrine, reconciled and accommodated to the notions of the Corpuscular physics.

If it be said that I have left divers things unmentioned which are wont to be largely treated of by the Aristotelians, and particularly have omitted the discussion of several questions about which they are wont very solemnly and eagerly to contend, I readily acknowledge it to be true: but I answer, further, that to do otherwise than I have done were not agreeable to the nature of my design, as is declared in the Preface to Pyrophilus; and that, though most readers will not take notice of it, yet such as are conversant in that sort of authors will, I presume, easily find that I have not left them

unconsulted, but have had the curiosity to resort to several – both of
the more, and of the less, recent – scholastical writers about physics,
and to some of the best metaphysicians to boot, that I might the
better inform myself both what their opinions are, and upon what
arguments they are grounded. But as I found those enquiries far
more troublesome than useful, so I doubt not that my omissions will
not much displease that sort of readers for whose sake chiefly it is
that these papers are permitted to be made public. For if I should
increase the obscurity of the things themselves I treat of, by adding
the several obscurer comments (rather than explications), and the
perplexed and contradictious opinions, I have met with among
scholastic writers, I doubt that such persons as I chiefly write for
would, instead of better comprehending what I should *so* deliver,
absolutely forbear to read it. And there being many doctrines, to
which number this we are speaking of seems to belong, wherein the
same innate light or other arguments that discover the truth do
likewise sufficiently show the erroneousness of dissenting opinions, I
hope it may suffice to propose and establish the notions that are to
be embraced, without solicitously disproving what cannot be true if
those be so. And indeed there are many opinions and arguments of
good repute in the Schools, which do so entirely rely upon the
authority of Aristotle or some of his more celebrated followers, that,
where that authority is not acknowledged, to fall upon a solemn
confutation of what has been so precariously advanced were not only
unnecessary, but indiscreet, even in a discourse not confined to the
brevity challenged by the nature of this of ours. And there are very
many questions and controversies which, though hotly and
clamorously contended about, and indeed pertinent and fit enough
to be debated in their philosophy, do yet so much suppose the truth
of several of their tenents which the new philosophers reject, or are
grounded upon technical terms or forms of speaking that suppose
the truth of such opinions, or are expressions whereof we neither do
nor need make any use, that to have inserted such debates into such
a discourse as mine would have been not only tedious, but
impertinent – as (for instance) those grand disputes whether the four
elements are endowed with distinct substantial forms or have only
their proper qualities instead of them, and whether they remain in
mixed bodies according to their forms or according to their qualities,
and whether the former or the latter of those be or be not refracted.
These, I say, and divers other controversies about the four elements

and their manner of mixtion, are quite out of doors in their philosophy that acknowledge neither that there are four elements, nor that cold, heat, dryness, and moisture are, in the Peripatetic sense, first qualities, or that there are any such things as substantial forms *in rerum natura*. And it made me the more unwilling to stuff these papers with any needless School controversies, because I found upon perusal of several scholastic writers (especially the recenter, who may probably be supposed to be the most refined) that they do not always mean the same things by the same terms, but some employ them in one sense, others in another, and sometimes the same writer uses them in very differing senses: which I am obliged to take notice of, that such readers as have consulted some of those authors may not accuse me of mistaking or injuring some of the scholastical terms and notions he may meet with in these papers, when I have only employed them in the sense of other School writers which I judged preferable. And this puts me in mind of intimating that, whereas, on the contrary, I sometimes employ[3] variety of terms and phrases to express the same thing, I did it purposely, though perhaps to the prejudice of my own reputation, for the advantage of Pyrophilus: both I and others having observed that, the same unobvious notions being several ways expressed, some readers even among the ingeniouser sort of them will take it up much better in one of those expressions, and some in another.

But perhaps it will be wondered at, even by some of the new philosophers, that, dissenting so much as I do from Aristotle and the schoolmen, I should overlook or decline some arguments which some very ingenious men think to be of[4] great force against the doctrine I oppose. But divers of these arguments being such as the logicians call *ad hominem*, I thought I might well enough spare them. For I have observed Aristotle in his physics to write very often in so dark and ambiguous a way, that it is far more difficult than one would think to be sure what his opinion was, and the unlearned and too frequently jarring glosses of his interpreters have often made the comment darker than the text, so that (though in most it be, yet) in divers cases it is not easy (especially without the expense of many words) to lay open the contradictions of the Peripatetic doctrine: besides that the urging such contradictions are oftentimes fitter to silence an unwary adversary than satisfy a wary and judicious reader, it being very possible that a man may contradict himself in two several places of his works and yet not be in both of them in the wrong; for one of his assertions, though inconsistent with the other, may yet be consistent with truth. But this is not all I have to say on this occasion. For besides that, having for many reasons, elsewhere mentioned, purposely forborne the reading of some very much and, for aught I know, very justly esteemed discourses about general *hypotheses*, it is very possible that I may be a stranger to some of those arguments – besides this, I say, I confess I have purposely forborne to make use of others which I have sufficiently taken notice of. For some of those ratiocinations would engage him that should employ them to adopt a hypothesis or theory in which, perhaps, I am not so thoroughly satisfied, and of which I do not conceive myself to have, on this occasion, any necessity to make use: and accordingly I have forborne to employ arguments that are either grounded on, or suppose, indivisible corpuscles called *atoms*, or any *innate motion* belonging to them; or that the essence of bodies consists in extension; or that a vacuum is impossible; or that there are such *globuli caelestes*, or such a *materia subtilis*, as the Cartesians employ to explicate most of the phenomena of nature. For these, and divers other notions, I (who here write rather for the Corpuscularians in general, than any party of them) thought it improper needlessly to take in, discoursing *either* against those to whom these things appear as disputable as the Peripatetic tenets seem to me, *or* for to satisfy an ingenious person whom it were not fair to impose upon with *notions* that I did not myself think proper.

And on the like account I forbore such *arguments* as those that suppose, in nature and bodies inanimate, designs and passions proper to living and perhaps peculiar to intelligent beings, and (such as) some proofs that are drawn from the theology of the Schools (which I wish less interwoven with Aristotle's philosophy). For though there be some things which seem to be of this sort (as arguments drawn from final causes in divers particulars that concern animals), which, in a sound sense, I not only admit but maintain, yet since, as they are wont to be proposed, they are liable enough to be questioned, I thought it expedient for my present design to pretermit them, as things that I do not absolutely need, though the employing some of them would facilitate my task. And this I did the rather because I also forbear to answer arguments that, however vehemently and subtly urged by many of the modern schoolmen of the Roman Catholic communion, are either confessedly, or at least really, built upon some theological tenets of theirs which, being opposed by the divines of other churches and not left unquestioned by some acute ones of their own, would not be proper to be solemnly taken notice of by me – whose business in this tract is to discourse of natural things as a naturalist, without invading the province of divines by intermeddling with supernatural mysteries – such as those upon which divers of the physico-theological tenents of the schoolmen, especially about real qualities and the separableness of accidents from subjects of inhesion, are *manifestly*, if not also *avowedly*, grounded.[a5] But to return to the other things I was owning to have left unmentioned, notwithstanding all that I have been saying I readily acknowledge that, in some recent authors that have been embracers of the new philosophy, I have met with some passages that might well and pertinently be taken into the following discourse; but that having been (as I formerly intimated) transcribed some years ago, I cannot now so conveniently alter it: which I am the less troubled at, because these few additional arguments, thought fit to illustrate or confirm, being not necessary to make out what has been delivered, may safely be let alone, unless there happen (as it is not unlikely there may) an occasion of reprinting these notes, with such enlargements as may make them the more fit to be an introduction into the Corpuscular philosophy.

I hope then, upon the whole matter, that I have pitched upon that way that was the most conducive to my design – partly by insisting only on those opinions, whether true or false, which for their importance or difficulty seemed to deserve to be particularly either explicated or disproved; and partly by choosing to employ such arguments as I thought the clearest and cogentest, and, by their assuming the least of any, seemed the easiest to be vindicated from exceptions – without troubling myself to answer objections that appeared rather to be drawn from metaphysical or logical subtleties, or to be grounded upon the authority of men, than to be physical ratiocinations, founded upon experience or the nature of the things

---

[a] '*Atque haec sententia* [of the distinction and separableness of quantity from matter] *est omnino tenenda: quanquam enim non possit ratione naturali sufficienter demonstrari, tamen ex principiis theologiae convincitur esse vera, maxime propter mysterium Eucharistiae. . . . Prima ratio pro hac sententia est, quia in mysterio Eucharistiae Deus separavit quantitatem a substantiis panis et vini, &c.*' – F. Suarez, *Disputationes Metaphysicae*, disp. 40, sect. 2, subs. 8. '*Haec responsio et sententia* [adversariorum] *sic explicata non potest facile et evidenter impugnari, sistendo in puro naturali. Nihilominus tamen, partim ratione naturali, partim adiuncto mysterio, sufficientissime improbatur.*' – ibid., subs. 12–13.

under debate: especially having, in the proposal and confirmation of the truth, so laid the grounds, and intimated the ways of answering what is like to be colourably objected against it, that an ingenious man may well enough furnish himself with weapons to defend the truth out of the notions, hints, and experiments, wherewith in this tract care has been taken to accompany it. And my forbearing to prosecute some of the Peripatetic controversies any further than I have done will not, I hope, be blamed by them that have observed, as well as I, how much those disputes are wont to be lengthened by such frivolous distinctions as do not deserve to be solemnly examined, especially in such a compendious treatise as ours. For an attentive reader needs not be much conversant with the writings of the modern Peripatetics, about such subjects as substantial forms, generation, corruption, &c., to take notice that it is their custom, when they find themselves distressed by a solid argument, to endeavour to elude it by some pitiful distinction or other, which is usually so groundless and so unintelligible, or so nugatory, or so impertinent to the subject, or at least so insufficient for the purpose it is alleged for, that to vouchsafe it a solicitous confutation might question a writer's judgement with intelligent readers, who by such insignificant distinctions are satisfied of nothing so much as that the framers of them had rather say (that which indeed amounts to) nothing, than not seem to say something. And of such evasions they may probably be emboldened to make use by the practice of Aristotle himself, to whom such obscure and unsatisfactory distinctions are so familiar that I remember one of his own commentators (and he one of the most judicious) could not forbear, upon a certain text of his master's, to complain of it, and particularly to take notice that that one distinction of *actu* and *potentia* runs through almost all Aristotle's philosophy, and is employed to shift off those difficulties he could not clearly explicate.[b]

By which, nevertheless, I would not be understood to censure or decry the whole Peripatetic philosophy, much less to despise

---

[b] The author here meant is the inquisitive Peripatetic Cabaeus, who in one place hath these words: '*Ut hanc quaestionem solvat, recurrit ad illam distinctionem sibi valde familiarem, qua utitur Aristoteles in tota sua philosophia, quoties obviam habet aliquam gravem difficultatem; distinguit enim* actu *vel* potentia, *&c.*' In another, these, '*Quae est distinctio quaedam familiaris Aristoteli, quam applicat omnibus rebus ubi difficultates urgent, et videtur istis vocibus quasi fatali gladio omnes rescindere difficultatis nodos; vix enim est difficultas, cui non putat se satisfacere distinguendo* actu *et* potentia.'

Aristotle himself, whose own writings give me sometimes cause a little to wonder, to find some absurdities so confidently fathered upon him by his scholastic interpreters. For I look upon Aristotle as *one* (though but as *one amongst many*) of those famed ancients whose learning about Alexander's time ennobled Greece; and I readily allow him most of the praises due to great wits, excepting those which belong to clear-headed naturalists. And I here declare, once for all, that where in the following tract, or any other of my writings, I do *indefinitely* depreciate Aristotle's doctrine, I would be understood to speak of *his physics*, or rather of the speculative part of them (for his historical writings concerning animals I much esteem); nor do I say that even these may not have their use among scholars, and even in universities, if they be retained and studied with due cautions and limitations (of which I have elsewhere spoken).

But to resume the discourse whence the Peripatetic distinctions tempted me to digress, by anything I formerly said I would not in the least disparage those excellent and especially those modern authors that have professedly opposed the Aristotelian physics (such as Lucretius, Verulam, Basso, Descartes and his followers, Gassendus, the two Boates, Magnenus, Pemble, Helmont), nor be thought to have made no use of any of their cogitations or arguments. For, though some of their books I could not procure when I had occasion to have recourse to them, and though the weakness of my eyes discouraged me from perusing those parts of others that concerned not the subject I was treating of, yet I hope I have been benefited by those I have consulted, and might have been more so by the learned Gassendus's little, but ingenious, *Syntagma Philosophiae Epicuri*, if I had more seasonably been acquainted with it.

But whether we have treated of the nature and origin of forms and qualities in a more comprehensive way than others, whether we have by new and fit similitudes and examples and other means rendered it more intelligible than they have done, whether we have added any considerable number of notions and arguments towards the completing and confirming of the proposed hypothesis, whether we have with reason dismissed arguments unfit to be relied on, and whether we have proposed some notions and arguments so warily as to keep them from being liable to exceptions or evasions whereto they were obnoxious as others have proposed them – whether (I say) we have done all or any of these in the first or speculative part of this treatise, we willingly leave the reader to judge. But in the second or historical part of it, perhaps he will be invited to grant that we have done that part of physics we have been treating of some little service: since by the lovers of real learning it was very much wished that the doctrines of the new philosophy (as it is called) were backed by particular experiments, the want of which I have endeavoured to supply, by annexing some whose nature and novelty I am made believe will render them as well acceptable as instructive. For though, that I might not anticipate what belongs to other papers, I did not make the last section consist of above a decade of them – and though, for the reasons intimated in the advertisements premised to them, I did not expressly mention to Pyrophilus all that I could have told him about them – yet I have been careful so to choose them, and to interweave hints in delivering them, that a sagacious reader who shall have the curiosity to try them heedfully, and make reflections on the several phenomena that in likelihood will occur to him, will (if I mistake not) receive no contemptible information, as of some other things, so particularly about the nature of mixtions (which I take to be one of the most important and useful, though neglected and ill understood, doctrines of the practical part of physics), and may probably light upon more than he expects, or I have fully delivered, and perhaps too more than I foresaw.

And though some virtuosi, more conversant perhaps with things than books, presuming the decay of the Peripatetic philosophy to be everywhere as great as it is among them in England, may think that a doctrine which they look on as expiring need not have been so solicitously confuted, yet those that know how deep rooting this philosophy has taken (both elsewhere, and particularly) in those academies where it has flourished for many ages – and in some of which it is, exclusively to the Mechanical philosophy, watered and fenced by their statutes or their superiors – and he that also knows how much more easy some (more subtle than candid) wits find it plausibly to defend an error than ingenuously to confess it, will not wonder that I should think that a doctrine so advantaged, though it be too erroneous to be feared, is yet too considerable to be despised. And not to question whether several of those that most contemn the favourers of the Peripatetic hypothesis, as the later discoveries have reduced them to reform it, be not the least provided to answer their arguments – (not to question this, I say) there are divers of our adversaries (misled only by education, and morally harmless pre-judices) who do so much deserve a better cause, than that which needs all their subtlety without being worthy of it, that I shall think more pains than I have taken very usefully bestowed, if my arguments and experiments prove so happy as to undeceive persons whose parts, too unluckily confined to narrow and fruitless notions, would render them illustrious champions for the truths they are able so subtly to oppose; and who might questionless perform considerable things, if they employed as much dexterity to expound the mysteries of Nature as the riddles of the schoolmen, and laid out their wit and industry to surmount the obscurity of her works instead of that of Aristotle's.

There might be a few other particulars fit to be taken notice of in this preface, but, finding that I had already mentioned them in that which I had addressed to Pyrophilus, my haste makes me willing rather to refer the reader thither for them, than alter that or lengthen this (which I should think much too long already, if it were not possible that it may hereafter prove preliminary to more papers than these it is now premised to). So that there remains but one advertisement necessary to be given here, namely that, whereas in the following notes I several times speak of the author of the *Essay of Saltpetre* as of a third person, the occasion of that was that when these notes, and some about particular qualities, were written, I had a design to make two distinct sorts of annotations upon that essay, in the *former* whereof (which now comes forth) I assumed the person of a Corpuscularian, and discoursed at that rate; but I had thoughts too (in case God were pleased to grant me life and opportunity) to take a *second* review, both of the treatise itself and of the notes on it, and on that occasion to add what my riper thoughts and further experience might suggest unto me. And that in my animadversions I might, with the more freedom and conveniency, add, explain, alter, and even retract, as I should see cause, I thought it not amiss to write them as if they were made on the work of another: by which intimation the reader may be assisted to guess how much I intended in the following discourse (in which, as in the prefaces belonging to it, I play the Corpuscularian) to reserve myself the freedom of questioning and correcting, upon the designed review, anything delivered in these notes; and how much more it was in them my design to bring Pyrophilus experiments and queries to illustrate obscure matters, than by hasty assertions to dogmatize about them.

THE PREFACE

The origin, Pyrophilus, and nature of the qualities of bodies is a subject that I have long looked upon as one of the most important and useful that the naturalist can pitch upon for his contemplation. For the knowledge we have of the bodies without us being, for the most part, fetched from the informations the mind receives by the senses, we scarce know anything else in bodies, upon whose account they can work upon our senses, save their qualities; for as to the substantial forms which some imagine to be in all natural bodies, it is not half so evident that there are such, as it is that the wisest of those that do admit them confess that they do not well know them.[c] And as it is by their qualities that bodies act immediately upon our senses, so it is by virtue of those attributes likewise that they act upon other bodies, and by that action produce in them, and oftentimes in themselves, those changes that sometimes we call *alterations*,° and sometimes *generation*° or *corruption*.° | And it is chiefly by the knowledge, such as it is, that experience (not art) hath taught us of these differing qualities of bodies, that we are enabled, by a due application of agents to patients, to exercise the little empire that we have either acquired or regained over the creatures. +

But I think not the contemplation of qualities more noble and useful than I find it difficult; for what is wont to be taught us of qualities in the Schools is so slight and ill-grounded that it may be doubted whether they have not rather obscured than illustrated the things they should have explained. And I was quickly discouraged from expecting to learn much from them of the nature of divers particular qualities, when I found that, except some few which they tell you in general may be deduced (by ways they leave those to guess at that can) from those four qualities they are pleased to call the *first*,° they confess that the rest spring from those forms of bodies whose particular natures the judiciousest of them acknowledge they cannot comprehend. And Aristotle himself not only doth (as we shall see anon) give us of quality in general (which yet seems far more easily definable than many a particular quality) no other than

---

[c] '*Nego tibi ullam esse formam nobis notam plene et plane, nostramque scientiam esse umbram in sole.*' – Scaliger (of whose confessions to the same purpose more are cited hereafter).

such a definition as is as obscure as the thing to be declared by it; but I observe, not without some wonder, that in his eight books of *Physics*, where he professedly treats of the general affections of natural things, he leaves out the doctrine of qualities, as after him Magirus and divers other writers of the Peripatetic physiology have done: which (by the way) I cannot but look upon as an omission, since qualities do as well seem to belong to natural bodies, generally considered, as place, time, motion, and those other things which upon that account are wont to be treated of in the general part of natural philosophy. The most ingenious Descartes has something concerning some qualities: but though, for reasons elsewhere expressed, I have purposely forborne to peruse his system of philosophy, yet I find by turning over the leaves that he has left most of the other qualities untreated of; and of those that are more properly called *sensible*,° he speaks but very briefly and generally, rather considering what they do upon the organs of sense, than what changes happen in the objects themselves to make them cause in us a perception sometimes of one quality and sometimes of another. Besides that his explications do many of them so depend upon his peculiar notions (of a *materia subtilis, globuli secundi elementi*, and the like), and these, as it became so great a person, he has so interwoven with the rest of his hypothesis, that they can seldom be made use of without adopting his whole philosophy. Epicurus indeed, and his scholiast Lucretius, have given some good hints concerning the nature of some few qualities. But beside that even these explications are divers of them either doubtful, or imperfect, or both, there are many other qualities which are left for others to treat of.+

And this is the second and main difficulty which I find in investigating the nature of qualities: namely, that whatever be to be thought of the general theories of Aristotle or other philosophers concerning qualities, we evidently want that upon which a theory, to be solid and useful, must be built – I mean an experimental history of them. And this we so want that, except perhaps what mathematicians have done concerning sounds, and the observations (rather than experiments) that our illustrious Verulam hath (in some few pages) said of heat in his short essay *De Forma Calidi*, I know not any one quality of which any author has yet given us an anything competent history. These things I mention to you, Pyrophilus, not at all to derogate from those great men, whose design seems rather to have been to deliver principles and summaries of philosophy than to insist upon particulars: but for this purpose, that, since the nature of qualities is so *beneficial* a speculation, my labours may not be looked upon as wholly useless, though I can contribute but a little to the clearing of it; and that, since it is so *abstruse* a subject, I may be pardoned if I sometimes miss the mark and leave divers things uncompleted, that being but what such great philosophers have done before me.

But, Pyrophilus, before I proceed to give you my notes upon this part of our author's essay, that you may rightly understand my intention in them it will be requisite to give you three or four advertisements.

And first: Whenever I shall speak indefinitely of substantial forms, I would always be understood to except the reasonable soul that is said to inform the human body, which declaration I here desire may be taken notice of once for all.

Secondly: Nor am I willing to treat of the origin of qualities in beasts, partly because I would not be engaged to examine of what nature their souls are, and partly because it is difficult in most cases (at least for one that is compassionate enough) either to make experiments upon living animals, or to judge what influence their life may have upon the change of qualities produced by such experiments.

Thirdly: The occasion of the following reflections being only this, that our author, in that part of his *Essay concerning Saltpetre* whereto these notes refer, does briefly intimate some notions about the nature and origin of qualities, you must not expect that I, whose method leads me but to write some notes upon this and some other parts of this essay, should make solemn or elaborate discourses concerning the nature of particular qualities, and that I should fully deliver my own apprehensions concerning those subjects. For, as I elsewhere sufficiently intimate that in these first notes I write as a *Corpuscularian*, and set down those things only that seem to have a tendency to illustrate or countenance the notions or fancies implied in our author's essay, so I must here tell you that I neither have now the leisure, nor pretend to the skill, to deliver fully the history or to explicate particularly the nature of each several quality.

Fourthly: But I consider that the Schools have of late much amused the world with a way they have got of referring all natural effects to certain entities that they call *real qualities*, and accordingly attribute to them a nature distinct from the modification of the matter they belong to, and in some cases separable from all matter whatsoever: by which means they have, as far forth as their doctrine is acquiesced in, made it thought needless or hopeless for men to employ their industry in searching into the nature of particular qualities and their effects. As, if (for instance) it be demanded how snow comes to dazzle the eyes, they will answer that it is by a *quality* of whiteness that is in it, which makes all very white bodies produce the same effect; and if you ask what this whiteness is, they will tell you no more in substance than that it is a *real entity*, which denominates the parcel of matter to which it is joined *white*;° and if you further enquire what this real entity which they call a *quality*° is, you will find, as we shall see anon, that they either speak of it much after the same rate that they do of their substantial forms (as indeed some of the modernest teach that a quality affects the matter it belongs to *per modum formae secundariae*, as they speak), or at least they will not explicate it more intelligibly.| And accordingly, if you further ask them how white bodies in general do rather produce this effect of dazzling the eyes than green or blue ones, instead of being told that the former sort of bodies reflect outwards – and so to the eye – far more of the incident light than the latter, you shall perchance be told that it is their respective natures so to act: by which way of dispatching difficulties they make it very *easy* to solve all the phenomena of nature in general, but make men think it *impossible* to explicate almost any of them in particular.

And though the unsatisfactoriness and barrenness of the School philosophy have persuaded a great many learned men, especially physicians, to substitute the chemists' three principles instead of those of the Schools, and though I have a very good opinion of chemistry itself, as it is a practical art, yet, as it is by chemists pretended to contain a system of theorical principles of philosophy, I fear it will afford but[6] very little satisfaction to a severe enquirer into the nature of qualities. For besides that, as we shall more particularly see anon, there are many qualities which cannot with any probability be deduced from any of the three principles, those that are ascribed to one or other of them cannot intelligibly be explicated without recourse to the more comprehensive principles of the Corpuscularian philosophy: to tell us, for instance, that all solidity proceeds from salt only informing us (where it can plausibly be pretended) *in what* material principle or *ingredient* that quality *resides*, not *how* it is *produced*; for this doth not teach us (for example)

how water even in exactly-closed vessels comes to be frozen into ice –
that is, turned from a fluid to a solid body, without the accession of a
saline ingredient (which I have not yet found pretended, especially
glass being held impervious to salts). Wherefore, Pyrophilus, I
thought it might much conduce to the understanding the nature of
qualities to show how they are generated; and by the same way I
hoped it might remove in some measure the obstacle that these dark
and narrow theories of the Peripatetics and chemists may prove to
the advancement of solid and useful philosophy. +

That, then, which I chiefly aim at is to make it probable to you by
experiments (which I think hath not yet been done) that almost all
sorts of qualities, most of which have been by the Schools either left
unexplicated, or generally referred to I know not what
incomprehensible substantial forms, *may* be produced mechanically
– I mean by such corporeal agents as do not appear either to work
otherwise than by virtue of the motion, size, figure, and contrivance,
of their own parts (which attributes I call the *mechanical affections*° of
matter, because to them men willingly refer the various operations of
mechanical engines); or to produce the new qualities, exhibited by
those bodies their action changes, by any other way than by
changing the *texture*, or *motion*, or some other *mechanical affection*, of the
body wrought upon. And this if I can in any passable measure do,
though but in a general way, in some or other of each of these three
sorts into which the Peripatetics are wont to divide the qualities of
bodies, I hope I shall have done no useless piece of service to natural
philosophy: partly by exciting you and your learned friends to
enquire after more intelligible and satisfactory ways of explicating
qualities, and partly by *beginning* such a collection of materials
towards the *history* of those qualities that I shall the most largely
insist on – as heat, colours, fluidity, and firmness – as may invite you
and other ingenious men to contribute also their experiments and
observations to so useful a work, and thereby lay a foundation
whereon you, and perhaps I, may superstruct a more distinct and
explicit theory of qualities than I shall at present adventure at. And
though I know that some of the things my experiments tend to
manifest may likewise be confirmed by the more obvious phenomena
of nature, yet I presume you will not dislike my choosing to entertain
you with the former (though without at all despising or so much as
strictly forbearing to employ the latter), because the changes of
qualities made by our experiments will, for the most part, be more

quick and conspicuous; and the agents made use of to produce them being of our own applying, and oftentimes of our own preparation, we may be thereby assisted the better to judge of what they are, and to make an estimate of what it is they do.

CONSIDERATIONS AND EXPERIMENTS TOUCHING THE ORIGIN OF QUALITIES AND FORMS: THE THEORICAL PART

That before I descend to particulars I may, Pyrophilus, furnish you with some general apprehension of the doctrine (or rather the *hypothesis*) which is to be collated with, and to be either confirmed or disproved by, the historical truths that will be delivered concerning particular qualities (and forms), I will assume the person of a Corpuscularian, and here at the entrance give you (in a general way) a brief account of the hypothesis itself, as it concerns the origin of qualities (and forms); and for distinction's sake, I shall comprise it in the eight following particulars, which, that the whole scheme may be the better comprehended and, as it were, surveyed under one prospect, I shall do little more than barely propose them that either seem evident enough by their own light, or may without prejudice have divers of their proofs reserved for proper places in the following part of this treatise.[7]

I. I agree with the generality of philosophers, so far as to allow that there is one catholic or universal matter common to all bodies, by which I mean a substance extended, divisible, and impenetrable.

II. But because, this matter being in its own nature but one, the diversity we see in bodies must necessarily arise from somewhat else than the matter they consist of, and since we see not how there could be any change in matter if all its (actual or designable) parts were perpetually at rest among themselves, it will follow that, to discriminate the catholic matter into variety of natural bodies, it must have motion in some or all its designable parts; and that motion must have various tendencies, that which is in this part of the matter tending one way, and that which is in that part tending another: as we plainly see in the universe or general mass of matter there is really a great quantity of motion, and that variously determined, and that yet divers portions of matter are at rest.

That there is local motion in many parts of matter is manifest to sense, but how matter came by this motion was of old, and is still, hotly disputed of. For the ancient Corpuscularian philosophers (whose doctrine in most other points, though not in all, we are the most inclinable to), not acknowledging an Author of the universe, were thereby reduced to make motion congenite to matter, and consequently coeval with it: but since local motion, or an endeavour at it, is not included in the nature of matter, which is as much matter when it rests as when it moves, and since we see that the same portion of matter may from motion be reduced to rest, and, after it hath continued at rest as long as other bodies do not put it out of that state, may by external agents be set a-moving again, I, who am not wont to think a man the worse naturalist for not being an atheist, shall not scruple to say with an eminent philosopher of old – whom I find to have proposed among the Greeks that opinion (for the main) that the excellent Descartes hath revived amongst us – that the origin of motion in matter is from God; and not only so, but that thinking it very unfit to be believed that matter, barely put into motion and then left to itself, should casually constitute this beautiful and orderly world, I think also further that the wise Author of things did, by establishing the laws of motion among bodies, and by guiding the first motions of the small parts of matter, bring them to convene after the manner requisite to compose the world, and especially did contrive those curious and elaborate engines, the bodies of living creatures, endowing most of them with a power of propagating their species. But though these things are my persuasions, yet, because they are not necessary to be supposed here – where I do not pretend to deliver any complete discourse of the principles of natural philosophy, but only to touch upon such notions as are requisite to explicate the origin of qualities and forms – I shall pass on to what remains, as soon as I have taken notice that *local motion seems to be indeed the principal amongst second causes, and the grand agent of all that happens in nature.* For though bulk, figure, rest, situation, and texture, do concur to the phenomena of nature, yet in comparison of motion they seem to be in many cases effects, and in many others little better than *conditions*, or *requisites*, or causes *sine quibus non*, which modify the operation that one part of matter by virtue of its motion hath upon another: as in a watch the number, the figure, and coaptation, of the wheels and other parts, is requisite to the showing the hour and doing the other things that may be performed by the watch, but till these parts be actually put into

motion all their other affections remain inefficacious; and so in a
key, though if[8] it were too big or too little, or if its shape were
incongruous to that of the cavity of the lock, it would be unfit to be
used as a key though it were put into motion, yet, let its bigness and
figure be never so fit, unless actual motion intervene it will never lock
or unlock anything, as without the like actual motion neither a knife
nor razor will actually cut, how much soever their shape and other
qualities may fit them to do so. And so brimstone, what disposition
of parts soever it have to be turned into flame, would never be
kindled unless some actual fire or other parcel of vehemently and
variously agitated matter should put the sulphureous corpuscles into
a very brisk motion.

III. These two grand and most catholic principles of bodies,
matter and motion, being thus established, it will follow both that
matter must be actually divided into parts, that being the genuine
effect of variously determined motion; and that each of the primitive
fragments, or other distinct and entire masses of matter, must have
two attributes – its own magnitude, or rather *size*, and its own *figure*
or *shape*. And since experience shows us (especially that which is
afforded us by chemical operations, in many of which matter is
divided into parts too small to be singly sensible) that this division of
matter is frequently made into insensible corpuscles or particles, we
may conclude that the minutest fragments, as well as the biggest
masses, of the universal matter are likewise endowed each with its
peculiar bulk and shape. For, being a finite body, its dimensions
must be terminated and measurable; and though it may change its
figure, yet for the same reason it must necessarily have *some figure* or
other. So that now we have found out and must admit three essential
properties of each entire or undivided, though insensible, part of
matter: namely, *magnitude* (by which I mean not quantity in general,
but a determined quantity, which we in English oftentimes call the
size of a body), *shape*, and either *motion* or *rest* (for betwixt them two
there is no mean), the two first of which may be called *inseparable
accidents* of each distinct part of matter – *inseparable* because, being
extended and yet finite, it is physically impossible that it should be
devoid of some bulk or other and some determinate shape or other,
and yet *accidents* because that, whether or no the shape can by
physical agents be altered, or the body subdivided, yet mentally
both the one and the other may be done, the whole essence of matter
remaining undestroyed.

Whether these accidents may not conveniently enough be called the *moods*° or *primary affections*° of bodies, to distinguish them from those less simple qualities (as colours, tastes, and odours) that belong to bodies upon their account, or whether, with the Epicureans, they may not be called the *conjuncts*° of the smallest parts of matter, I shall not now stay to consider; but one thing the modern Schools are wont to teach concerning accidents[9] is too repugnant to our present doctrine to be in this place quite omitted: namely, that there are in natural bodies store of *real qualities* and other *real accidents*, which not only are no moods of matter, but are real entities distinct from it, and, according to the doctrine of many modern schoolmen, may *exist separate* from all matter whatsoever.+

To clear this point a little, we must take notice that *accident* is among logicians and philosophers used in two several senses. For sometimes it is opposed to the 4th predicable (*property*), and is then defined 'that which may be present or absent without the destruction of the subject' – as a man may be sick or well, and a wall white or not white, and yet the one be still a man, the other a wall. And this is called in the Schools *accidens praedicabile*, to distinguish it from what they call *accidens praedicamentale*, which is opposed to substance. For when things are divided by logicians into 10 predicaments or highest genuses of things, substance making one of them, all the nine other are of accidents: and as substance is commonly defined to be a thing that subsists of itself and is the subject of accidents (or, more plainly, a real entity or thing that needs not any (*created*) being, that it may exist), so an accident is said commonly to be *id cuius esse est inesse*; and therefore Aristotle, who usually calls substances simply ὄντα, *entities*,° most commonly calls accidents ὄντος ὄντα, *entities of entities*,° these needing the existence of some substance or other in which they may be, as in their subject of inhesion. And because logicians make it the discriminating note of substance and accident that the former is a thing that cannot be in another as in its subject of inhesion, it is requisite to know that, according to them, that is said to *be in a subject* which hath these three conditions: that, however it (1) *be in another thing*, (2) *is not in it as a part*, and (3) *cannot exist separately* from the thing or subject wherein it is: as a white wall is the subject of inhesion of the whiteness we see in it, which selfsame whiteness though it be not in the wall as a part of it, yet cannot the selfsame whiteness, according to our logicians, exist anywhere out of the wall, though many other bodies may have the like degree of whiteness. +

This premised, it will not be hard to discover the falsity of the lately-mentioned scholastic opinion touching real qualities and accidents, their doctrine about which does, I confess, appear to me to be either unintelligible or manifestly contradictious. For, speaking in a physical sense, if they will not allow these accidents to be modes of matter, but entities really distinct from it and in some cases separable from all matter, they make them indeed accidents in name, but represent them under such a notion as belongs only to substances – the nature of a substance consisting in this, that it can subsist of itself without being in anything else as in a subject of inhesion – so that to tell us that a quality or other accident may subsist without a subject is indeed, whatever they please to call it, to allow it the true nature of substance; nor will their groundless distinctions do any more than keep them from seeming to contradict themselves in words, whilst unprepossessed persons see that they do it in effect. Nor could I ever find it intelligibly made out what these real qualities may be, that they deny to be either matter, or modes of matter, or immaterial substances. When a bowl runs along or lies still, that *motion*, or *rest*, or *globous figure*, of the bowl is not *nothing*, and yet it[10] is not any *part* of the bowl, whose whole substance would remain though it wanted which you please of these accidents; and to make them *real* and *physical* entities (for we have not here to do either with *logical* or *metaphysical* ones) is as if, because we may consider the same man sitting, standing, running, thirsty, hungry, weary, &c., we should make each of these a distinct entity, as we do give some of them (as hunger, weariness, &c.) distinct names: whereas the subject of all these qualities is but the same man, as he is considered with circumstances that make him appear different in one case from what he appears in another. And it may be very useful to our present scope to observe that not only diversity of *names*, but even diversity of *definitions*, doth not always infer a diversity of *physical entities* in the subject whereunto they are attributed. For it happens in many of the physical attributes of a body, as in those other cases wherein a man that is a father, a husband, a master, a prince, &c., may have a peculiar definition (such as the nature of the thing will bear) belong unto him in each of these capacities; and yet the man in himself considered is but the same man, who, in respect of differing capacities or relations to other things, is called by differing names, and described by various definitions, which yet (as I was saying) conclude not so many real and distinct entities in the person so variously denominated.

An excursion about the relative nature of physical qualities

But because I take this notion to be of no small importance towards the avoiding of the grand mistake that hath hitherto obtained about the nature of qualities, it will be worth while to illustrate it a little farther.+

We may consider, then, that when Tubal Cain, or whoever else were the smith that invented *locks* and *keys*, had made his first lock (for we may reasonably suppose him to have made that before the *key*, though the comparison may be made use of without that supposition), that was only a piece of iron contrived into such a shape; and when afterwards he made a key to that lock, that also in itself considered was nothing but a piece of iron of such a determinate figure. But in regard that these two pieces of iron might now be applied to one another after a certain manner, and that there was a congruity betwixt the wards of the lock and those of the key, the lock and the key did each of them now obtain a new capacity; and it became a main part of the notion and description of a *lock*° that it was capable of being made to lock or unlock by that other piece of iron we call a *key*,° and it was looked upon as a peculiar faculty and power in the key that it was fitted to open and shut the lock: and yet by these new attributes there was not added any real or physical entity either to the lock or to the key, each of them remaining indeed nothing but the same piece of iron, just so shaped as it was before. And when our smith made other keys of differing bignesses or with differing wards, though the first lock was not to be opened by any of those keys, yet that indisposition, however it might be considered as a peculiar power of resisting this or that key, and might serve to discriminate it sufficiently from the locks those keys belonged to, was nothing new in the lock, or distinct from the figure it had before those keys were made. To carry this comparison a little further, let me add that, though one that would have defined the first lock and the first key would have given them distinct definitions with reference to each other,[11] yet (as I was saying) these definitions, being given but upon the score of certain respects which the defined bodies had one to another, would not infer that these two iron instruments did physically differ otherwise than in the figure, size, or contrivement, of the iron whereof each of them consisted. And proportionably hereunto, I do not see why we may not conceive that, as to those qualities (for instance) which we call *sensible*,° though, by virtue of a certain congruity or incongruity in point of figure or texture (or other mechanical attributes) to our sensories, the portions of matter they modify are enabled to produce various effects upon whose account we make bodies to be endowed with qualities, yet they are not in the bodies that are endowed with them any real or distinct entities, or differing from the matter itself furnished with such a determinate bigness, shape, or other mechanical modifications. Thus, though the modern goldsmiths and refiners reckon amongst the most distinguishing qualities of gold, by which men may be certain of its being true and not sophisticated, that it[12] is easily dissoluble in *aqua regis*, and that *aqua fortis* will not work upon it, yet these attributes are not in the gold anything distinct from its peculiar texture; nor is the gold we have now of any other nature than it was in Pliny's time, when *aqua fortis* and *aqua regis* had not been found out (at least in these parts of the world), and were utterly unknown to the Roman goldsmiths.+

And this example I have the rather pitched upon, because it affords me an opportunity to represent that, unless we admit the doctrine I have been proposing, we must admit that a body may have an almost infinite number of new real entities accruing to it without the intervention of any physical change in the body itself: as, for example, gold was the same natural body immediately before *aqua regis* and *aqua fortis* were first made, as it was immediately after, and yet now it is reckoned amongst its principal properties that it is dissoluble by the former of those two menstruums, and that it is not, like other metals, dissoluble or corrodible by the latter. And if one should invent another menstruum (as possibly I may think myself master of such a one), that will but in part dissolve pure gold, and change some part of it into another metalline body, there will then arise another new property whereby to distinguish that from other metals; and yet the nature of gold is not a whit other now than it was before this last menstruum was first made. There are some bodies not cathartic nor sudorific, with some of which gold being joined acquires a purgative virtue, and with others a power to procure sweat. And, in a word, nature herself doth sometimes otherwise, and sometimes by chance, produce so many things that have new relations unto others; and art, especially assisted by chemistry, may, by variously dissipating natural bodies, or compounding either them or their constituent parts with one another, make such an innumerable company of new productions, that will each of them have new operations either immediately upon our sensories or upon other bodies whose changes we are able to perceive, that no man can know but that the most familiar bodies may have multitudes of qualities that he dreams not of: and a considering man will hardly imagine that so numerous a crowd of real physical entities can accrue to a body, whilst in the judgement of all our senses it remains unchanged and the same that it was before.

To clear this a little farther, we may add that beaten glass is commonly reckoned among poisons; and (to skip what is mentioned out of Sanctorius of the dysentery procured by the fragments of it) I remember Cardan hath a story that, in a cloister where he had a patient then like to die of torments in the stomach, two other nuns had been already killed by a distracted woman that, having casually got free, had mixed beaten glass with peas that were eaten by these three, and divers others[13] of the sisters (who yet escaped unharmed).[d] Now though the powers of poisons be not only looked upon as *real* qualities, but are reckoned among the *abstrusest* ones, yet this deleterious faculty, which is supposed to be a peculiar and superadded entity in the beaten glass, is really nothing distinct from the glass itself (which, though a concrete made up of those innocent ingredients, salt and ashes, is yet a hard and stiff body), as it is furnished with that determinate bigness and figure of parts which have been acquired by comminution. For these glassy fragments, being many and rigid and somewhat small (without yet being so small as dust), and endowed with sharp points and cutting edges, are enabled by these mechanical affections to pierce or wound the tender membranes of the stomach and guts, and cut the slender vessels that they meet with there: whereby naturally ensue great gripings and contortions of the injured parts, and oftentimes bloody fluxes, occasioned by the perforation of the capillary arteries and the great irritation of the expulsive faculty, and sometimes also not only horrid convulsions, by consent of the brain and cerebellum with some of the nervous or membranous parts that happen to be hurt, but also dropsies, occasioned by the great loss of blood we were just now speaking of. And it agrees very well with this conjecture, that

[d] G. Cardano, *Contradicentes Medici*, lib. II, tract. v, contradict. 9.

beaten glass hath divers times been observed to have done no mischief to animals that have swallowed it. For there is no reason it should, in case the corpuscles of the powder[14] chance to be so small as not to be fit to wound the guts – which are usually lined with a slimy substance, wherein very minute powders may be as it were sheathed, and by that means hindered from hurting the guts (insomuch that a fragment of glass with three very sharp corners hath been observed to have for above eighteen months lain inoffensive even in a nervous and very sensible part of the body[e]) – out of which they may, with the grosser excrements of the lower belly, be harmlessly excluded, especially in some individuals whose guts and stomach too may be of a much stronger texture, and better lined or stuffed with gross and slimy matter, than those of others. And accordingly we see that the fragments of sapphires, crystals, and even rubies, which are much harder than glass, are innocently though perhaps not very effectually used by physicians (and I have several times taken that without inconvenience) in cordial compositions, because of their being, by grinding, reduced to a powder too subtle to excoriate or grate upon the stomach or guts; and probably it was upon some such account that that happened which is related by Cardan in the same place: namely, that though the three nuns we have been speaking of were poisoned by the glass, yet many others who ate of the other portions of the same mingled peas received no mischief thereby. (But of this subject more elsewhere.[f])

And this puts me in mind to add that the multiplicity of qualities that are sometimes to be met with in the same natural bodies needs not make men reject the opinion we have been proposing, by persuading them that so many differing attributes as may be sometimes found in one and the same natural body cannot proceed from the bare texture and other mechanical affections of its matter. For we must consider each body not barely as it is in itself an entire and distinct portion of matter, but as it is a part of the universe, and

---

[e] This memorable accident happened to a senator of Berne, who was cured by the experienced Fabricius Hildanus, that gives a long account of it to the learned Horstius, among whose *Observations* it is extant (lib. II, observ. 35), who ascribes the indolence of the part, whilst uncompressed, to some slimy juice (familiar enough to those tendinous parts) wherein the glassy fragment was, as it were, bedded.

[f] In those *Notes about Occult Qualities* where the deleterious faculty attributed to diamonds is considered.

consequently placed among a great number and variety of other bodies, upon which it may act and by which it may be acted on in many ways (or upon many accounts), each of which men are wont to fancy as a distinct power or quality in the body by which those actions, or in which those passions, are produced. For if we thus consider things, we shall not much wonder that a portion of matter, that is indeed endowed but with a very few mechanical affections – as such a determinate texture and motion – but is placed among a multitude of other bodies that differ in those attributes from it and one another, should be capable of having a great number and variety of relations to those other bodies, and consequently should be thought to have many distinct inherent qualities, by such as look upon those several relations or respects it may have to bodies without it as real and distinct entities implanted in the body itself. When a curious watch is going, though the spring be that which puts all the parts into motion, yet we do not fancy (as an Indian or Chinese would perchance do) in this spring one faculty to move the index uniformly round the dial-plate, another to strike the hour, and perhaps a third to give an alarm, or show the age of the moon or the tides: all the action of the spring (which is but a flexible piece of steel forcibly coiled together) being but an endeavour to dilate or unbind itself, and the rest being performed by the various respects it hath to the several bodies (that compose the watch) among which it is placed, and which they have one to another. We all know that the sun hath a power to harden clay, and soften wax, and melt butter, and thaw ice, and turn water into vapours, and make air expand itself in weather-glasses, and contribute to blanch linen, and make the white skin of the face swarthy and mowed grass yellow, and ripen fruit, hatch the eggs of silk-worms, caterpillars and the like insects, and perform I know not how many other things, divers of which seem contrary effects; and yet these are not distinct powers or faculties in the sun, but only the productions of its heat (which itself is but the brisk and confused local motion of the minute parts of a body), diversified by the differing textures of the body that it chances to work upon, and the condition of the other bodies that are concerned in the operation. And therefore, whether the sun in some cases have any influence at all distinct from its light and heat, we see that all those phenomena we have thought fit to name are producible by the heat of the common culinary fire duly applied and regulated. And so, to give an instance of another kind, when, some years since, to try some experiments about the propagation of motion with bodies less capable of being battered by one another than those that have been formerly employed, I caused some solid balls of iron, skilfully hardened and exquisitely shaped and glazed, to be purposely made, each of these polished balls was a spherical looking-glass, which, placed in the midst of a room, would exhibit the images of the objects round about it in a very regular and pleasing perspective. It would contract the image and reflect the beams of the sun after a manner differing from flat and from convex looking-glasses. It would in a neat perspective lessen the image of him that looked upon it, and bend it, and it would show that image as if it were behind the surface and within the solid substance of the sphere; and, in sum, it had all those distinct and some of them wonderful properties which either ancient or modern writers of catoptrics have demonstrated to belong to spherical specula as such. And yet the globe, furnished with all these properties and affections, was but the iron itself reduced by the artificer to a spherical figure (for the glass that made it specular was not distinct from the superficial parts of the iron, reduced all of them to a physically equal distance from the centre). And of specula, spherical enough as to sense, you may make store in a trice, by breaking a large drop of quicksilver into several little ones, each of which will serve for objects placed pretty near it, and the smaller of which (being the least depressed in the middle by their own weight, and consequently more perfectly globous) may, with a good microscope placed in a window, afford you no unpleasant prospect of the neighbouring objects; and yet to reduce a parcel of stagnant quicksilver, which will much emulate a flat looking-glass, into many of these little spherical specula, whose properties are so differing from those of plane ones, there intervenes nothing but a slight local motion which, in the twinkling of an eye, changeth the figure of the selfsame matter.

I have said thus much, Pyrophilus, to remove the mistake that *everything men are wont to call a quality* must needs be a real and physical entity, because of the importance of the subject. And yet I have omitted some things that might have been pertinently added, partly because I may hereafter have opportunity to take them in, and partly because I would not any farther lengthen this *excursion*, which yet I must not conclude till I have added this short advertisement:| that I have chosen to declare what I mean by *qualities*° rather by examples than definitions, partly because, being immediately or reductively the objects of sense, men generally understand pretty well what one another mean when they are spoken of (as to say that the taste of such a thing is saline or sour, or that such a sound is melodious, shrill, or jarring (especially if, when we speak of sensible qualities, we add some enumeration of particular subjects wherein they do the most eminently reside), will make a man as soon understood as if he should go about to give logical definitions of those qualities); and partly because the notions of things are not yet so well stated and agreed on but that it is many times difficult to assign their true genuses. And Aristotle himself doth not only define *accidents* without setting down their genus, but when he comes to define *qualities*, he tells us that *quality is that by which a thing is said to be qualis* – where I would have you take notice both that in his definition he omits the genus, and that it is no such easy thing to give a very good definition of qualities, since he that is reputed the great master of logic, where he pretends to give us one, doth but upon the matter define the thing by the same thing; for it is supposed to be as little known what *qualis* is as what *qualitas* is, and methinks he does just as if I should define whiteness to be that for which a thing is called white, or virtue that for which a man is said to be virtuous.[g] Besides that I much doubt whether his definition be not untrue as well as obscure. For to the question '*qualis res est?*' answer may be returned out of *some*, if not *all*, of the other *predicaments of accidents*: which some of the modern logicians being aware of, they have endeavoured to salve the matter with certain cautions and limitations, which however they may argue the devisers to be

[g] Since the writing of this the author found that some of the eminentest of the modern schoolmen themselves have been, as well as he, unsatisfied with the Aristotelian definition of quality, concerning which (not to mention Revius, a learned Protestant annotator upon Suarez) Arriaga says (*Disputationes Metaphysicae*, disp. 5, sect. 2, subs. 1): '*Per hanc nihil explicatur, nam de hoc quaerimus quid sit esse quale: dices, habere qualitatem. Bonus circulus: qualitas est id quo quis fit qualis, et esse qualem est habere qualitatem.*' And even the famous Jesuit Suarez, though he endeavours to excuse it, yet confesseth that it leaves the proper notion of quality as obscure to us as before: '*Quae definitio,*' saith he, '*licet ea ratione essentialis videatur, quod detur per habitudinem ad effectum formalem, quem omnis forma essentialiter respicit, tamen quod ad nos spectat, aeque obscura nobis manet propria ratio qualitatis.*' – Suarez, *Disputationes Metaphysicae*, disp. 42, sect. 1, subs. 1. But Hurtadus (*Disputationes Metaphysicae*, disp. 14, sect. 1) speaks more boldly, telling us roundly that it is '*non tam definitio, quam inanis quaedam nugatio*' – which makes me the more wonder that a famous Cartesian (whom I forbear to name) should content himself to give us such an insignificant, or at least superficial, definition of quality.

ingenious, do, for aught I can discern, leave us still to seek for a right and intelligible definition of quality in general; though to give such a one be probably a much easier task than to define many qualities that may be named in particular, as saltness, sourness, green, blue, and many others, which when we hear named, every man knows what is meant by them, though no man (that I know of) hath been able to give accurate definitions of them.

IV. And if we should conceive that all the rest of the universe were annihilated, except any of these entire and undivided corpuscles (treated of in the 3rd particular foregoing), it is hard to say what could be attributed to it besides matter, motion (or rest), bulk, and shape (whence, by the way, you may take notice that bulk, though usually taken in a comparative sense, is in our sense an absolute thing, since a body would have it though there were no other in the world). But now, there being actually in the universe great multitudes of corpuscles mingled among themselves, there arise, in any distinct portion of matter which a number of them make up, two new accidents or events: the one doth more relate to each particular corpuscle in reference to the (really or supposedly) stable bodies about it, namely its *posture* (whether erected, inclined, or horizontal); and when two or more of such bodies are placed one by another, the manner of their being so placed, as one besides another or one behind another, may be called their *order* – as, I remember, Aristotle, in his *Metaphysics*, lib. I, cap. 4, recites this example out of the ancient Corpuscularians, that **A** *and* **N** *differ in figure, and* **AN** *and* **NA** *in order,* **Z** *and* **N** *in situation* – and indeed posture and order seem both of them reducible to situation. And when many corpuscles do so convene together as to compose any distinct body, as a stone or a metal, then from their other accidents (or modes), and from these two last mentioned, there doth emerge a certain disposition or contrivance of parts in the whole, which we may call the *texture* of it.

V. And if we should conceive all the rest of the universe to be annihilated, save one such body – suppose a metal or a stone – it were hard to show that there is physically anything more in it than matter and the accidents we have already named. But now we are to consider that there are *de facto* in the world certain sensible and rational beings that we call men, and the body of man having several of its external parts, as the eye, the ear, &c., each of a distinct and peculiar texture, whereby it is capable to receive impressions from the bodies about it, and upon that account it is called an organ of sense – we must consider, I say, that these sensories may be wrought upon by the figure, shape, motion and texture of bodies without them after several ways, some of those external bodies being fitted to affect the eye, others the ear, others the nostrils, &c. And to these operations of the objects on the sensories, the mind of man, which upon the account of its union with the body perceives them, giveth distinct names, calling the one *light*° or *colour*,° the other *sound*,° the other *odour*,° &c. And because also each organ of sense, as the eye or the palate, may be itself differingly affected by external objects, the mind likewise gives the objects of the same sense distinct appellations, calling one colour *green*,° the other *blue*,° and one taste *sweet*° and another *bitter*,° &c.: whence men have been induced to frame a long catalogue of such things as, for their relating to our senses, we call *sensible*° qualities. And because we have been conversant with them before we had the use of reason, and the mind of man is prone to conceive almost everything (nay, even privations, as blindness, death, &c.) under the notion of a true entity or substance, as itself is, we have been from our infancy apt to imagine that these sensible qualities are real beings in the objects they denominate, and have the faculty or power to work such and such things, as gravity hath a power to stop the motion of a bullet shot upwards and carry that solid globe of matter toward the centre of the earth: whereas indeed (according to what we have largely shown above) there is in the body to which these sensible qualities are attributed nothing of real and physical but the size, shape, and motion or rest, of its component particles, together with that texture of the whole which results from their being so contrived as they are. Nor is it necessary they should have in them anything more, like to the ideas they occasion in us – those ideas being either the effects of our prejudices or inconsiderateness, or else to be fetched from the relation that happens to be betwixt those primary accidents of the sensible object and the peculiar texture of the organ it affects: as, when a pin being run into my finger causeth pain, there is no distinct quality in the pin answerable to what I am apt to fancy pain to be; but the pin in itself is only slender, stiff, and sharp, and by those qualities happens to make a solution of continuity in my organ of touching, upon which, by reason of the fabric of the body and the intimate union of the soul with it, there ariseth that troublesome kind of perception which we call *pain*,° and I shall anon more particularly show how much that depends upon the peculiar fabric of the body.

VI. But here I foresee a difficulty, which being perhaps the chiefest that we shall meet with against the Corpuscular hypothesis, it will deserve to be, before we proceed any farther, taken notice of. And it is this, that whereas we explicate colours, odours, and the like sensible qualities, by a *relation to our senses*, it seems evident that they have an *absolute* being irrelative to *us*; for snow (for instance) would be white, and a glowing coal would be hot, though there were no man or any other animal in the world. And it is plain that bodies do not only by their qualities work upon *our senses*, but upon *other*, and those inanimate, *bodies*: as the coal will not only heat or burn a *man's hand* if he touch it, but would likewise heat wax (even so much as to melt it and make it flow), and thaw ice into water, though[15] all the men and sensitive beings in the world were annihilated. To clear this difficulty, I have several things to represent: and

1. I say not that there are no other accidents in bodies than colours, odours and the like: for I have already taught that there are simpler and more primitive affections of matter, from which these secondary qualities, if I may so call them, do depend; and that the operations of bodies upon one another spring from the same, we shall see by and by.

2. Nor do I say that all qualities of bodies are *directly sensible*: but I observe that, when one body works upon another, the knowledge we have of their operation proceeds either from some sensible quality, or some more catholic affection of matter, as motion, rest, or texture, generated or destroyed in one of them; for else it is hard to conceive how we should[16] come to discover what passes betwixt them.

3. We must not look upon every distinct body that works upon our senses as a bare lump of matter of that bigness and outward shape that it appears of: many of them having their parts curiously contrived, and most of them perhaps in motion too. Nor must we look upon the universe that surrounds us as upon a moveless and undistinguished heap of matter, but as upon a great engine, which having either no vacuity, or none that is considerable, betwixt its parts (known to us), the actions of particular bodies upon one another must not be barely estimated as if two portions of matter of their bulk and figure were placed in some imaginary space beyond the world, but as being situated[17] in the world constituted as it now is, and consequently as having their action upon each other liable to

be promoted or hindered or modified by the actions of other bodies besides them: as in a clock, a small force applied to move the index to the figure of 12 will make the hammer strike often and forcibly against the bell, and will make a far greater commotion among the wheels and weights than a far greater force would do, if the texture and contrivance of the clock did not abundantly contribute to the production of so great an effect. And in agitating water into froth, the whiteness would never be produced by that motion, were it not that the sun or other lucid body, shining upon that aggregate of small bubbles, enables them to reflect confusedly great store of little and, as it were, contiguous lucid images to the eye. And so the giving to a large metalline speculum a concave figure would never enable it to set wood on fire, and even to melt down metals readily, if the sunbeams that in cloudless days do, as to sense, fill the air were not, by the help of that concavity, thrown together to a point. And to show you, by an eminent instance, how various and how differing effects the same action of a natural agent may produce, according to the several dispositions of the bodies it works upon, do but consider that in two eggs, the one prolific, the other barren, the sense can perhaps distinguish before incubation no difference at all; and yet these bodies, outwardly so like, do so differ in the internal disposition of their parts that, if they be both exposed to the same degree of heat (whether of a hen or an artificial oven), that heat will change the one into a putrid and stinking substance, and the other into a chick, furnished with great variety of organical parts of very differing consistences and curious as well as differing textures.

4. I do not deny but that bodies may be said in a very favourable sense to have those qualities we call *sensible*,° though there were no animals in the world. For a body in that case may differ from those bodies which now are quite devoid of quality, in its having such a disposition of its constituent corpuscles that, in case it were duly applied to the sensory of an animal, it would produce such a sensible quality which a body of another texture would not: as, though if there were no animals there would be no such thing as pain, yet a pin may, upon the account of its figure, be fitted to cause pain, in case it were moved against a man's finger; whereas a bullet or other blunt body, moved against it with no greater force, will not cause any such perception of pain. And thus snow, though, if there were no lucid body nor organ of sight in the world, it would exhibit no colour at all (for I could not find it had any in places exactly darkened), yet

it hath a greater disposition than a coal or soot to reflect store of light outwards, when the sun shines upon them all three. And so we say that a lute is in tune, whether it be actually played upon or no, if the strings be all so duly stretched as that it would appear to be in tune if it were played upon. But as, if you should thrust a pin into a man's finger, both a while before and after his death, though the pin be as sharp at one time as at another and maketh in both cases alike a solution of continuity, yet in the former case the action of the pin will produce pain, and not in the latter, because in this the pricked body wants the soul and consequently the perceptive faculty: so, if there were no sensitive beings, those bodies that are now the objects of our senses would be but *dispositively*, if I may so speak, endowed with colours, tastes, and the like, and *actually* but only with those more catholic affections of bodies – figure, motion, texture, &c.

To illustrate this yet a little farther, suppose a man should beat a drum at some distance from the mouth of a cave, conveniently situated to return the noise he makes. Although men will presently conclude that that cave hath an echo, and will be apt to fancy upon that account some real property in the place to which the echo is said to belong – and although indeed the same noise made in many other of the neighbouring places would not be reflected to the ear, and consequently would manifest those places to have no echoes – yet, to speak physically of things, this peculiar quality or property we fancy in the cave is in it nothing else but the hollowness of its figure, whereby it is so disposed as, when the air beats against it, to reflect the motion towards the place whence that motion began. And that which passeth on this occasion is indeed but this, that the drum-stick, falling upon the drum, makes a percussion of the air, and puts that fluid body into an undulating motion; and the airy waves, thrusting on one another till they arrive at the hollow superficies of the cave, have, by reason of its resistance and figure, their motion determined the contrary way, namely backwards towards that part where the drum was when it was struck: so that, in that which here happens, there intervenes nothing but the figure of one body and the motion of another, though, if a man's ear chance to be in the way of these motions of the air forwards and backwards, it gives him a perception of them which he calls *sound*.° And because these perceptions, which are supposed to proceed from the same percussion of the drum, and thereby of the air, are made at distinct times one after another, that hollow body from whence the last sound is conceived to come to the air is imagined to have a peculiar faculty, upon whose account men are wont to say that such a place hath an *echo*.°

5. And whereas one body doth often seem to produce in another divers such qualities as we call *sensible*,° which qualities therefore seem not to need any reference to our senses, I consider that, when one inanimate body works upon another, there is nothing really produced by the agent in the patient, save some local motion of its parts or some change of texture consequent upon that motion; and so, if the patient come to have any sensible quality that it had not before, it acquires it upon the same account upon which other bodies have it, and it is but a consequent to this mechanical change of texture that, by means of its effects upon our organs of sense, we are induced to attribute this or that sensible quality to it. As, in case a pin should chance by some inanimate body to be driven against a man's finger, that which the agent doth is but to put a sharp and slender body into such a kind of motion, and that which the pin doth is to pierce into a body that it meets with, not hard enough to resist its motion – and so, that upon this there should ensue such a thing as pain, is but a consequent that superadds nothing of real to the pin that occasions that pain – so, if a piece of transparent ice be, by the falling of some heavy and hard body upon it, broken into a gross powder that looks whitish, the falling body doth nothing to the ice but break it into very small fragments, lying confusedly upon one another, though, by reason of the fabric of the world and of our eyes, there doth in the daytime, upon this comminution, ensue such a kind of copious reflection of the incident light to our eyes as we call *whiteness*.° And when the sun, by thawing this broken ice, destroys the whiteness of that portion of matter, and makes it become diaphanous, which it was not before, it doth no more than alter the texture of the component parts by putting them into motion, and thereby into a new order, in which, by reason of the disposition of the pores intercepted betwixt them, they reflect but few of the incident beams of light, and transmit most of them. Thus, when with a burnisher you polish a rough piece of silver, that which is really done is but the depression of the little protuberant parts into one level with the rest of the superficies: though, upon this mechanical change of the texture of the superficial parts, we men say that it hath lost the quality of roughness and acquired that of smoothness, because that, whereas before the little exstancies by their figure

resisted a little the motion of our fingers,[18] and grated upon them a little, our fingers now meet with no such offensive resistance. It is true that the fire doth thaw ice, and also both make wax flow and enable it to burn a man's hand; and yet this doth not necessarily argue in it any inherent quality of heat, distinct from the power it hath of putting the small parts of the wax into such a motion as that their agitation surmounts their cohesion: which motion, together with their gravity, is enough to make them *pro tempore* constitute a fluid body. And *aqua fortis*, without any (sensible) heat, will make camphor cast on it assume the form of a liquor distinct from it, as I have tried that a strong fire will also make camphor fluid – not to add that I know a liquor, into which certain bodies being put, when both itself (as well as they) is *actually cold* (and consequently when you would not suspect it of an actual inherent heat), will not only speedily dissipate many of their parts into smoke, but leave the rest black and burnt almost like a coal. So that, though we suppose the fire to do no more than variously and briskly to agitate the insensible parts of the wax, that may suffice to make us think the wax endowed with a quality of heat: because, if such an agitation be greater than that of the spirit and other parts of our organs of touching, that is enough to produce in us that sensation we call *heat*,° which is so much a relative to the sensory which apprehends it that we see that the same lukewarm water – that is, whose corpuscles are moderately agitated by the fire – will appear hot to one of a man's hands, if that be very cold, and cold to the other, in case it be very hot, though both of them be the same man's hands.+

To be short, if we fancy any two of the bodies about us, as a stone, a metal, &c., to have nothing at all to do with any other body in the universe, it is not easy to conceive either how one can act upon the other, but by local motion (of the whole body or its corporeal effluvia); or how by motion it can do any more than put the parts of the other body into motion too, and thereby produce in them a change of situation and texture, or of some other of its mechanical affections: though this (passive) body, being placed among other bodies in a world constituted as ours now is, and being brought to act upon the most curiously contrived sensories of animals, may upon both these accounts exhibit many differing sensible phenomena, which, however we look upon them as distinct qualities, are consequently but the effects of the often-mentioned catholic affections of matter, and deducible from the size, shape, motion (or rest), posture, order, and the resulting texture, of the insensible parts of bodies. And therefore, though, for shortness of speech, I shall not scruple to make use of the word *qualities*, since it is already so generally received, yet I would be understood to mean them in a sense suitable to the doctrine above delivered: as, if I should say that roughness is apt to grate and offend the skin, I should mean that a file or other body, by having upon its surface a multitude of little hard and exstant parts, and of an angular or sharp figure, is qualified to work the mentioned effect; and so, if I should say that heat melts metals, I should mean that this fusion is effected by fire or some other body, which, by the various and vehement motion of its insensible parts, does to us appear hot. And hence (by the way) I presume you will easily guess at what I think of the controversy so hotly disputed of late betwixt two parties of learned men, whereof the one would have all accidents to work only in virtue of the matter they reside in, and the other would have the matter to act only in virtue of its accidents: for, considering that, on the one side, the qualities we here speak of do so depend upon matter that they cannot so much as have a being but in and by it, and, on the other side, if all matter were but quite devoid of motion (to name now no other accidents), I do not readily conceive how it could operate at all, I think it is safest to conclude that neither matter nor qualities apart, but both of them conjointly, do perform what we see done by bodies to one another, according to the doctrine of qualities just now delivered.

VII. *Of the Nature of a. Form.* We may now advance somewhat farther, and consider that, men having taken notice that certain conspicuous accidents were to be found associated in some bodies, and other conventions of accidents in other bodies, they did for conveniency and for the more expeditious expression of their conceptions agree to distinguish them into several sorts, which they call *genders* or *species*, according as they referred them either upwards, to a more comprehensive sort of bodies, or downward, to a narrower species or to individuals: as, observing many bodies to agree in being fusible, malleable, heavy, and the like, they gave to that sort of body the name of *metal*, which is a *genus* in reference to gold, silver, lead, and but a *species* in reference to that sort of mixed bodies they call *fossilia* – this *superior genus* comprehending both metals, stones, and divers other concretions, though itself be but a *species* in respect of mixed bodies. Now when any body is referred to any particular species (as of a metal, a stone, or the like), because men have for their convenience agreed to signify all the essentials requisite to constitute such a body by one name, most of the writers of physics have been apt to think that, besides the common matter of all bodies, there is but one thing that discriminates it from other kinds and makes it what it is, and this, for brevity's sake, they call a *form*: which, because all the qualities and other accidents of the body must depend on it, they also imagine to be a very substance, and indeed a kind of soul, which, united to the gross matter, composes with it a natural body, and acts in it by the several qualities to be found therein, which men are wont to ascribe to the creature so composed.+

But as to this affair, I observe that if (for instance) you ask a man what gold is, if he cannot show you a piece of gold and tell you 'This is gold', he will describe it to you as a body that is extremely ponderous, very malleable and ductile, fusible and yet fixed in the fire, and of a yellowish colour; and if you offer to put off to him a piece of brass for a piece of gold, he will presently refuse it, and (if he understand metals) tell you that, though your brass be coloured like it, it is not so heavy nor so malleable, neither will it like gold resist the utmost brunt of the fire, or resist *aqua fortis*. And if you ask men what they mean by a ruby, or nitre, or a pearl, they will still make you such answers that you may clearly perceive that, whatever men talk in theory of substantial forms, yet that upon whose account they really distinguish any one body from others, and refer it to this or that species of bodies, is nothing but an aggregate or convention of such accidents as most men do by a kind of agreement (for the thing is more arbitrary than we are aware of) think necessary or sufficient to make a portion of the universal matter belong to this or that determinate genus or species of natural bodies. And therefore not only the generality of chemists, but divers philosophers, and, what is more, some schoolmen themselves, maintain it to be possible to transmute the ignobler metals into gold: which argues that, if a man could bring any parcel of matter to be yellow and malleable and ponderous, and fixed in the fire, and, upon the test,[19] indissoluble in *aqua fortis*, and in sum to have a concurrence of all those accidents by which men try true gold from false, they would take it for true gold without scruple. And in this case the generality of mankind would leave the School doctors to dispute whether, being a factitious body (as made by the chemist's art), it have the substantial form of gold, and would upon the account of the convention of the freshly-mentioned accidents let it pass current amongst them, notwithstanding most men's greater care not to be deceived in a matter of this nature than in any other. And indeed, since to every determinate species of bodies there doth belong more than one quality, and for the most part a concurrence of many is so essential to that sort of bodies that the want of any[20] of them is sufficient to exclude it from belonging to that species, there needs no more to discriminate sufficiently any one kind of bodies from all the bodies in the world that are not of that kind: as the chemists' *luna fixa*, which they tell us wants not the weight, the malleableness, nor the fixedness, nor any other property of gold except the yellowness (which makes them call it *white gold*°), would by reason of that want of colour be easily known from true gold. And you will not wonder at this if you consider that, though[21] spheres and parallelepipedons differ but in shape, yet this difference alone is the ground of so many others, that Euclid and other geometricians have demonstrated I know not how many properties of the one, which do no way belong to the other; and Aristotle himself somewhere tells us that a sphere is composed of brass and roundness.[h] And I suppose it would be thought a man's own fault if he could not distinguish a needle from a file, or a key from a pair of scissors, though these, being all made of iron, and differing but in bigness and shape, are less remarkably diverse than natural bodies, the most part of which differ from each other in far more accidents than two.+

Nor need we think that, qualities being but accidents, they cannot be *essential* to a natural body; for *accident*,° as I formerly noted, is sometimes opposed to *substance*,° and sometimes to *essence*.° And though an accident can[22] be but accidental to matter, as it is a substantial thing, yet it may be essential to this or that particular body: as in Aristotle's newly-mentioned example, though roundness is but accidental to brass, yet it is essential to a brazen sphere, because, though the brass were devoid of roundness (as if it were cubical, or of any other figure), it would still be a corporeal substance, yet without that roundness it could not be a sphere. Wherefore, since an aggregate or convention of qualities is enough to make the portion of matter it is found in what it is, and denominate it of this or that determinate sort of bodies, and since those qualities,

[h] Aristotle, *Metaphysics*, lib. VII, cap. 8.

as we have seen already, do themselves proceed from those more primary and catholic affections of matter – bulk, shape, motion or rest – and the texture thence resulting, why may we not say that the form of a body, being made up of those qualities united in one subject, doth likewise consist in such a convention of those newly-named mechanical affections of matter as is necessary to constitute a body of that determinate kind? And so, though I shall for brevity's sake retain the word *form*, yet I would be understood to mean by it not a real *substance* distinct from matter, but only the matter itself of a natural body, considered with its peculiar manner of existence, which I think may not inconveniently be called either its *specifical* or its *denominating state*, or its *essential modification* – or, if you would have me express it in one word, its *stamp*. For such a convention of accidents is sufficient to perform the offices that are necessarily required in what men call a *form*,° since it makes the body such as it is, making it appertain to this or that determinate species of bodies, and discriminating it from all other species of bodies whatsoever: as, for instance, ponderousness, ductility, fixedness, yellowness, and some other qualities, concurring in a portion of matter, do with it constitute gold, and, making it belong to that species we call *metals*,° and to that sort of metals we call *gold*,° do both denominate and discriminate it from stones, salts, marcasites, and all other sorts of bodies that are not metals, and from silver, brass, copper, and all metals except gold.⁺

And whereas it is said by some that the form also of a body ought to be the principle of its operations,[23] we shall hereafter consider in what sense that is to be admitted or rejected; in the meantime it may suffice us that, even in the vulgar philosophy, it is acknowledged that natural things for the most part operate by their qualities, as snow dazzles the eyes by its whiteness, and water scattered into drops of rain falls from the clouds upon the account of its gravity: to which I shall add that how great the power may be, which a body may exercise by virtue of a single quality, may appear by the various and oftentimes prodigious effects which fire produces by its heat, when thereby it melts metals, calcines stones, destroys whole woods and cities, &c. And if several active qualities convene in one body (as that which in our hypothesis is meant by *form*° usually comprises several of them), what great things may be thereby performed may be somewhat guessed at by the strange things we see done by some engines, which, being as engines undoubtedly devoid of substantial forms, must do those strange things they are admired for by virtue of those accidents, the shape, size, motion, and contrivance, of their parts. Not to mention that in our hypothesis, besides those operations that proceed from the essential modification of the matter, as the body (composed of matter and necessary accidents) is considered *per modum unius* – as one entire corporeal agent – it may in divers cases have other operations upon the account of those particular corpuscles, which, though they concur to compose it and are, in reference to the whole, considered but as its parts, may yet retain their own particular nature and divers of the peculiar qualities: as in a watch, besides those things which the watch performs as such, the several parts whereof it consists, as the spring, the wheels, the string, the pins, &c., may have each of them its peculiar bulk, shape, and other attributes, upon the account of one or more of which the wheel or spring, &c., may do other things than what it doth as merely a constituent part of the watch. And so, in the milk of a nurse that hath some hours before taken a potion, though the corpuscles of the purging medicine appear not to sense distinct from the other parts of the milk, which in far greater numbers concur with them to constitute that white liquor, yet these purgative particles, that seem but[24] to be part of the matter whereof the milk consists, do yet so retain their own nature and qualities that, being sucked in with the rest by the infant, they quickly discriminate and discover themselves by purging him. But of this subject more hereafter.

VIII. *Of Generation, Corruption and Alteration.* It now remains that we declare what, according to the tenor of our hypothesis, is to be meant by *generation, corruption,* and *alteration* (three names that have very much puzzled and divided philosophers). In order hereunto we may consider:

1. That there are in the world great store of particles of matter, each of which is too small to be, whilst single, sensible, and, being entire or undivided, must needs both have its determinate shape and be very solid: insomuch that, though it be *mentally,* and by divine omnipotence, divisible, yet by reason of its smallness and solidity nature doth scarce ever actually divide it; and these may in this sense be called *minima* or *prima naturalia.*

2. That there are also multitudes of corpuscles which are made up of the coalition of several of the former *minima naturalia,* and whose bulk is so small, and their adhesion so close and strict, that

each of these little primitive concretions or clusters (if I may so call them) of particles is singly below the discernment of sense; and, though not absolutely indivisible by nature into the *prima naturalia* that composed it, or perhaps into other little fragments, yet, for the reasons freshly intimated, they very rarely happen to be actually dissolved or broken, but remain entire in great variety of sensible bodies, and under various forms or disguises: as, not to repeat what we lately mentioned of the undestroyed purging corpuscles of milk, we see that even grosser and more compounded corpuscles may have such a permanent texture; for quicksilver, for instance, may be turned into a red powder for a fusible and malleable body, or a fugitive smoke, and disguised I know not how many other ways, and yet remain true and recoverable mercury. And these are, as it were, the seeds or immediate principles of many sorts of natural bodies, as earth, water, salt, &c., and those singly insensible become capable, when united, to affect the sense: as I have tried that, if good camphor be kept awhile in pure spirit of wine, it will thereby be reduced into such little parts as totally to disappear in the liquor, without making it look less clear than fair water; and yet, if into this mixture you pour a competent quantity of water, in a moment the scattered corpuscles of the camphor will, by reuniting themselves, become white and consequently visible, as before their dispersion.

3. That as well each of the *minima naturalia* as each of the primary clusters above mentioned having its own determinate bulk and shape, when these come to adhere to one another, it must *always* happen that the size, and *often* that the figure, of the corpuscle composed by their juxtaposition and cohesion will be changed; and *not seldom*, too, the motion either of the one or the other, or both, will receive a new tendency, or be altered as to its velocity or otherwise. And the like will happen when the corpuscles that compose a cluster of particles are disjoined, or anything of the little mass is broken off. And whether anything of matter be added to a corpuscle or taken from it, in either case (as we just now intimated) the size of it must necessarily be altered, and for the most part the figure will be so too: whereby it will both acquire a congruity to the pores of some bodies (and perhaps some of our sensories), and become incongruous to those of others, and consequently be qualified, as I shall more fully show you hereafter, to operate on divers occasions much otherwise than it was fitted to do before.

4. That when many of these insensible corpuscles come to be

associated into one visible body, if many or most of them be put into motion, from what cause soever the motion proceeds, that itself may produce great changes and new qualities in the body they compose. For not only motion may perform much, even when it makes not any visible alteration in it – as air put into swift motion (as when it is blown out of bellows) acquires a new name and is called *wind*, and to the touch appears far colder than the same *air* not so formed into a stream, and iron, by being briskly rubbed against wood or other iron, hath its small parts so agitated as to appear hot to our sense – but this motion oftentimes makes visible alterations in the texture of the body into which it is received. For always the moved parts strive to communicate their motion, or somewhat of the degree of it, to some parts that were before either at rest or otherwise moved, and oftentimes the same moved parts do thereby either disjoin or break some of the corpuscles they hit against, and thereby change their bulk or shape, or both, and either drive some of them quite out of the body, and perhaps lodge themselves in their places, or else associate them anew with others: whence it usually follows that the texture is, for a while at least – and, unless it be very stable and permanent, for good and all – very much altered, and especially in that the pores or little intervals intercepted betwixt the component particles will be changed as to bigness or figure, or both, and so will cease to be commensurate to the corpuscles that were fit for them before, and become commensurate to such corpuscles of other sizes and shapes as, till then, were incongruous to them. Thus we see that water, by losing the wonted agitation of its parts, may acquire the firmness and brittleness we find in ice, and lose much of the transparency it had whilst it was a liquor. Thus also, by very hard rubbing two pieces of resinous wood against one another, we may make them throw out divers of their looser parts into steams and visible smoke, and may, if the attrition be duly continued, make that commotion of the parts so change the texture of the whole as afterwards to turn the superficial parts into a kind of coal. And thus milk, especially in hot weather, will, by the intestine though languid motions of its parts, be in a short time turned into a thinner sort of liquor than milk, and into cream; and this (last named) will, by being barely agitated in a churn, be turned in a shorter time into that unctuous and consistent body we call butter, and into thin, fluid, and sour buttermilk. And thus (to dispatch) by the bruising of fruit, the texture is commonly so changed that, as we see particularly in apples,[25] the bruised part soon comes to be of another nature than the sound part, the one differing from the other both in colour, taste, smell, and consistence. So that (as we have already inculcated) *local motion* hath, of all other affections of matter, the greatest interest in the altering and modifying of it, since it is not only the grand *agent* or *efficient* among second causes, but is also oftentimes one of the principal things that *constitutes the form* of bodies: as, when two sticks are set on fire by long and vehement attrition, local *motion* is not only that which kindles the wood, and so as an efficient produces the fire, but is that which principally concurs to give the produced stream of shining matter the name and nature of flame; and so it concurs also to constitute all fluid bodies.

5. And that, since we have formerly seen that it is from the size, shape, and motion, of the small parts of matter, and the texture that results from the manner of their being disposed in any one body, that the colour, odour, taste and other qualities of that body are to be derived, it will be easy for us to recollect that such changes cannot happen in a portion of matter without so much varying the nature of it, that we need not deride the ancient atomists for attempting to deduce the *generation* and *corruption* of bodies from the famed σύγκρισις καὶ διάκρισις, the *convention* and *dissolution*, and the *alterations* of them from the *transposition*, of their (supposed) atoms. For though indeed nature is wont, in the changes she makes among things corporeal, to employ all the *three* ways as well in *alterations* as *generations* and *corruptions*, yet if they only meant, as probably enough they did, that, of the *three* ways proposed, the first was wont to be the principal in the *generation* of bodies, the second in the *corruption*, and the third in their *alterations*, I shall not much oppose this doctrine: though I take the local motion or *transposition* of parts in the same portion of matter to bear a great stroke as well in reference to *generation* and *corruption* as to *alteration*, as we see when milk, or flesh, or fruit, without any remarkable addition or loss of parts, turns into maggots or other insects; and as we may more conspicuously observe in the precipitation of mercury, without addition, in the vitrification of metals, and other chemical experiments to be hereafter mentioned.

These things premised, it will not now be difficult to comprise in few words such a doctrine touching the *generation, corruption,* and *alteration,* of bodies as is suitable to our hypothesis and the former discourse. For if in a parcel of matter there happen to be produced (it imports not much how) a concurrence of all those accidents (whether those only or more) that men by tacit agreement have thought *necessary* and *sufficient* to constitute any one determinate species of things corporeal, then we say that a body belonging to that species, as suppose a stone or a metal, is *generated* or produced *de novo* – not that there is really anything of *substantial* produced, but that those parts of matter that did indeed before pre-exist, but were either scattered and shared among other bodies, or at least otherwise disposed of, are now brought together and disposed of after the manner requisite to entitle the body that results from them to a *new denomination*, and make it appertain to such a determinate species of natural bodies, so that no new *substance* is in generation *produced*, but only that which was *pre-existent* obtains a new *modification* or manner of existence. Thus when the spring and wheels and string and balance and index, &c., necessary to a watch, which lay before scattered, some in one part, some in another, of the artificer's shop, are first set together in the order requisite to make such an engine to show how the time passes, a watch is said to be *made* – not that any of the mentioned material parts is *produced de novo*, but that till then the divided matter was not so *contrived* and put together as was requisite to constitute such a thing as we call a *watch*.° And so, when sand and ashes are well melted together and suffered to cool, there is generated by the colliquation that sort of concretion we call *glass*, though it be evident that its ingredients were both pre-existent and do but by their *association* obtain a new manner of existing together. And so when, by the churning of cream, butter and buttermilk are generated, we find not anything substantial produced *de novo* in either of them, but only that the serum and the fat corpuscles, being put into local motion, do by their frequent occursions extricate themselves from each other, and associate themselves in the new manner requisite to constitute the bodies whose names are given them.

And as a body is said to be *generated*, when it first appears clothed with all those qualities upon whose account men have been pleased to call some bodies *stones*, others *metals*, others *salts*, &c., so, when a body comes to lose *all* or *any* of those accidents that are *essential* and necessary to the constituting of such a body, it is then said to be *corrupted* or destroyed, and is no more a body of *that kind*, but loses its title to its former denomination – not that anything *corporeal* or substantial *perishes* in this *change*, but only that the essential modification of the matter is destroyed; and though the body be still a *body* (no natural agent being able to *annihilate* matter), yet it is no longer *such a body* as it was before, but perisheth in the capacity of a body of that kind. Thus, if a stone falling upon a watch break it to pieces, as, when the watch was made, there was no new substance produced – all the material parts (as the steel, brass, string, &c.) being pre-existent somewhere or other (as in iron and copper mines, in the bellies of those animals of whose guts men use to make strings) – so not the least part of the substance of the watch is lost, but only displaced and scattered; and yet that portion of matter ceases to be a *watch* as it was before. And so (to resume our late example) when cream is by churning turned into butter and a serous liquor, the parts of the milk remain associated into those two bodies, but the white liquor perisheth in the capacity of *milk*.° And so when ice comes to be thawed in exactly-closed vessels, though the corruption be produced only (for aught appears) by introducing a new motion and disposition into the parts of the frozen water, yet it thereupon ceases to be *ice*, however it be as much *water*, and consequently as much a *body*, as before it was frozen or thawed. These and the like examples may teach us rightly to understand that common axiom of naturalists, '*Corruptio unius est generatio alterius, et e contra*'; for since it is acknowledged on all hands that matter cannot be annihilated, and since it appears by what we have said above that there are some properties, namely *size*, *shape*, *motion* (or, in its absence, *rest*), that are inseparable from the actual parts of matter, and since also the coalition of any competent number of these parts is sufficient to constitute a natural body endowed with divers sensible qualities, it can *scarce* be otherwise but that the same agents that shatter the frame, or *destroy* the texture, of one body will, by shuffling them together and disposing them after a new manner, bring them to *constitute* some new sort of bodies: as the same thing that by burning destroys wood turns it into flame, soot, and ashes. Only I doubt whether the axiom do generally hold true, if it be meant that *every corruption must end in the generation of a body belonging to some particular species of things*, unless we take powders and fluid bodies indefinitely for species of natural bodies: since it is plain there are multitudes of vegetables and other concretions which, when they rot, do not, as some others do, turn into worms, but either into some slimy or watery substance, or else (which is the most usual) they crumble into a kind of dust or powder, which, though looked upon as being the earth into which rotten bodies are at length resolved, is very far from being of an elementary nature, but as yet a compounded body, retaining some if not many qualities, which often makes the dust of one sort of plant or animal differ much from that of another. And this will supply me with this argument *ad hominem*, viz. that since, in those *violent corruptions* of bodies that are made by outward agents shattering them into pieces, if the axiom hold true the new *bodies emergent* upon the dissolution of the former must be really *natural bodies* (as indeed divers of the moderns hold them to be) and generated according to the course of nature – as when wood is destroyed by fire, and turned partly into flame, partly into soot, partly into coals, and partly into ashes – I hope we may be allowed to conclude that those *chemical productions*, which so many would have to be but *factitious bodies*, are *natural ones*, and regularly generated. For it being the same agent, the fire, that operates upon bodies, whether they be exposed to it in close glasses or in chimneys, I see no sufficient reason why the chemical oils and volatile salts, and other things which spagyrites obtain from mixed bodies, should not be accounted natural bodies, as well as the soot and ashes and charcoal that by the same fire are obtained from kindled wood.

But before we pass away from the mention of the corruption of bodies, I must take some notice of what is called their *putrefaction*. This is but a peculiar kind of corruption, wrought slowly (whereby it may be distinguished from destruction by fire and other nimble agents) in bodies. It happens to them for the most part by means of the air or some other ambient fluid, which, by penetrating into the pores of the body, and by its agitation in them, doth usually call out some of the more agile and less entangled parts of the body, and doth almost ever loosen and dislocate the parts in general, and thereby so change the texture, and perhaps too the figure of the corpuscles that compose it, that the body thus changed acquires qualities unsuitable to its former nature and for the most part offensive to our senses, especially of smelling and tasting: which last clause I therefore add, not only because the vulgar look not upon the change of an egg into a chick as a *corruption*, but as a *perfection*, of the egg; but because also I think it not improbable that if, by such slow changes of bodies as make them lose their former nature and might otherwise pass for *putrefaction*, many bodies should acquire better scents or tastes than before – or if nature, custom, or any other cause, should much alter the texture of our organs of tasting and smelling – it would not perhaps be so well agreed on what should be called *putrefaction,*° as that imports an *impairing alteration,* but men would find some favourabler notion for such changes. For I observe that medlars, though they acquire in length of time such a colour and softness as rotten apples and other putrefied fruits do, yet, because their taste is not then harsh as before, we call that *ripeness* in them which otherwise we should call *rottenness.* And though, upon the death of a four-footed beast, we generally call that change which happens to the flesh or blood *putrefaction,*° yet we pass a more favourable judgement upon that which happens to the flesh and other softer parts of that animal (whether it be a kind of large rabbits or very small and hornless deer) of which in China and in the Levant they make musk, because, by the change that ensues the animal's death, the flesh acquires not an *odious* but a *grateful smell.* And we see that some men, whose appetites are gratified by rotten cheese, think it then not to have *degenerated* but to have attained its *best state,* when – having lost its former colour, smell, and taste, and, which is more, being in great part turned into those insects called mites – it is both in a philosophical sense *corrupted,* and in the estimate of the generality of men grown *putrid.* But because it very seldom happens that a body by generation acquires no other qualities than just those that are absolutely *necessary* to make it belong to the species that denominates it, therefore in most bodies there are divers other qualities that may *be* there, or may be *missing,* without essentially changing the subject: as water may be clear or muddy, odorous or stinking, and still remain water; and butter may be white or yellow, sweet or rancid, consistent or melted, and still be called butter. Now therefore, whensoever a parcel of matter does *acquire* or *lose* a quality that is not *essential* to it, that acquisition or loss is distinctly called *alteration* (or by some *mutation*): the acquist only of the qualities that are absolutely *necessary* to constitute its essential and specifical difference, or the loss of any of *those* qualities, being such a change as must not be called mere *alteration,* but have the particular name of *generation*° or *corruption;*° both which, according to this doctrine, appear to be but several *kinds of alteration,* taken in a large sense, though they are distinguished from it in a more strict and limited acception of that term.

And here we have a fair occasion to take notice of the fruitfulness and extent of our Mechanical hypothesis. For since, according to our doctrine, the world we live in is not a moveless or indigested mass of matter, but an αὐτόματον or *self-moving engine*, wherein the greatest part of the common matter of all bodies is always (though not still the same parts of it) in motion, and wherein bodies are so close set by one another that (unless in some very few and extraordinary and, as it were, preternatural cases) they have either no vacuities betwixt them, or only here and there interposed and very small ones; and since, according to us, the various *manner* of the *coalition* of several *corpuscles* into one visible *body* is enough to give them a peculiar texture, and thereby fit them to exhibit divers sensible qualities, and to become a body sometimes of one denomination and sometimes of another: it will very naturally follow that, from the various occursions of those innumerable swarms of little bodies that are moved to and fro in the world, there will be many fitted to stick to one another and so compose concretions, and many (though not in the selfsame place) disjoined from one another and agitated apart, and multitudes also that will be driven to associate themselves, now with one body, and presently with another. And if we also consider, on the one side, that the sizes of the small particles of matter may be very *various*, their figures almost *innumerable*, and that if a parcel of matter do but happen to stick to one body it may chance to give it a new quality, and if it adhere to another or hit against some of its parts it may constitute a body of another kind, or if a parcel of matter be knocked off from another it may barely by that leave it and become itself of another nature than before – if, I say, we consider these things on the one side, and, on the other side, that (to use Lucretius's comparison) all that innumerable multitude of words that are contained in all the languages of the world are made of the various combinations of some of the 24 letters of the alphabet, it will not be hard to conceive that there may be an incomprehensible variety of associations and textures of the minute parts of bodies, and consequently a vast multitude of portions of matter endowed with store enough of differing qualities to deserve distinct appellations, though for want of heedfulness and fit words men have not yet taken so much notice of their less obvious varieties as to sort them as they deserve and give them distinct and proper names. So that, though I would not say that any thing can immediately be made of every thing – as a gold ring of a *wedge* of gold, or oil or fire of water – yet, since bodies, having but one common matter, can be differenced but by accidents, which seem all of them to be the effects and consequents of local motion, I see not why it should be absurd to think that (at least among inanimate bodies), by the intervention of some very small *addition* or *subtraction* of matter (which yet in most cases will scarce be needed), and of an orderly *series of alterations*, disposing by degrees the matter to be transmuted, almost of any thing may at length be made any thing: as, though out of a *wedge* of gold one cannot immediately make a *ring*, yet by either wire-drawing that wedge by degrees, or by melting it and casting a little of it into a mould, that thing may easily be effected. And so, though water cannot immediately be transmuted into oil, and much less into fire, yet if you nourish certain plants with water alone (as I have done), till they have assimilated a great quantity of water into their own nature, you may, by committing this transmuted water (which you may distinguish and separate from that part of the vegetable you first put in) to distillation in convenient glasses, obtain, besides other things, a true oil, and a black combustible coal (and consequently fire): both of which may be so copious, as to leave no just cause to suspect that they could be anything near afforded by any little spirituous parts which may be presumed to have been communicated, by that part of the vegetable that is first put into the water, to that far greater part of it which was committed to distillation.

But, Pyrophilus, I perceive the difficulty and fruitfulness of my subject have made me so much more prolix than I intended, that it will not now be amiss to contract the summary of our hypothesis, and give you the main points of it with little or no illustration, and without particular proofs, in a few words. We teach, then (but without peremptorily asserting it):

1.[26] That the matter of all natural bodies is the same, namely, a substance extended and impenetrable.

2. That all bodies thus agreeing in the same common matter, their distinction is to be taken from those accidents that do diversify it.

3. That motion, not belonging to the essence of matter (which retains its whole nature when it is at rest), and not being originally producible by other accidents as they are from it, may be looked upon as the first and chief *mood* or affection of matter.

4. That motion, variously determined, doth naturally divide the matter it belongs to into actual fragments or parts; and this division obvious experience (and, more eminently, chemical operations)

manifest to have been made into parts exceedingly *minute*, and very often too minute to be singly perceivable by our senses.

5. Whence it must necessarily follow that each of these minute parts or *minima naturalia* (as well as every particular body made up by the coalition of any number of them) must have its determinate *bigness* or *size*, and its own *shape*. And these three, namely *bulk, figure*, and either *motion* or *rest* (there being no mean between these two), are the three *primary* and most *catholic moods* or affections of the *insensible* parts of matter, considered *each* of them *apart*.

6. That when *divers* of them are considered *together*, there will necessarily follow here below both a certain *position* or *posture* in reference to the horizon (as erected, inclining, or level) of each of them, and a certain *order* or placing before or behind or besides one another (as, when in a company of soldiers one stands *upright*, the other *stoops*, the other *lies along* upon the ground, they have various *postures*, and their being placed *besides* one another in ranks and *behind* one another in files are varieties of their *order*); and when many of these small parts are brought to convene into one body from their *primary affections* and their disposition or *contrivance* as to *posture* and *order*, there results that which by one comprehensive name we call the *texture* of that body. And indeed these several kinds of *location* (to borrow a scholastical term), attributed (in this 6th number) to the minute particles of bodies, are so near of kin that they seem all of them referable to (that one event of their convening) *situation* or *position*. And these are the affections that belong to a body, as it is considered in itself, without relation to *sensitive* beings or to other natural bodies.

7. That yet there being men in the world, whose organs of sense are contrived in such differing ways that one sensory is fitted to receive impressions from some, and another from other sorts of external objects or bodies without them (whether these act as entire bodies, or by *emission* of their corpuscles, or by *propagating* some motion to the sensory), the perceptions of these impressions are by men called by several names, as *heat*, *colour*, *sound*, *odour*, and are commonly imagined to proceed from certain distinct and peculiar qualities in the external object which have some resemblance to the ideas their action upon the senses excites in the mind: though indeed all these sensible qualities, and the rest that are to be met with in the bodies without us, are but the effects or consequents of the above-mentioned *primary affections* of matter, whose operations are

diversified according to the nature of the sensories or other bodies they work upon.

8. That when a portion of matter, either by the *accession* or *recess* of corpuscles, or by the *transposition* of those it consisted of before, or by any *two* or *all* of these ways, happens to obtain a *concurrence of all* those qualities which men commonly agree to be *necessary* and *sufficient* to denominate the body which hath them either a *metal*, or a *stone*, or the like, and to rank it in any peculiar and determinate species of bodies, then a body of that denomination is said to be *generated*.

9. This *convention of essential accidents*, being taken (not any of them apart, but all) *together* for the specifical difference that *constitutes* the body and *discriminates* it from all other sorts of bodies, is by one name, because considered as one *collective* thing, called its *form* (as beauty, which is made up both[27] of symmetry of parts and agreeableness of colours): which is consequently but a certain *character* (as I sometimes call it), or a *peculiar state of matter*, or, if I may so name it, an *essential modification* – a *modification*, because it is indeed but a determinate *manner of existence* of the matter, and yet an *essential modification*, because that, though the concurrent qualities be but accidental to matter (which with others instead of them would be matter still), yet they are *essentially necessary* to the particular *body*, which, without those accidents, would not be a body of that denomination, as a *metal* or a *stone*, but of some other.

10. Now a body being capable of many *other* qualities *besides* those whose convention is *necessary* to make up its form, the *acquisition* or *loss* of any such quality is by naturalists, in the more strict sense of that term, named *alteration*, as when oil comes to be frozen, or to change colour, or to grow rancid; but if all or any of the qualities that are reputed *essential* to such a body come to be *lost* or *destroyed*, that notable change is called *corruption*: as, when oil being boiled takes fire, the oil is not said to be *altered* in the former sense, but *corrupted* or *destroyed*, and the emergent fire *generated*; and when it so happens that the body is *slowly corrupted*, and thereby also acquires *qualities offensive to our senses*, especially of *smell* and *taste* (as when flesh or fruit grows rotten), that kind of corruption is by a more particular name called *putrefaction*. But neither in this nor in any other kind of corruption is there anything *substantial* destroyed (no such thing having been produced in generation, and matter itself being on all hands acknowledged *incorruptible*), but only that *special connexion of the parts*, or *manner of their co-existence*, upon whose account the matter,

whilst it was in its former state, was, and was called, a stone or a metal, or did belong to any other determinate species of bodies.

OF THE ORIGIN OF FORMS[28]

The origin of forms, Pyrophilus, as it is thought the *noblest*, so, if I mistake not, it hath been found one of the most *perplexed* enquiries that belong to natural philosophy; and I confess it is one of the things that has invited me to look about for some more satisfactory account than the Schools usually give of this matter, that I have observed that the wisest that have busied themselves in explicating forms according to the Peripatetic notions of them have either knowingly confessed themselves unable to explain them, or unwittingly proved themselves to be so, by giving but unsatisfactory explications of them.

It will not (I presume) be expected that I, who now write but *notes*, should enumerate, much less examine, all the various opinions touching the origin and nature of forms – it being enough for our purpose if, having already intimated in our hypothesis what, according to that, may be thought of this subject, we now briefly consider the general opinion of our modern Aristotelians and the Schools concerning it. I say the *modern* Aristotelians, because divers of the *ancient*, especially Greek, commentators of Aristotle seem to have understood their master's doctrine of forms much otherwise and less incongruously than his Latin followers, the schoolmen, and others have since done. Nor do I expressly mention Aristotle himself among the champions of substantial forms, because, though he seem in a place or two expressly enough to reckon forms among *substances*, yet elsewhere, the examples he employs to set forth the *forms* of natural things by being taken from the *figures* of artificial things (as of a statue, &c.) which are confessedly but *accidents*, and making very little use, if any, of substantial forms to explain the phenomena of nature, he seems to me upon the whole matter either to have been irresolved whether there were any such substances or no, or to speak ambiguously and obscurely enough of them to make it questionable what his opinions of them were.

But the sum of the controversy betwixt us and the Schools is this: whether or no the forms of natural things (the souls of men always excepted) be in generation *educed*, as they speak, *out of the power of the matter*, and whether these forms be true *substantial entities*, distinct from the other substantial principle of natural bodies, namely matter.

The reasons that move me to embrace the negative are principally these three. *First*, that I see no necessity of admitting in natural things any such substantial forms, matter and the accidents of matter being sufficient to explicate as much of the phenomena of nature as we either do or are like to understand. *The next*, that I see not what use this puzzling doctrine of substantial forms is of in natural philosophy, the acute Scaliger and those that have most busied themselves in the indagation of them having freely acknowledged (as the more candid of the Peripatetics generally do) that the true knowledge of forms is too difficult and abstruse to be attained by them.[i][29] And how like it is that particular phenomena will be explained by a principle whose nature is confessedly ignored, I leave you to judge; but because to these considerations I often have had, and shall have here and there, occasion to say something in the body of these notes, I shall at present insist upon the *third*, which is that I cannot conceive neither how forms can be generated, as the Peripatetics would have it, nor how the things they ascribe to them are consistent with the principles of true philosophy, or even with what themselves otherwise teach.

The manner how forms are educed out of the power of the matter, according to that part of the doctrine of forms wherein the Schools generally enough agree, is a thing so inexplicable that I wonder not it hath put acute men upon several hypotheses to make it out. And indeed the number of these is of late grown too great to be fit to be here recited, especially since I find them all so very unsatisfactory that I cannot but think the acute sticklers for any of them are rather driven to embrace it by the palpable inconveniences of the ways they reject, than by anything they find to satisfy them in that which they make choice of; and for my part, I confess I find so much reason in what each party says against the explications of the rest, that I think they all confute well, and none does well establish. | But my present way of writing forbidding me to insist on many arguments against

[i] '*Formarum cognitio est rudis, confusa, nec nisi per* περιστάσεις *; neque verum est, formae substantialis speciem recipi in intellectum, non enim in sensu usquam fuit.*' – J. C. Scaliger. '*Formae substantiales sunt incognitae nobis, quia insensiles: ideo per qualitates, quae sunt principia immediata transmutationis, exprimuntur.*' – Aquinas, *ad* 1 *De Gen. & Corr.* '*In hac humanae mentis caligine aeque forma ignis ac magnetis nobis ignota est.*' – Sennertus.

the doctrine wherein they most agree, I shall only urge that which I confess chiefly sticks with me, namely, that I find it not *comprehensible*.

I know the modern schoolmen fly here to their wonted refuge of an obscure distinction, and tell us that the power of matter in reference to forms is partly eductive, as the agent can make the form out of it, and partly receptive, whereby it can receive the form so made; but since those that say this will not allow that the form of a generated body was actually pre-existent in its matter, or indeed anywhere else, it is hard to conceive how a substance can be educed out of another substance totally distinct in nature from it, without being before such eduction actually existent in it. And as for the receptive power of the matter, *that* but fitting it to receive or lodge a form when brought to be united with it, how can it be intelligibly made out to contribute to the production of a new substance of a quite differing nature from that matter, though it harbours it when produced? And it is plain that the human body hath a receptive power in reference to the human soul, which yet themselves confess both to be a substantial form and not to be educed out of the power of matter. Indeed, if they would admit the form of a natural body to be but a more fine and subtle part of the matter, as spirit of wine is of wine, which upon its recess remains no longer wine, but phlegm or vinegar, then the eductive power of matter might signify something – and so it might if, with us, they would allow the form to be but a modification of the matter; for then it would import but that the matter may be so ordered or disposed by fit agents as to constitute a body of such a sort and denomination, and so (to resume that example) the form of a sphere may be said to lurk potentially in a piece of brass, inasmuch as that brass may, by casting, turning, or otherwise, be so figured as to become a sphere. But *this* they will not admit, lest they should make forms to be but accidents: though it is, for aught I know, as little intelligible how what is educed out of any matter, without being either pre-existent or being any part of the matter, can be a true substance, as how that roundness that makes a piece of brass become a sphere can be a new substance in it. Nor can they admit the *other way* of educing a form out of matter, as spirit is out of wine, because then not only matter will be corruptible against their grounds, but matter and form would not be two differing and substantial principles but one and the same, though diversified by firmness and[30] grossness, &c., which are but accidental differences. I know they speak much of the efficacy of the agent upon the matter in the generation of natural bodies, and tell us strange things of his manner of working. But not to spend time in examining those obscure niceties, I answer in short that, since the agent, be he what he will, is but a physical and finite agent, and since what way soever he works he can do nothing repugnant to the nature of things, the difficulty that sticks with me will still remain. For if the form produced in generation be, as they would have it, a substance that was not before to be found anywhere out of that portion of matter wherewith it constitutes the generated body, I say that either it must be produced by refining or subtiliating some parts of the matter into form, or else it must be produced out of nothing – that is, created (for I see no third way how a substance can be produced *de novo*). If they allow the first, then will the form be indeed a substance, but not, as they hold it is, distinct from matter, since matter however subtiliated is matter still, as the finest spirit of wine is as truly a body as was the wine itself that yielded it, or as is the grosser phlegm from which it was extracted: besides that the Peripatetics teach that the form is not made of anything of the matter; nor indeed is it conceivable how a physical agent can turn a material into an immaterial substance, especially matter being, as they themselves confess, as well incorruptible as ingenerable. But if they will not allow, as indeed they do not, that the substantial form is made of anything that is material, they must give me leave to believe that it is produced out of nothing, till they show me how a substance can be produced otherwise, that existed nowhere before. And at this rate every natural body of a special denomination, as gold, marble, nitre, &c., must not be produced barely by generation, but partly by generation and partly by creation. And since it is confessed on all sides that no natural agent can produce the least atom of matter, it is strange they should in generation allow every physical agent the power of producing a form – which, according to them, is not only a substance but a far nobler one than matter – and thereby attribute to the meanest creatures that power of creating substances which the ancient naturalists thought too great to be ascribed to God himself, and which indeed is too great to be ascribed to any other than him; and therefore some schoolmen and philosophers have derived forms immediately from God, but this is not only to desert Aristotle and the Peripatetic philosophy they would seem to maintain, but to put Omnipotence upon working I know not how many thousand miracles every hour, to perform that (I mean the generation of bodies of new denominations) in a supernatural way which seems the most familiar effect of nature in her ordinary course.

And as the production of forms out of the power of matter is for these reasons incomprehensible to me, so those things which the Peripatetics ascribe to their substantial forms are some of them such as I confess I cannot reconcile my reason to. For they tell us positively that these forms are substances; and yet at the same time they teach that they depend upon matter both *in fieri* and *in esse*, as they speak, so that out of the matter that supports them they cannot so much as exist (whence they are usually called *material forms°*), which is to make them substances in name and but accidents in truth: for, not to ask how (among physical things) one substance can be said to depend upon another *in fieri* that is not made of any part of it, the very notion of a substance is to be a self-subsisting entity, or that which needs no other created being to support it or to make it exist. Besides that, there being but two sorts of substances – material and immaterial – a substantial form must appertain to one of the two, and yet they ascribe things to it that make it very unfit to be referred to either. To all this I add that these imaginary material forms do almost as much trouble the doctrine of corruption as that of generation. For if a form be a true substance really distinct from matter, it must, as I lately noted, be able to exist of itself without any other substance to support it – as those I reason with confess that the soul of man survives the body it did before death inform – whereas they will have it that in corruption the form is quite abolished and utterly perishes, as not being capable of existing separated from the matter whereunto it was united; so that here again what they call a substance they make indeed an accident, and, besides, contradict their own vulgar doctrine that natural things are upon their corruption resolved into the first matter: since, at this rate, they should say that such things are but partly resolved into the first matter, and partly either into nothing, or into forms which, being as well immaterial as the souls of men, must, for aught appears, be also like them accounted immortal.

I should now examine those arguments that are wont to be employed by the Schools to evince their substantial forms, but, besides that the nature and scope of my present work enjoins me brevity, I confess that, one or two excepted, the arguments I have found mentioned as the chief are rather metaphysical or logical, than grounded upon the principles and phenomena of nature, and respect rather words than things; and therefore I, who have neither inclination nor leisure to wrangle about terms, shall content myself to propose, and very briefly answer, two or three of those that are thought the plausiblest.

First, then, they thus argue: *Omne compositum substantiale* (for it is hard to English well such uncouth terms) *requirit materiam et formam substantialem, ex quibus componatur. Omne corpus naturale est compositum substantiale. Ergo*, &c. In this syllogism some do plausibly enough deny the consequence, but for brevity's sake I shall rather choose to deny the minor, and desire the proposers to prove it. For I know not anything in nature that is composed of matter and a substance distinct from matter, except man, who alone is made up of an immaterial form and a human body; and if it be urged that then other bodies cannot be properly said to be *composita substantialia*, I shall, rather than wrangle with them, give them leave to find out some other name for other natural things.

But then they argue, in the next place, that if there were no substantial forms, all bodies would be but *entia per accidens*, as they speak: which is absurd. To which I answer that, in the notion that divers learned men have of an *ens per accidens* – namely, that it is that which consists of those things *quae non ordinantur ad unum* – it may be said that, though we do not admit substantial forms, yet we need not admit natural bodies to be *entia per accidens*: because in them the several things that concur to constitute the body, as matter, shape, situation, and motion, *ordinantur per se et intrinsece* to constitute one natural body. But if this answer satisfy not, I shall add that, for my part, that which I am solicitous about is what nature hath made things to be in themselves, not what a logician or metaphysician will call them in the terms of his art: it being much fitter, in my judgement, to alter words that they may better fit the nature of things, than to affix a wrong nature to things, that they may be accommodated to forms of words that were probably devised when the things themselves were not known, or well understood, if at all thought on.

Wherefore I shall but add one argument more of this sort, and that is that, if there were no substantial forms, neither could there be any substantial definitions: but the consequent is absurd, and therefore so is the antecedent. To which I reply that, since the Peripatetics themselves confess the forms of bodies to be of themselves unknown, all that this argument seems to me to conclude is but this, that if we do not admit some things that are not *in rerum natura* we cannot build our definitions upon them; nor indeed could we, if we should admit substantial forms, give substantial definitions of natural things, unless we could also define natural bodies by things that we know not: for such the substantial forms are (as we have seen already) confessed to be by the wisest Peripatetics,ʲ who pretend not to give the substantial definition of any natural *compositum* except man. But it may suffice us to have, instead of *substantial*, *essential* definitions of things – I mean such as are taken from the essential differences of things, which constitute them in such a sort of natural bodies and discriminate them from all those of any other sort.

These three arguments, Pyrophilus, for substantial forms, you may possibly, as well as I, find variously proposed and, perhaps with some light alterations, multiplied in the writings of the Peripatetics and schoolmen; but all the arguments of this kind that I have met with may, if I mistake not, be sufficiently solved by the answers we have given to these, or at least by the grounds upon which those answers are built: those seemingly various arguments agreeing in this, that either they respect rather words than things, or that they are grounded upon precarious suppositions, or lastly that they urge that as an absurdity which, whether it be one or not in those that admit the Peripatetic philosophy, to me, that do as little acquiesce in many of their other principles as I do in their substantial forms, doth not appear any absurdity at all. And it is, perhaps, for fear that arguments of this sort should not much prevail with naturalists, that some of the modern assertors of the forms we question have thought it requisite to add some more physical arguments, which (though I have not found them all in the same writers, yet) being in all but few, I shall here briefly consider them.

First, then, among the physical arguments that are brought to prove substantial forms, I find that the most confidently insisted on, which is taken from the spontaneous return of heated water to coldness: which effects, say they, must necessarily be ascribed to the action of the substantial form, whose office it is to preserve the body in its natural state, and, when there is occasion, to reduce it

---

ʲ '*Nego tibi ullam esse formam nobis notam plene et plane, nostramque scientiam esse umbram in sole.*' – Scaliger.

thereunto. And the argument indeed might be plausible, if we were sure that heated water would grow cold again (without the avolation of any parts more agitated than the rest), supposing it to be removed into some of the imaginary spaces beyond the world; but as the case is, I see no necessity of flying to a substantial form, the matter seeming to be easily explicable otherwise. The water we heat is surrounded with our air, or with some vessel or other body contiguous to the air, and both the air and the water in these climates are most commonly less agitated than the juices in our hands, or other organs of touching, which makes us esteem and call those fluids cold. Now when the water is exposed to the fire, it is thereby put into a new agitation more vehement than that of the parts of our sensory, which you will easily grant if you consider that, when the heat is intense, it makes the water boil and smoke and oftentimes run over the vessel; but when the liquor is removed from the fire, this acquired agitation must needs by degrees be lost, either by the avolation of such fiery corpuscles as the Epicureans imagine to be got into heated water, or by the water's communicating the agitation of its parts to the contiguous air, or to the vessel that contains it, till it have lost its surplusage of motion, or by the ingress of those frigorific atoms wherewith (if any such be to be granted) the air in these climates is wont to abound, and so be reduced into its former temperature: which may as well be done without a substantial form, as, if a ship swimming slowly down a river should by a sudden gust of wind, blowing the same way the stream runs, be driven on much faster than before, the vessel upon the ceasing of the wind may, without any such internal principle, return after a while to its former slowness of motion. So that in this phenomenon we need not have recourse to an internal principle, the temperature of the external air being sufficient to give an account of it. And if water be kept (as is usual in poor men's houses that want cellars) in the upper rooms of the house, in case the climate be hot the water will, in spite of the form, continue far less cold than according to the Peripatetics its nature requires, all the summer long. And let me here represent to the champions of forms that, according to their doctrine, the fluidity of water must at least as much proceed from its form as the coldness; and yet this does so much depend upon the temperature of the air, that in Nova Zembla vast quantities of water are kept in the hard and solid form of ice all the year long by the sharp cold of the ambient air, notwithstanding all the pretended office and power of the substantial form to keep it fluid: which it will never be reduced to be, unless by such a thawing temperature of the air as would itself, for aught appears, make it flow again, although there were no substantial form *in rerum natura*.

There is another argument much urged of late by some learned men, the substance whereof is this: that, matter being indifferent to one sort of accidents as well as to another, it is necessary there should be a substantial form to keep those accidents which are said to constitute it, united to the matter they belong to, and preserve both them and the body in their natural state; for since it is confessed that matter hath no appetite to these accidents more than to any others, they demand how, without a substantial form, these accidents can be contained and preserved. To this I might represent that I am not so well satisfied with the notion wont to be taken for granted, not only by the vulgar but by philosophers, of the natural state of bodies: as if it were undeniable that every natural body (for as to some I shall not *now* question it) has a certain state wherein nature endeavours to preserve it, and out of which it cannot be put but by being put into a preternatural state. For the world being once constituted by the great Author of things as it now is, I look upon the phenomena of nature to be caused by the local motion of one part of matter hitting against another, and am not so fully convinced that there is such a thing as nature's designing to keep such a parcel of matter in such a state that is clothed with just such accidents, rather than with any other. But I look upon many bodies, especially fluid ones, as frequently changing their state, according as they happen to be more or less agitated or otherwise wrought upon by the sun and other considerable agents in nature: as the air, water, and other fluids, if the temperature as to cold or heat, and rarefaction or condensation, which they are in at the beginning of the spring here at London, be pitched upon as their natural state, then not only in the torrid and frozen zones they must have other and very differing natural states, but here itself they will almost all the summer and all the winter, as our weather-glasses inform us, be in a varying preternatural state, because they will be in those seasons either more hot and rarefied, or more cold and condensed, than in the beginning of the spring. And in more stable and constant bodies, I take in many cases the natural state to be but either *the most usual state*, or *that wherein that which produces a notable change in them finds them*: as, when a slender piece of silver, that is most commonly flexible and will stand bent every way, comes to be well hammered, I count that flexibility to be the natural state of that metal, because most commonly silver is found to be flexible, and because it was so before it was hammered; but the springiness it acquires by hammering is a state which is properly no more unnatural to the silver than the other, and would continue with the metal as long as it, if both pieces of silver – the one flexible, the other springy – were let alone and kept from outward violence. And as the silver, to be deprived of its flexibleness, needed the violent motion of the hammer, so to deprive it of its spring it needs the violent agitation of a nealing fire. These things and much more I might here represent; but to come close to the objection, I answer that the accidents spoken of are introduced into the matter by the agents or efficient causes, whatever they be that produce in it what, in the sense formerly explained, we call an *essential* (though not a *substantial*) form. And these accidents being once thus introduced into the matter, we need not seek for a new substantial principle to preserve them there, since, by the general law or common course of nature, the matter qualified by them must continue in the state such accidents have put it into, till by some agent or other it be forcibly put out of it and so divested of those accidents: as, in the formerly-mentioned example, borrowed from Aristotle, of a brazen sphere, when once the motion of tools impelled and guided by the artificer have turned a piece of brass into a sphere, there needs no new substance to preserve that round figure, since the brass must retain it till it be destroyed by the artificer himself, or some other agent able to overcome the resistance of the matter to be put into another figure.+

And on this occasion let me confirm this *ad hominem*, by representing that there is not an inconsiderable party among the Peripatetics themselves who maintain that in the elements the first qualities (as they call them) are instead of forms, and that the fire (for instance) hath no other form than heat and dryness, and the water than coldness and moisture. Now if these bodies, that are the vastest and the most important of the sublunary world, consist but of the universal matter and the few accidents, and if in these there needs no substantial form to keep the qualities of the matter united to it and conjoined among themselves, and preserve them in that state as long as the law of nature requires – though, besides the four qualities that are called *first*, the elements have divers others, as gravity and levity, firmness and fluidity, opacousness and transparency, &c. – why should the favourers of this opinion deny that in other bodies, besides the elements, qualities may be preserved and kept united to the matter they belong to without the band or support of a substantial form? And as, when there is no competent destructive cause, the accidents of a body will by the law of nature remain such as they were, so, if there be, it cannot with reason be pretended that the substantial form is able to preserve all those accidents of a body that are said to flow from it and to be, as it were, under its care and tuition. For if, for instance, you expose a sphere or bullet of lead to a strong fire, it will quickly lose (not to mention its figure) both its coldness, its consistence, its malleableness, its colour (for it will appear of the colour of fire), its flexibility, and some other qualities – and all this in spite of the imaginary substantial form, which, according to the Peripatetical principles, in this case must still remain in it without being able to help it. And though, upon the taking the lead from off the fire, it is wont to be reduced to most of its former qualities (for it will not of itself recover its sphericity), yet that may well be ascribed partly to its peculiar texture, and partly to the coldness of the ambient air – according to what we lately discoursed touching heated and refrigerated water – which temperature of the air is an extrinsical thing to the lead: and indeed it is but accidental that the lead upon refrigeration regains its former qualities, for in case the lead have been exposed long enough to a sufficiently intense fire, it will (as we have purposely tried) be turned into glass, and lose its colour, its opacity, its malleableness, and (former degree of) flexibleness, and acquire a reddishness, a degree of transparency, a brittleness, and some other qualities that it had not before; and let the supposed substantial form do what it can, even when the vessel is removed from the fire, to reduce or restore the body to its natural state and accidents, yet the former qualities will remain lost as long as these preternatural ones introduced by the fire continue in the matter, and neither the one will be restored nor the other destroyed till some sufficiently powerful extrinsic agent effect the change. And on the other side, I consider that the fruit, when severed from the tree it grew on, is confessed to be no longer animated (at least the kernels or seeds excepted) by the vegetative soul or substantial form of the plant; yet in an orange or lemon (for instance), plucked from the tree, we see that the same colour, the same odour, the same taste, the same figure, the same consistence, and, for aught we know, the same other qualities – whether sensible or even occult, as are its antidotal and antiscorbutical virtues – that must before be said to have flowed from the soul of the tree, will continue many months, perhaps some years, after the fruit has ceased to have any commerce with the tree (nay, though the tree whereon it grew be perhaps in the meantime hewn down or burnt, and though consequently its vegetative soul or form be destroyed), as when it grew thereon and made up one plant with it. And we find that tamarinds, rhubarb, senna, and many other simples, will, for divers years after they have been deprived of their former vegetative soul, retain their purgative and other specific properties.

I find it likewise urged that there can be no reason why whiteness should be separable from a wall, and not from snow or milk, unless we have recourse to substantial forms. But in case men have agreed to call a thing by such a name, because it has such a particular quality that differences it from others, we need go no farther to find a reason why one quality is essential to one thing and not to another. As in our former example of a brass sphere, the figure is that for which we give it that name; and therefore, though you may alter the figure of the matter, yet by that very alteration the body perishes in the capacity of a sphere, whereas its coldness may be exchanged for heat without the making it the less a sphere, because it is not for any such quality, but for roundness, that a body is said to be a *sphere*.° And so firmness is an inseparable quality of ice, though this or that particular figure be not, because that it is for want of fluidity that anything that was immediately before a liquor is called *ice*.° And congruously hereunto, though whiteness were inseparable from snow and milk, yet that would not necessarily infer that there must be a substantial form to make it so: for the firmness of the corpuscles that compose snow is as inseparable from it as the whiteness, and yet[31] is not pretended to be the effect of the substantial form of the water, but of the excess of the coldness of the air, which (to use vulgar though perhaps inaccurate expressions) puts the water out of its natural state of fluidity and into a preternatural one of firmness and brittleness. And the reason why snow seldom loses its whiteness, but with its nature, seems to be that its component particles are so disposed that the same heat of the ambient air that is fit to turn it into a transparent body is also fit to make it a fluid one, which when it is become, we no longer call it *snow*,° but *water*:° so that the water loses its whiteness, though the snow do not. But if there be a cause proper to make a convenient alteration of texture in the snow without melting or resolving it into water, it may then exchange its whiteness for yellowness without losing its right to be called *snow*:° as I remember I have read in an eminent writer that *de facto*, in the northern regions towards the pole, those parcels of snow that have lain very long on the ground degenerate[32] in time into a yellowish colour, very differing from that pure whiteness to be observed in the neighbouring snow lately fallen.

But there yet remains an argument for substantial forms, which, though (perhaps because physical) wont to be overlooked or slightly answered by their opposers, will for the same reason deserve to be taken notice of here; and it is that there seems to be a necessity of admitting substantial forms in bodies, that from thence we may derive all the various changes to which they are subject, and the differing effects they produce – the preservation and restitution of the state requisite to each particular body, as also the keeping of its several parts united into one *totum*. To the answering of this argument so many things will be found applicable, both in the past and subsequent parts of these notes, that I shall at present but point the chief particulars on which the solution is grounded.

I consider, then, first, that many and great alterations may happen to bodies, which seem manifestly to proceed from their peculiar texture and the action of outward agents upon them, and of which it cannot be shown that they would happen otherwise though there were no substantial forms *in rerum natura*: as we see that tallow (for instance), being melted by the fire, loses its coldness, firmness, and its whiteness, and acquires heat, fluidity, and some transparency, all which, being suffered to cool, it presently exchanges for the three first-named qualities. And yet divers of these changes are plainly enough the effects partly of the fire, partly of the ambient air, and not of I know not what substantial form; and it is both evident and remarkable what great variety of changes in qualities, and productions of new ones, the fire (that is, a body consisting of insensible parts that are variously and vehemently moved) doth effect by its heat – that is, *by a modified local motion*. I consider, further, that various operations of a body may be derived from the peculiar texture of the whole and the mechanical affections of the particular corpuscles or other parts that compose it: as we have often occasion to declare here and there in this treatise, and particularly by an instance ere long to be further insisted on, namely, that though vitriol made of iron with a corrosive liquor be but a factitious body, made by a convenient apposition of the small parts of the saline menstruum to those of the metal, yet this vitriol will do most, if not all, of the same things that vitriol made by nature in the bowels of the earth, and digged out thence, will perform; and each of these bodies may be endowed with variety of differing qualities, which I see not why they must flow in the native vitriol from a substantial form, since in the factitious vitriol the same qualities belong to a form that does plainly emerge from the coalition of metalline and saline corpuscles associated together and disposed of after a certain manner.

And lastly, as to what is very confidently as well as plausibly pretended, that a substantial form is requisite to keep the parts of a body united, without which it would not be one body, I answer that the contrivance of conveniently figured parts, and in some cases their juxtaposition, may, without the assistance of a substantial form, be sufficient for this matter. For not to repeat what I just now mentioned concerning vitriol made by art, whose parts are as well united and kept together as those of the native vitriol, I observe that a pear grafted upon a thorn, or a plum inoculated upon an apricot, will bear good fruit and grow up with the stock, as though they both made but one tree and were animated but by the same common form: whereas indeed both the stock and the inoculated or grafted plant have each of them its own form, as may appear by the differing leaves and fruits and seeds they bear. And that which makes to our present purpose is that even vegetation and the distribution of aliments are in such cases well made, though the nourished parts of the total plant, if I may so call it, have not one common soul or form: which is yet more remarkable in the mistletoes that I have seen growing upon old hazel trees, crab trees, apple trees, and other plants, in which the mistletoe often differs very widely from that kind of plant on which it grows and prospers. And for the durableness of the union betwixt bodies, that a substantial form is not requisite to procure it, I have been induced to think by considering that silver and gold, being barely mingled by infusion, will have their minute parts more closely united than those of any plant or animal that we know of. And there is scarce any natural body wherein the form makes so strict, durable, and indissoluble, a union of the parts it consists of, as that which in that factitious concrete we call glass arises from the bare commixtion of the corpuscles of sand with those saline ones wherewith they are colliquated by the violence of the fire; and the like may be said of the union of the proper accidents of glass with the matter of it, and betwixt one another.

To draw towards a conclusion: I know it is alleged as a main consideration on the behalf of substantial forms that, these being in natural bodies the true principles of their properties and consequently of their operations, their natural philosophy must needs be very imperfect and defective, who will not take in such forms; but, for my part, I confess that this very consideration does rather indispose than incline me to admit them. For if indeed there were in every natural body such a thing as a substantial form, from which all its properties and qualities immediately flow, since we see that the actions of bodies upon one another are for the most part (if not all) immediately performed by their qualities or accidents, it would scarce be possible to explicate very many of the explicable phenomena of nature without having recourse to them, and it would be strange if many of the abstruser phenomena were not explicable by them only: whereas indeed almost all the rational accounts to be met with of difficult phenomena are given by such as either do not *acknowledge*, or at least do not *take notice of*, substantial forms. And it is evident by the clear solutions (untouched by many vulgar philosophers) we meet with of many phenomena in the statics and other parts of the mechanics, and especially in the hydrostatics and pneumatics, how clearly many phenomena may be solved without employing a substantial form. And on the other side, I do not remember that either Aristotle himself (who perhaps scarce ever attempted it), or any of his followers, has given a solid and intelligible solution of any one phenomenon of nature by the help of substantial forms: which you need not think it strange I should say, since, the greatest patrons of forms acknowledging[33] their nature to be unknown to us,[k] to explain any effect by a substantial form must be to declare (as they speak) *ignotum per ignotius*, or at least *per aeque ignotum*. And indeed, to explicate a phenomenon being to deduce it from something else in nature more known to us than the thing to be explained by it, how can the employing of incomprehensible (or at least uncomprehended) substantial forms help us to explain intelligibly this or that particular phenomenon? For to say that such

---

[k] '*Nomina tu lapidis, qui quotidie tuis oculis observatur, formam, et Phyllida solus habeto.*' – Scaliger, *contra* Cardan.

an effect proceeds not from this or that quality of the agent, but from its substantial form, is to take an easy way to resolve all difficulties in general without rightly resolving any one in particular, and would make a rare philosophy if it were not far more easy than satisfactory. For if it be demanded why jet attracts straws, rhubarb purges choler, snow dazzles the eyes rather than grass, &c., to say that these and the like effects are performed by the substantial forms of the respective bodies is, at best, but to tell me what is the agent, not how the effect is wrought; and seems to be but such a kind of general way of answering, as leaves the curious enquirer as much to seek for the *causes* and *manner* of particular things, as men commonly are for the particular causes of the several strange things performed by witchcraft, though they be told that it is some devil that does them all. Wherefore I do not think but that natural philosophy, without being for that the more defective, may well enough spare the doctrine of substantial forms as a useless theory – not that men are yet[34] arrived to be able to explicate all the phenomena of nature without them, but because whatever we cannot explicate without them, we cannot neither intelligibly explicate *by* them.

And thus, Pyrophilus, I have offered you some of those many things that indisposed me to acquiesce in the received doctrine of substantial forms; but in case any more piercing enquirer shall persuade himself that he understands it thoroughly and can explicate it clearly, I shall congratulate him for such happy intellectuals, and be very ready to be informed by him. But since what the Schools are wont to teach of the origin and attributes of substantial forms is that which I confess I cannot yet comprehend – and since I have some of the eminentest persons among the modern philosophers to join with me, though perhaps not for the same considerations, in the like confession, that it is not necessary the reason of my not finding this doctrine conceivable must be rather a defectiveness in my understanding than the unconceivable nature of the thing itself – I, who love not (in matters purely philosophical) to acquiesce in what I do not understand, nor to go about to explicate things to others by what appears to me itself inexplicable, shall, I hope, be excused if, leaving those that contend for them the liberty of making what use they can of substantial forms, I do till I be better satisfied decline employing them myself, and endeavour to solve those phenomena I attempt to give an account of without them, as not scrupling to confess that those that I cannot explicate, at least in a general way, by intelligible principles, I am not yet arrived to the distinct and particular knowledge of.

Now for our doctrine touching the origin of forms, it will not be difficult to collect it from what we formerly discoursed about qualities and forms together. For the form of a natural body being, according to us, but an essential modification and, as it were, the *stamp* of its matter, or such a convention of the bigness, shape, motion (or rest), situation, and contexture (together with the thence-resulting qualities) of the small parts that compose the body, as is necessary to constitute and denominate such a particular body, and all these accidents being producible in matter by local motion, it is agreeable to our hypothesis to say that the first and universal, though not immediate, cause of forms is none other but God, who *put matter into motion* (which belongs not to its essence), and *established the laws of motion* amongst bodies, and also, according to my opinion, *guided it in divers cases at the beginning of things*; and that, among second causes, the grand efficient of forms is *local motion*, which, by variously dividing, sequestering, transposing, and so connecting, the parts of matter, produces in them those accidents and qualities upon whose account the portion of matter they diversify comes to belong to this or that determinate species of natural bodies: which yet is not so to be understood as if *motion* were only an efficient cause in the generation of bodies, but very often (as in water, fire, &c.) it is also one of the chief *accidents* that concur to make up the form.

But in this last summary account of the origin of forms, I think myself obliged to declare to you a little more distinctly what I just now intimated to be my own opinion. And this I shall do by advertising you that, though I agree with our Epicureans in thinking it probable that the world is made up of an innumerable multitude of singly insensible corpuscles, endowed with their own sizes, shapes, and motions, and though I agree with the Cartesians in believing (as I find that Anaxagoras[l] did of old) that matter hath not its motion from itself, but originally from God, yet in this I differ[ʹ] both from Epicurus and Descartes, that – whereas the former of them plainly denies that the world was made by any deity (for deities he owned), and the latter of them, for aught I can find in his

---

[l] Aristotle, speaking of Anaxagoras in the first chapter of the last Book of his *Physics*, hath this passage: '*Dicit* [Anaxagoras] *cum omnia simul essent atque* quiescerent *tempore infinito, mentem* movisse *ac segregasse.*'

writings or those of some of his eminentest disciples, thought that God, having once put matter into motion and established the laws of that motion, needed not more particularly interpose for the production of things corporeal, nor even of plants or animals, which according to him are but enginès – I do not at all believe that either these *Cartesian laws of motion*, or the *Epicurean casual concourse* of atoms, could bring mere matter into so orderly and well contrived a fabric as this world. And therefore I think that the wise Author of nature did not only *put matter into motion*, but, when he resolved to make the world, did so regulate and *guide the motions* of the small parts of the universal matter as to reduce the greater systems of them into the order they were to continue in, and did more particularly contrive some portions of that matter into seminal rudiments or principles, lodged in convenient receptacles (and, as it were, wombs), and others into the bodies of plants and animals: one main part of whose contrivance did, as I apprehend, consist in this, that some of their organs were so framed that, supposing the fabric of the greater bodies of the universe and the laws he had established in nature, some juicy and spirituous parts of these living creatures must be fit to be turned into prolific seeds, whereby they may have a power, by generating their like, to propagate their species. So that, according to my apprehension, it was *at the beginning* necessary that an intelligent and wise Agent should contrive the universal matter into the world (and especially some portions of it into seminal organs and principles) and settle the laws according to which the motions and actions of its parts upon one another should be regulated: without which interposition of the world's Architect, however *moving matter* may, with some *probability* (for I see not in the notion any certainty), be conceived to be able, after numberless occursions of its insensible parts, to cast itself into such grand conventions and convolutions as the Cartesians call *vortices*, and as I remember Epicurus speaks of under the name of προσκρίσεις καὶ δινήσεις,[m] yet I think it utterly improbable that *brute* and *unguided*, though *moving*, matter should ever convene into such admirable structures as the bodies of perfect animals. But the world being once framed, and the course of nature established, the naturalist (except in some few cases where God or incorporeal agents interpose) has recourse to the first cause but for its general and ordinary support and influence, whereby it

[m] Epicurus in his *Epistle to Pythocles*.

preserves matter and motion from annihilation or desition; and in explicating *particular phenomena* considers only the *size, shape, motion* (or *want of it*), *texture,* and the resulting qualities and attributes, of the small particles of matter. And thus in this great *automaton,* the world (as in a watch or clock), the materials it consists of being left to themselves could never at the first convene into so curious an engine: and yet, when the skilful artist has once made and set it a-going, the phenomena it exhibits are to be accounted for by the *number, bigness, proportion, shape, motion* (or *endeavour*), *rest, coaptation,* and other mechanical affections, of the spring, wheels, pillars, and other parts it is made up of; and those effects of such a watch that cannot this way be explicated must, for aught I yet know, be confessed not to be sufficiently understood.

But to return thither, whence my duty to the Author of nature obliged me to make this short digression:| the hitherto proposed hypothesis touching the origination of forms *hath*, I hope, been rendered probable by divers particulars in the past discourses, and *will* be both exemplified and confirmed by some of the experiments that make the latter part of this present treatise (especially the fifth and seventh of them), which, containing experiments of the changing the form of a salt and a metal, do chiefly belong to the historical or experimental part of what we deliver touching the origin of forms. And indeed, besides the *two kinds* of experiments presently to be mentioned, we might here present you a third sort, consisting partly of divers relations of metalline transmutations delivered, upon their own credit, by credible men that are not alchemists, and partly of some experiments (some made, some directed, by us) of changing both bodies totally *inflammable* almost totally into *water*, and a good part even of *distilled rain-water* without additament into *earth*, and distilled liquors readily and totally mingleable with water *pro parte* into a true *oil* that will not mix with it. This sort of experiments, I say, I might here annex, if I thought fit in this place either to lay any stress upon those that I cannot myself make out, or to transfer hither those experiments of changes amongst bodies not metalline that belong to another treatise.[n] But over and above what the past notes and the experiments that are to follow them contain towards the making of what we teach concerning forms, we will here for further confirmation proceed to

[n] *The Sceptical Chemist.*

add two sorts of experiments (besides the third already mentioned): the *one*, wherein it appears that bodies of very differing natures, being put together like the wheels and other pieces of a watch, and by their connexion acquiring a new texture, and so new qualities, may, without having recourse to a substantial form, compose such a new concrete as may as well deserve to have a substantial form attributed to it, by virtue of that new disposition of its parts, as other bodies that are said to be endowed therewith; and the *other*, that a natural body, being dissipated and, as it were, taken in pieces like a watch, may have its parts so associated as to constitute new bodies, of natures very differing from its own and from each other, and yet these dissipated and scattered parts, by being re-collected and put together again like the pieces of a watch in the like order as before, may recompose (almost, if not more than almost) such another body as that they made up before they were taken asunder.

1. Experiments and Thoughts about the Production and Reproduction of Forms

It was not at random that I spoke when, in the foregoing notes about the origin of qualities, I intimated that it was very much by a kind of tacit agreement that men had distinguished the species of bodies, and that those distinctions were more arbitrary than we are wont to be aware of. For I confess that I have not yet, either in Aristotle or any other writer, met with any genuine and sufficient diagnostic and boundary for the discriminating and limiting the species of things; or, to speak more plainly, I have not found that any naturalist has laid down a determinate number and sort of qualities or other attributes, which is *sufficient* and *necessary* to constitute all portions of matter endowed with them distinct kinds of natural bodies. And therefore I observe that most commonly men look upon these as distinct species of bodies, that have had the luck to have distinct names found out for them, though perhaps divers of them differ much less from one another than other bodies which (because they have been huddled up under one name) have been looked upon as but one sort of bodies. But not to lay any weight on this intimation about names, I found that, for want of a true characteristic or discriminating notes, it hath been and is still both very *uncertain*, as to divers bodies, whether they are of different species or of the same, and very *difficult* to give a sufficient reason why divers bodies wherein nature is assisted by art should not as well pass for distinct kinds of bodies as others that are generally reckoned to be so.

Whether (for instance) water and ice be not to be esteemed distinct kinds of bodies is so little evident, that some that pretend to be very well versed in Aristotle's writings and opinions affirm him to teach that water loses not its own nature by being turned into ice, and indeed I remember I have read a text of his that seems express enough to this purpose;[o] and the thing itself is made plausible by the reducibleness of ice back again into water. And yet I remember Galen is affirmed to make these two distinct species of bodies, which doctrine is favoured by the differing qualities of ice and water; for not only the one is fluid and the other solid and even brittle, but ice is also commonly more or less opacous in comparison of water, being also lighter than it *in specie*, since it swims upon it: to which may be added that ice beaten with common salt will freeze other bodies, when water mingled with salt will not. And on this occasion I would propose to be resolved whether must, wine, spirit of wine, vinegar, tartar, and vappa, be specifically distinct bodies. And the like question[35] I would ask concerning a hen's egg and the chick that is afterwards hatched out of it, as also concerning wood, ashes, soot; and likewise the eggs of silkworms, which are first small caterpillars or (as some think them) but worms, when they are newly hatched, and then aurelias (or husked maggots), and then butterflies – which I have observed, with pleasure, to be the successive production of the prolific seed of silkworms. And whether the answer to these queries be affirmative or negative, I doubt the reason that will be given for either of the two will not hold in divers cases whereto I might apply it. And a more puzzling question it may be to some whether a charcoal, being thoroughly kindled, do specifically differ from another charcoal: for according to those I argue with, the fire has *penetrated* it quite through; and therefore some of the recent Aristotelians are so convinced of its being transmuted, that all the satisfaction I could find from a very subtle modern schoolman, to the objection that if the glowing coal were plunged into water it would

---

[o] See *De Generatione & Corruptione*, lib. I, cap. 9. 'Idem corpus,' says he there, '*quanquam continuum, alias liquidum, alias concretum videmus, non divisione aut compositione hoc passum, aut conversione aut attactu, sicuti Democritus asserit: nam neque transpositione, neque naturae demutatione* (οὐ τὸ μεταβάλλον τὴν φύσιν) *ex liquido concretum evadere solet.*'

be a black coal again, was that, notwithstanding that reduction, the form of a charcoal had been once abolished by the fire, and was reproduced by God upon the regained disposition of the matter to receive it.

Nor is it very easy to determine whether clouds and rain and hail and snow be bodies specifically distinct from water and from each other, and the writers of meteors are wont to handle them as distinct. And[36] if such slight differences as those that discriminate these bodies, or that which distinguishes wind from exhalations whose course makes it, be sufficient to constitute differing kinds of bodies, it will be hard to give a satisfactory reason why other bodies that differ in more, or more considerable, particulars should not enjoy the same privilege. And I presume that snow differs less from rain than paper doth from rags, or glass made of wood-ashes does from wood. And indeed, men having by tacit consent agreed to look upon paper, and glass, and soap, and sugar, and brass, and ink, and pewter, and gunpowder, and I know not how many others, to be distinct sorts of bodies, I see not why they may not be thought to have done it on as good grounds as those upon which divers other differing species of bodies have been constituted. Nor will it suffice to object that these bodies are *factitious*; for it is the present nature of bodies that ought to be considered in referring them to species, which way soever they came by that nature. For salt, that is in many countries made by boiling sea-water in cauldrons and other vessels, is as well true sea-salt as that which is made in the Isle of Man (as navigators call it), without any co-operation of man, by the bare action of the sun upon those parts of the sea-water which chance to be left behind in hollow places after a high spring-tide; and silkworms which will hatch by the heat of human bodies, and chickens that are hatched in Egypt by the heat of ovens or dunghills, are no less true silkworms or chickens than those that are hatched by the sun or by hens.

As for what may be objected, that we must distinguish betwixt factitious bodies and natural, I will not now stay to examine how far that distinction may be allowed. For it may suffice for our present purpose to represent that, whatever may be said of factitious bodies where man does, by instruments of his own providing, only give figure, or also contexture, to the *sensible* (not insensible) parts of the matter he works upon – as when a joiner makes a stool, or a statuary makes an image, or a turner a bowl – yet the case may be very differing in those other factitious productions wherein the *insensible* parts of matter are altered by natural agents, who perform the greatest part of the work among themselves, though the artificer be an assistant by putting them together after a due manner. And therefore I know not why all the productions of the fire made by chemists should be looked upon as not natural but artificial bodies, since the fire, which is the grand agent in these changes, doth not, by being employed by the chemist, cease to be and to work as a natural agent; and since nature herself doth, by the help of the fire, sometimes afford us the like productions that the alchemist's art presents us: as in Etna, Vesuvius, and other burning mountains (some of whose productions I can show you), stones are sometimes turned into lime (and so an alkalizate salt is produced), and sometimes, if they be more disposed to be fluxed than calcined, brought to vitrification; metalline and mineral bodies are by the violence of the fire colliquated into masses of very strange and compounded natures; ashes and metalline flowers of divers kinds are scattered about the neighbouring places, and copious flowers of sulphur, sublimed by the internal fire, have been several times found about the vents at which the fumes are discharged into the air (as I have been assured by ingenious visitors of such places, whom I purposely enquired of touching these *flores*, for of these travellers more than one answered me they had themselves gathered and had brought some very good). Not to add that I have sometimes suspected, upon no absurd grounds, that divers of the minerals and other bodies we meet with in the lower parts of the earth, and think to have been formed and lodged there ever since the beginning of things, have been since produced there by the help of subterraneal fires or other heats, which may either, by their immediate action and exceedingly long application, very much alter some bodies by changing their texture – as when lead is turned into minium, and tin into putty, by the operation of the fire in a few hours – or by elevating, in the form of exhalations or vapours, divers saline and sulphureous corpuscles or particles of unripe (or, to use a chemical term of art, embryonated) minerals, and perhaps metals, which may very much alter the nature, and thereby vary the kind, of other subterraneal bodies which they pervade and in which they often come to be incorporated; or else may, by convening among themselves, constitute particular concretions, as we see that the fumes of sulphur and those of mercury unite into that lovely red

mass which in the shops they call *vermilion*,° and which is so like to
the mineral whence we usually obtain mercury that the Latins give
them both the same name, *cinnabaris*, and in that are imitated by the
French and Italians – in whose favour I shall add that, if we suppose
this mineral to consist of a stony concretion penetrated by such
mineral fumes as I have been speaking of, the appellation may be
better excused than perhaps you imagine, since from *cinnabaris nativa*
not only I obtained a considerable quantity of good running mercury
(which is that men are wont to seek for from it) but, to gratify my
curiosity somewhat further, I tried an easy way that came into my
mind, whereby the *caput mortuum* afforded me no despicable quantity
of good combustible sulphur. But this upon the bye, being not
obliged to set down here the grounds of my paradoxical conjecture
about the effects of subterraneal fires and heats, since I here lay no
stress upon it, but return to what I was saying about Etna and other
volcans. Since, then, these productions of the fire, being of nature's
own making, cannot be denied to be natural bodies, I see not why
the like productions of the fire should be thought unworthy that
name, only because the fire that made the former was kindled by
chance in a hill, and that which produced the latter was kindled by a
man in a furnace. And if flower of sulphur, lime, glass, and
colliquated mixtures of metals and minerals, are to be reckoned
among natural bodies, it seems to be but reasonable that, upon the
same grounds, we should admit flower of antimony, lime, and glass,
and pewter, and brass, and many other chemical concretes (if I may
so call them), to be taken into the same number; and then it will be
evident that, to distinguish the species of natural bodies, a concourse
of accidents will, without considering any substantial form, be
sufficient.

But because I need not on this occasion have recourse to instances
of a disputable nature, I will pitch, for the illustration of the
mechanical production of forms, upon vitriol. For since nature
herself, without the help of art, does oftentimes produce that
concrete (as I have elsewhere shown by experience), there is no
reason why vitriol, produced by easy chemical operations, should
not be looked upon as a body of the same nature and kind. And in
factitious vitriol, our knowing what ingredients we make use of, and
how we put them together, enables us to judge very well how vitriol
is produced. But because it is wont to be reckoned with saltpetre,
sea-salt, and sal-gem, among true salts, I think it requisite to take

notice in the first place that vitriol is not a mere salt, but that which
Paracelsus somewhere, and after him divers other spagyrists, call a
magistery,° which in their sense (for there are that use it in another)
commonly signifies a preparation wherein the body to be prepared
has not its *principles separated*, as in distillation, incineration, &c., but
wherein the *whole body* is brought into another form by the *addition* of
some salt or menstruum that is united *per minima* with it. And
agreeably to this notion, we find that from common vitriol, whether
native or factitious, may be obtained (by distillation and reduction)
an acid saline spirit and a metalline substance, as I elsewhere
mention that from blue vitriol copper may be (by more than one
way) separated. And I the rather give this advertisement, because
that, as there is a vitriol of iron which is usually green, and another
of copper which is wont to be blue, and also a white vitriol about
which it is disputed what it holds (though that it holds some copper
I have found), and yet all of these are without scruple reputed true
vitriols, notwithstanding that they differ so much in colour and (as I
have discovered) in several other qualities, so I see no reason why the
other minerals, being reduced by their proper menstruums into salt-
like magisteries, may not pass for the vitriols of those metals, and
consequently for natural bodies: which, if granted, will add some
confirmation to our doctrine, though its being granted is not
necessary to make it out. For to confine ourselves to vitriol, it is
known among chemists that, if upon the filings of mars one put a
convenient quantity of that acid distilled liquor which is (abusively)
wont to be called *oil of vitriol*,° diluting the mixture with rain or with
common water, it is easy, by filtrating the solution, by evaporating
the aqueous superfluity of it, and by leaving the rest for a competent
while in a cellar (or other cold place) to crystallize – it is easy, I say,
by this means to obtain a vitriol of iron, which agrees with the other
vitriol, of vitriol-stones or marcasites, presented us by nature
without the help of any other menstruum than the rain that falls
upon them from the clouds, in I know not how many qualities, part
obvious and part of them occult: as (of the *first sort*) in colour,
transparency, brittleness, easiness of fusion, styptical taste,
reducibleness to a red powder by calcination, and other qualities
more obvious to be taken notice of; to which may be annexed divers
qualities of the *second sort* (I mean the more abstruse ones), as the
power to turn in a trice an infusion of galls made in ordinary water
(as also to turn a certain clear mineral solution, elsewhere

mentioned) into an inky colour, to which in all probability we may add a faculty of causing vomits, even in a small dose, when taken into the stomach of a man, and that remarkable property of being endowed with as exact and curious a shape or figure as those for which salts have been, by modern philosophers especially, so much admired. But that no scruple might arise from hence that, in the *vitriolum martis* wont to be made by chemists, the menstruum that is employed is the oil of common vitriol, which may be suspected to have retained the nature of the concrete whence it proceeded – and so this factitious vitriol may not be barely a new production, but partly a recorporification, as they speak, of the vitriolate corpuscles contained in the menstruum – to prevent this scruple, I say (which yet perhaps would not much trouble a considering chemist), I thought fit to employ a quite other menstruum, that would not be suspected to have anything of vitriol in it. And though *aqua fortis* and spirit of nitre, however they *corrode* mars, are unfit for such a work, yet, having pitched upon spirit of salt instead of oil of vitriol, and proceeding the same way that has been already set down, it answered our expectation and afforded us a good green vitriol. Nor will the great disposition I have observed in this our vitriol, to resolve, by the moisture of the air, into a liquor, make it essentially differing from other vitriols, since it has been observed, and particularly by Guntherus Belichius more than once, that even the common vitriol he used in Germany will also, though not so easily as other salts, run (as the chemists phrase it) *per deliquium*. And to make the experiment more complete, though we did not find either oil of vitriol or spirit of salt good menstruums to make a blue venereal vitriol out of copper (however filed, or thinly laminated), and though upon more trials than one it appeared that *aqua fortis* and spirit of nitre, which we thought fit to substitute to the above-mentioned liquors, did indeed make a solution of copper, but so unctuous a one that it was very hard to bring any part of it to dryness without spoiling the colour and shape of the desired body, yet, repeating the experiment with care and watchfulness, we this way obtained one of the loveliest vitriols that hath perhaps been seen, and of which you yourself may be the judge by a parcel of it I keep by me for a rarity.

To apply now these experiments, especially that wherein spirit of salt is employed, to the purpose for which I have mentioned them, let us briefly consider these two things: the one, that our factitious vitriol is a body that, as well as the natural, is endowed with many qualities (manifest and occult), not only such as are common to it with other salts, as transparency, brittleness, solubleness in water, &c., but such as are properties peculiar to it, as greenness, easiness of fusion, stypticity of taste, a peculiar shape, a power to strike a black with infusion of galls, an emetic faculty, &c. | The other thing we are to consider is that, though these qualities are in common vitriol believed to flow from the substantial form of the concrete, and may, as justly as the qualities, whether manifest or occult, of other inanimate bodies, be employed as arguments to evince such a form, yet, in our vitriol made with spirit of salt, the same qualities and properties were produced by the associating and juxtaposition of the two ingredients of which the vitriol was compounded: the mystery being no more but this, that the steel being dissolved in the spirit, the saline particles of the former and the metalline ones of the latter, having each their determinate shapes, did by their association compose divers corpuscles of a mixed or compounded nature, from the convention of many whereof there resulted a new body, of such a texture as qualified it to affect our sensories, and work upon other bodies, after such a manner as common vitriol is wont to do. And indeed in our case, not only it cannot be made appear that there is any substantial form generated anew, but that there is not so much as an exquisite mixture, according to the common notion the Schools have of such a mixture. For both the ingredients retain their nature (though perhaps somewhat altered), so that there is, as we were saying, but a juxtaposition of the metalline and saline corpuscles; only they are associated so as, by the manner of their coalition, to acquire that new texture which denominates the magistery they compose *vitriol*.° For it is evident that the saline ingredient may either totally, or for much the greatest part, be separated by distillation, the metalline remaining behind. Nay, some of the qualities we have been ascribing to our vitriol do so much depend upon texture that the very beams of the sun (converged) will, as I have purposely tried, very easily alter its colour as well as spoil its transparency, turning it at first from green to white, and, if they be concentred by a good burning-glass, making it change that livery for a deep red.

Doubts and experiments touching the curious figures of salts

And here let me take notice that, though the exact and curious figures in which vitriol and other salts are wont to shoot be made arguments of the *presence*, and great instances of the *plastic skill*, of substantial forms and seminal powers, yet I confess I am not so fully satisfied in this matter as even the modern philosophers appear to be. It is not that I deny that Plato's excellent saying, 'γεωμετρεῖ ὁ Θεός', may be applied to these exquisite productions of nature. For though God has thought fit to make things corporeal after a much more facile and intelligible way than by the intervention of substantial forms, and though the plastic power of seeds, which in plants and animals I willingly admit, seem not in our case to be needful, yet is the divine Architect's geometry (if I may so call it) nevertheless to be acknowledged and admired, for having been pleased to make the *primary* and insensible corpuscles of salts and metals of such determinate, curious, and exact shapes that, as they happen to be associated together, they should naturally produce concretions which, though *differingly* figured according to the respective natures of their ingredients and the various manners of their convening, should yet be all of them very *curious*, and seem elaborate in their kinds. How little I think it fit to be allowed that the bodies of animals, which consist of so many curiously framed and wonderfully adapted organical parts (and whose structure is a thousand times more artificial than that of salts and stones and other minerals), can be reasonably supposed to have been produced by chance, or without the guidance of an intelligent Author of things, I have elsewhere largely declared. But I confess I look upon these figures we admire in salts and in some kinds of stones (which I have not been incurious to collect) as textures so simple and slight, in comparison of the bodies of animals, and oftentimes in comparison of some one organical part, that I think it cannot be in the least inferred that, because such slight figurations need not be ascribed to the plastic power of seeds, it is not necessary that the stupendious and incomparably more elaborate fabric and structure of animals themselves should be so. And this premised, I shall add that I have been inclined to the conjecture about the shapes of salts that I lately proposed, by these considerations:

First, that by a bare association of metalline and saline corpuscles, a concrete as finely figured as other vitriols may be produced, as we have lately seen.

Secondly, because that the figures of these salts are not constantly in all respects the same, but may in divers manners be somewhat varied, as they happen to be made to shoot more hastily or more leisurely, and as they shoot in a scanter or in a fuller proportion of liquor. This may be easily observed by any that will but with a little attention consider the difference that may be found in vitriolate crystals or grains, when quantities of them were taken out of the great coolers, as they call them, wherein that salt, at the works where it is boiled, is wont to be set to shoot. And accordingly, where the experienced mineralist Agricola describes the several ways of making vitriol in great quantities, he does not only more than once call the great grains or crystals, into which it coagulates, *cubes*;° but, speaking of the manner of their concretion about the cords or ropes that are wont (in Germany) to be hanged from certain cross-bars into the vitriolate water or solution for the vitriol to fasten itself to, he compares the concretions indifferently to cubes or clusters of grapes. '*Ex his*,' says he (speaking of the cross-bars), '*pendent restes lapillis extentae, ad quas humor spissus adhaerescens densatur in translucentes atramenti sutorii vel cubos, vel acinos, qui uvae speciem gerunt.*ᵖ I remember also that, having many years since a suspicion that the reason why alkalies, such as salt of tartar and potashes, are wont to be obtained in the form of white powders or calces, might be the way wherein the water or the lixiviums that contain them is wont to be drawn off, I fancied that, by leaving the saline corpuscles a competent quantity of water to swim in, and allowing them leisure for such a multitude of occursions as might suffice to make them hit upon more congruous coalitions than is usual, I might obtain crystals of them, as well as of other salts. Conjecturing this, I say, I caused some well-purified alkalies, dissolved in clear water, to be slowly evaporated, till the top was covered with a thin ice-like crust; then, taking care not to break that, lest they should (as in the ordinary way, where the water is all forced off) want a sufficient stock of liquor, I kept them in a very gentle heat for a good while, and then, breaking the above-mentioned ice-like cake, I had, as I wished, divers figured lumps of crystalline salt shot in the water, and transparent almost like white sugar-candy.

I likewise remember that, having on several occasions distilled a certain quantity of oil of vitriol with a strong solution of sea-salt till the remaining matter was left dry, that saline residue, being dissolved in fair water, filtered, and gently evaporated, would shoot

ᵖ G. Agricola, *De Re Metallica*, lib. XII, p. 462.

into crystals, sometimes of one figure, sometimes of another, according as the quantity or strength of the oil of vitriol and other substances determined. And yet these crystals, though sometimes they would shoot into prism-like figures, as roched petre, and sometimes into shapes more like to alum or vitriol – nay, though oftentimes the same *caput mortuum* dissolved would in the same glass shoot into crystals whereof some would be of one shape, some of another – yet would these differing grains or crystals appear, for the most part, more exquisitely figured than oftentimes vitriol does. From spirit of urine and spirit of nitre, when I have suffered them to remain long together before coagulation and freed the mixture from the superfluous moisture very slowly, I have sometimes obtained fine long crystals (some of which I can show you) so shaped that most beholders would take them for crystals of saltpetre. And I have likewise tried that, whereas silver is wont to shoot into plates exceeding thin almost like those of Moscovia glass, when I have dissolved a pretty quantity of it in *aqua fortis* or spirit of nitre and suffered it to shoot very leisurely, I have obtained lunar crystals (several of which I have yet by me), whose figure, though so pretty as to have given some wonder even to an excellent geometrician, is differing enough from that of the thin plates formerly mentioned, each crystal being composed of many small and finely-shaped solids that stick so congruously to one another as to have one surface, that appeared plane enough, common to them all.

Thirdly, that insensible corpuscles of different but all of them exquisite shapes, and endowed with plane as well as smooth sides, will constitute bodies variously but all very finely figured, I have made use of several ways to manifest. And first, though hartshorn, blood, and urine, being resolved and (as the chemists speak) analysed by distillation, may well be supposed to have their substantial forms (if they had any) destroyed by the action of the fire, yet, in regard the saline particles they contain are endowed with such figures as we have been speaking of, when, in the liquor that abounds with either of these volatile salts, the dissolved particles do leisurely shoot into crystals, I have divers times observed in these many masses (some bigger and some less), whose surfaces had planes, some of figures as to sense exactly geometrical, and others very curious and pleasant. And of these finely-shaped crystals of various sizes, I have pretty store by me. And because (as it may be probably gathered from the event) the saline corpuscles of stillatitious acid liquors, and those of many of the bodies they are fitted to dissolve, have such kind of figures as we have been speaking of, when the solutions of these bodies upon the recess of the superfluous moisture shoot into crystals,[37] though they will sometimes be differing enough according to the particular natures of the dissolved bodies and the menstruum, yet either the crystals themselves, or their surfaces, or both, will oftentimes have fine and exquisite figures: as I have tried by a menstruum wherewith I was able to dissolve some gems, as also with a solution of coral made with spirit of verdigris, to omit other examples. And for the same reason, when I tried whether the particles of silver, dissolved in *aqua fortis*, would not, without concoagulating with the salts, convene upon the account of their own shapes into little concretions of smooth and flat surfaces, I found that having (to afford the metalline corpuscles scope to move in) diluted one part of the solution with a great many parts of distilled rain-water (for common water will oftentimes make such solutions become white or turbid), a plate of copper being suspended in the liquor and suffered to lie quiet there awhile (for it need not be long), there would settle all about it swarms of little metalline and undiaphanous bodies, shining in the water like the scales of small fishes, but formed into little plates extremely thin, with surfaces not only flat but exceeding glossy; and among those, divers of the larger were prettily figured at the edges. And as for gold, its corpuscles are sufficiently disposed to convene with those of fit or congruous salts into concretions of determinate shapes, as I have found in the crystals I obtained from gold dissolved in *aqua regis* and, after having been suffered to lose its superfluous moisture, kept in a cold place; and not only so, but also when, by a more powerful menstruum, I had subdivided the body of gold into such minute particles that they were sublimable (for that I can assure you is possible), these volatile particles of gold, with the salts wherewith they were elevated, afforded me (sometimes) store of crystals, which, though not all of them near of the same bigness, resembled one another in their shape, which was regular enough, and a very pretty one. But of this more elsewhere.

I remember I have also long since taken pleasure to dissolve two or more of those saline bodies, whose shapes we know already, in fair water, that by a very gentle evaporation I might obtain concretions whose shapes should be, though curious, yet differing from the figure of either of the ingredients. But we must not expect that in all cases the salts dissolved together should be *totally* compounded; for oftentimes they are of such different natures that one will shoot much sooner than another, and then it frequently happens that a good proportion of that will be first crystallized in its own shape – as is conspicuously to be observed in the refining of that impure petre (which, from the country that affords it, the purifiers call *Barbary* nitre) from the common salt it abounds with – and (also), as Agricola observes, that in some cases where a vitriolate matter is mingled with that which yields alum, those two kinds of salts will shoot separately in the same large vessel*q* (which the trials I have made with the compounded solutions of those two salts do not discountenance). Now in such cases, all that can be expected, or needs be desired, is that the remaining part of the mixture, or some portion of it, afford crystals or grains of compounded solid figures. Though the Venetian borax wont to be sold in shops be known to be a factitious body, compounded of several salts that I shall not now stay to enumerate, and though, when we buy it, we usually find it to consist of lumps and grains mis-shapen enough, yet when I dissolved some of it in a good quantity of fair water, and made it coagulate very leisurely, I had crystals upon whose surfaces I could perceive very exquisite and, as to sense, regular[38] geometrical figures. And one thing I must not here by any means pretermit, which is that, though the *caput mortuum* of common *aqua fortis* consists of bodies of very differing natures (for such are nitre and vitriol), and has been exposed to a great violence of the fire, yet I have sometimes admired the curiousness of those figures that might be obtained barely by frequent solutions and coagulations of the saline particles of this *caput mortuum* in fair water. But because the glasses wherein my concretions were made were too little to afford great crystals, and they ought to shoot very slowly, I choose[39] rather to show the curious some large crystals, which I took out of the laboratory of an ingenious person, who, without minding the figures, had upon my recommendation made great quantity of that salt in large vessels for a medicine (it being the *panacea duplicata*, so famous in Holstein). For *divers* of these crystals have not only triangles, hexagons, and rhomboids, and other figures, exquisitely cut on their smooth and specular surfaces, and *others* bodies of prismatical shapes: but some of them are no less accurately figured than the finest nitre or vitriol I

q G. Agricola, *De Re Metallica*, lib. XII.

remember myself to have observed, and some also terminate in bodies almost like pyramids, consisting of divers triangles, that meet in one vertical point, and are no less admirably shaped than the fairer sort of Cornish diamonds that have been brought me for rarities.+

Besides the producing of salts of new shapes by compounding of saline bodies, I have found it to be practicable not only in some gross, or, as they speak, corporal salts, such as sea-salt, saltpetre, but also in some natural and some chemical salts dissolved together, and which perhaps you will think more considerable in saline spirits made by distillation – not that all of them are fit for this purpose, but that I have found divers of those that work upon one another with ebullition to be so. For in that conflict the saline corpuscles come to be associated to one another, and thereby, or by their newly-acquired figure, whilst their coalition lasts, to lose much of their former volatility, so that upon evaporation of the superfluous liquor they will not fly, as otherwise they might, but concoagulate into finely-shaped crystals – as I have tried, among other saline liquors, with spirit of urine and spirit of nitre, and with oil of vitriol and spirit of fermented urine, with spirit of sheep's blood and spirit of salt, and also with the spirits of salt and of[40] urine: which last experiment I the rather mention because it shows, by the difference of the crystals afforded by those two liquors from the crystals resulting from one of them, namely the spirit of urine (or, if you please, the volatile salt wherewith it abounds) concoagulated with a fit dose of oil of vitriol, how much those compounded emergent figures depend upon the more simple figures of the saline corpuscles that happen to convene into those new concretes. For the spirit of urine, satiated with spirit of salt, and both very gently and not too far evaporated, often afforded me crystals that differed exceedingly in shape from those which I obtained from the same spirit of urine, satiated either with oil of vitriol or with spirit of nitre. For (to add that upon the bye) that salt, compounded of the two spirits of urine and of common salt, is wont to be very prettily figured, consisting of one long beam, as it were, whence on both sides issue out far shorter crystals, sometimes perpendicular to that and parallel to one another like the teeth in a comb, and sometimes so inclining as to make the whole appear almost like a feather: which is the more remarkable, because I have (many years ago) observed that common sal-ammoniac that is made of urine and common salt, both crude, with a proportion of soot, will, if warily dissolved and coagulated, shoot into crystals of the like shape. How far the unknown figure of a salt may possibly (for I fear it will not easily) be guessed at by that of the figure which it makes with some other salt whose figure is already known, I leave to geometricians to consider, having, I fear, insisted too long on this subject already. But yet I must add one particular more, which will as well illustrate and confirm much of what has been said above touching the origination of vitriol, as show that the shape of vitriol depends upon the textures of the bodies whereof it is composed.

Fourthly, then, when I considered that (as I formerly noted), vitriol being but a magistery made by the concoagulation of the corpuscles of a dissolved metal with those of the menstruum, the magisteries of other metals might without inconvenience be added, as other vitriolate concretes, to the green, the blue, and white, vitriol, that are without scruple referred to the same species – and when I considered that oil of vitriol was not a fit menstruum to *dissolve* divers of the metals, nor even all those that it will *corrode*, and that the like unfitness also is to be found in common spirit of salt – I pitched upon *aqua fortis*, or spirit of nitre, as that menstruum which was likeliest to afford variety of vitriols. And accordingly I found that, besides the lovely vitriol of copper formerly mentioned, that liquor would with quicksilver afford one sort of crystals, with silver another, and with lead a third: all which crystals of vitriol, as they differed from each other in other qualities (upon which score you will find this experiment elsewhere mentioned), so they did very manifestly and considerably differ in shape, the crystals of silver shooting in exceeding thin plates, and those of lead and quicksilver obtaining figures, though differing enough from each other, yet of a far greater depth and thickness, and less remote from the figure of common vitriol or sea-salt; and yet all these vitriols, especially that of crude lead, when it was happily made, had shapes curious and elaborate, as well as those we admire in common vitriol or sea-salt.

If, then, these curious shapes, which are believed to be of the admirablest effects and of the strongest proofs of substantial forms, may be the results of texture, and if art can produce vitriol itself as well as nature, why may we not think that in ordinary phenomena, that have much less of wonder, recourse is wont to be had to substantial forms without any necessity (matter and a convention of accidents being able to serve the turn without them)? and why should we wilfully exclude those productions of the fire, wherein the chemist is but a servant to nature, from the number of natural bodies? And indeed, since there is no certain diagnostic agreed on, whereby to discriminate natural and factitious bodies and constitute the species of both, I see not why we may not draw arguments from the qualities and operations of several of those that are called factitious, to show how much may be ascribed to, and performed by, the mechanical characterization or *stamp* of matter: of which we have a noble instance in gunpowder, wherein, by a bare comminution and blending the ingredients, nitre, charcoal, and brimstone, which have only a new and that an exceeding slight contexture – each retaining its own nature in the mixture, so that there is no colour afforded to the pretence of a substantial form – there is produced a new body, whose operations are more powerful and prodigious than those of almost any body of nature's own compounding. And though glass be but an artificial concrete, yet, besides that it is a very noble and useful one, nature herself has produced very few, if enough to make up a number more lasting and more unalterable. And indeed divers of those factitious bodies that chemistry is able to afford us are endowed with more various and more noble qualities than many of those that are unquestionably natural. And if we admit these productions into the number of natural bodies, they will afford us a multitude of instances to show that bodies may acquire many and noble qualities, barely by having mechanical affections introduced by outward agents into the matter, or destroyed there: as, though glass be such a noble body as we have lately taken notice of, yet since it is fusibility, transparency, and brittleness, that are its only constituent attributes, we can in less than an hour (or perhaps half that time) turn an opacous body into transparent glass without the addition of any other visible body, by a change of texture made in the same matter; and by another change of texture, made without addition, as formerly, we can in a trice reduce glass into, or obtain from it, a body not glassy but opacous, and otherwise of a very differing nature, as it had been before.+

And here let me add, what may not a little conduce to our present design, that even those that embrace Aristotle's principles do unawares confess that a slight change of texture, without the introduction of a substantial form, may not only make a specifical difference betwixt bodies, but so vast a one that they shall have differing genuses, and may (as the chemists speak) belong to differing kingdoms. For coral, to pass by all other plants of that kind that may be mentioned to the same purpose, whilst it grows in the bottom of the sea, is a real plant, and several times (which suffices for my present scope) hath been there found by an acquaintance of mine, as well as by other enquirers, soft and tender like another plant. Nay, I elsewhere[r] bring very good and recent authority to prove that it is oftentimes found very succulent, and does propagate its species as well as other shrubs. And yet coral being gathered and removed into the air, by the recess of its soul – no new lapidific form being so much as pretended to – turns into a concretion that is, by many eminent writers and others, reckoned among lapideous ones: as indeed coral does not burn like wood, nor obey distillation like it; and not only its calx is very differing from the ashes of vegetables, and is totally soluble in divers acid liquors and even spirit of vinegar, but the uncalcined coral itself will be easily corroded by good vinegar, after the same manner as I have seen *lapis stellaris* and other unquestionably mineral stones dissolved, some by that liquor, and some by the spirit of it.[+]

A much stranger thing may be seen in the East India island of Sombrero, not very far from Sumatra, if we may believe our country-man Sir James Lancaster, who relates it as an eye-witness: for which reason, and for the strangeness of the thing, I shall add the story in his own words. 'Here,' says he (speaking of the coast of Sombrero), 'we found upon the sand by the sea side a small twig growing up to a young tree; and offering to pluck up the same, it shrunk down into the ground, and sinketh, unless you hold very hard. And being plucked up, a great worm is the root of it: and look how the tree groweth in greatness, the worm diminisheth. Now as soon as the worm is wholly turned into the tree, it rooteth in the ground, and so groweth to be great. This transformation was one of the greatest wonders I saw in all my travels. This tree being plucked up a little, the leaves stripped off; and the peel, by that time it was dry, turned into a hard stone, much like to white coral. So that,' concludes he, 'this worm was twice transformed into different natures; of these we gathered and brought home many.'[s41] The industrious Piso in his excellent history of Brazil vouches a multitude of witnesses (not having opportunity to be one himself) for the ordinary

[r] In the essays about things supposed to be spontaneously generated.

[s] S. Purchas, *Pilgrims*, Part the first, Bk. III, p. 152.

transformation of a sort of animals (not much unlike grasshoppers) into vegetables, at a certain season of the year.[*l*]

But since I set down this relation of Sir James[42] Lancaster, I have met with another whose strangeness may much countenance it, in a small tract newly published by a Jesuit, Fr Michael Boym, whom a good critic much commended to me. For this author doth as an eyewitness affirm that which is little less to my present purpose: '*Je vis, &c.*,' i.e., 'I saw in a small freshwater and shallow lake of the island Hainan (which belongs to China) crabs or crawfishes, which, as soon as they were drawn out of the water, did in a moment lose both life and motion, and became petrified, though nothing appeared to be changed either in the external or internal figure of their bodies.'[*u*] What he further adds of these fishes is but of their virtues in physic, which not concerning our subject, I shall, Pyrophilus, willingly pretermit it; and even as to our countryman's relation, hoping by means of an ingenious correspondent in the East Indies to receive a further information about the strange plant he mentions, I shall at present urge only what has been taken notice of concerning coral, to countenance the observation for whose sake these narratives have been alleged. And so likewise as to what I was saying of glass and gunpowder, our receiving of those, and the generality of factitious bodies, into the catalogue of natural bodies, is not (which I formerly also intimated) necessary to my present argument, whereto it is sufficient that vitriol is granted on all hands to be a natural body, though it be also producible by art. And also to the argument it affords us we might add that memorable experiment delivered by Helmont, of turning oil of vitriol into alum by the odour (as he calls it) of mercury, if, however it be not despicable, we had found it fit to be relied on. But reserving an account of that for another place, we shall substitute the instance presented us by our author about the production of saltpetre: for if, having dissolved potashes in fair water, you coagulate the filtrated solution into a white salt, and on that pour spirit of nitre till they will not hiss any longer together,[43] there will shoot, when the superfluous water is evaporated, crystals,

---

[*l*] The passage, which is long, I do not here transcribe, having had occasion to do it elsewhere. It is extant, *De Indiae Utriusque Re Naturali et Medica*, lib. V, cap. 21; and at the close of his narrative he subjoins, '*Non est, quod quisquam de veritate dubitet, cum infinitos testes habeat Brasilia, &c.*'

[*u*] M. Boym, *Flora Sinensis, ou Traité des Fleurs, &c.*, under the title 'Lozméoques'.

that proclaim their nitrous nature by their prismatical (or at least prism-like) shape, their easy fusion, their accension and deflagration, and other qualities partly mentioned by our author, and partly discoverable by a little curiosity in making trials.

II. *Experimental Attempts about the Redintegration of Bodies*

The former of those two arguments, Pyrophilus, by which I proposed to confirm the origin of forms, was, as you may remember, grounded upon the manner by which such a convention of accidents as deserves to pass for a form may be produced; and that having been hitherto prosecuted, it now remains that we proceed to the second argument, drawn not (as the former) from the first production, but from the reproduction, of a physical body. And though both these arguments are valid, yet if this latter could, in spite of the difficulties intervening in making of the experiments that belong to it, be as clearly made out as the former, you would, I suppose, like it much the better of the two. For if we could reproduce a body which has been deprived of its substantial form, you would, I presume, think it highly probable, if not more than probable, that (to borrow our author's expression) that which is commonly called the *form*° of a concrete, which gives it its being and denomination and from whence all its qualities are, in the vulgar philosophy, by I know not what inexplicable ways, supposed to flow, may be in some bodies but a characterization or modification of the matter they consist of, whose parts, by being so and so disposed in relation to each other, constitute such a determinate kind of body, endowed with such and such properties: whereas, if the same parts were otherwise disposed, they would constitute other bodies of very differing natures from that of the concrete whose parts they formerly were, and which may again result or be produced after its dissipation and seeming destruction, by the reunion of the same component particles, associated according to their former disposition.

But though it were[44] impossible to make an adequate redintegration of a chemically analysed body – because some of the dissipated parts will either escape through the junctures of the vessels (though diligently closed), or, if they be very subtle, will fly away upon the disjoining of the vessels, or will irrecoverably stick to the inside of them – yet I see not why such a reproduction as is very possible to be effected may not suffice to manifest what we intend to make out by it. For, even in such experiments, it appears that, when the form of a natural body is abolished and its parts violently scattered, by the bare reunion of some parts after the former manner the very same matter the destroyed body was before made of may, without addition of other bodies, be brought again to constitute a body of the *like nature* with the former, though not of *equal bulk*. And indeed, the experiment recorded by our author about the reproduction of saltpetre, as it is the best and successfullest I have ever been able to make upon bodies that require a strong heat to dissipate them, so I hope it will suffice to give you those thoughts about this matter that the author designed in alleging it. And therefore, though, having premised thus much, I shall proceed to acquaint you with the success of some attempts he intimates (in that essay) his intention of making for the redintegration of some bodies, yet, doing it only out of some historical notes I find among my loose papers, that which I at present pretend to is but partly to show you the *difficulty* of such attempts – which, since our author's essay was communicated, have been represented (I fear by conjecture only) as *very easy* to be accurately enough done – and partly because our author does not without reason intimate the usefulness of redintegrations in case they can be effected, and does not causelessly intimate that such attempts, though they should not perfectly succeed, may increase the number of noble and active bodies, and consequently the inventory of mankind's goods.

Upon such considerations we attempted the dissipation and reunion of the parts of common amber; and though chemists, for fear of breaking their vessels, are wont when they commit it to distillation to add to it a *caput mortuum* (as they speak) of sand, brick, &c. (in whose room we sometimes choose to substitute beaten glass), which hinders them to judge of and employ the remanence of the amber after the distillation is finished, yet we supposed and found that if the retort were not too much filled, and if the fire were slowly and warily enough administered, the addition of any other body would be needless. Wherefore, having put into a glass retort four or five ounces of amber, and administered a gentle and gradual heat, we observed the amber to melt and bubble (which we therefore mention because ingenious men have lately questioned whether it can be melted), and having ended the operation and severed the vessels, we found that there was come over in the form partly of oil, partly of spirit and phlegm, and partly of volatile salt, near half the weight of the concrete. And having broken the retort, we found in the bottom of it a cake of coal-black matter, than whose upper surface I scarce remember to have seen in my whole life anything more exquisitely polished – insomuch that, notwithstanding the colour, as long as I kept it, it was fit to serve for a looking-glass; and this smooth mass being broken (for it was exceeding brittle), the larger fragments of it appeared adorned with an excellent lustre. All those parts of the amber, being put together into a glass body with a blind head luted to it, were placed in sand to be incorporated by a gentle heat: but whilst I stepped aside to receive a visit, the fire having been increased without my knowledge, the fumes ascended so copiously that they lifted up the vessel out of the sand, whereupon, falling against the side of the furnace, it broke at the top; but, being seasonably called, we saved all but the fumes, and the remaining matter looks not unlike tar, and with the least heat may be poured out like a liquor, sticking, even when it is cold, to the fingers. Yet this opened body doth not easily communicate so much as a tincture to spirit of wine (which therefore seems somewhat strange, because another time, presuming that this would be a good way to obtain a solution of some of the resinous parts of amber, we did, by pouring spirit of wine that (though rectified) was not of the very best, upon the reunited parts of amber, lightly digested into a mass, easily obtain a clear yellow solution very differing from the tincture of amber, and abounding (as I found by trial) in the dissolved substance of the amber); but in oil of turpentine we have in a short time dissolved it into a blood-red balsam, which may be of good use (at least) to surgeons. And having again made the former experiment with more wariness than before, we had the like success in our distillation, but the reunited parts of the amber being set to digest in a large bolt-head, the liquor that was drawn off did in a few hours, from its own *caput mortuum*, extract a blood-red tincture, or else made a solution of some part of it whereby it obtained a very deep red; but, having been by intervening accidents hindered from finishing the experiment, we missed the satisfaction of knowing to what it may be brought at last.

And as for what our author tells us of this design to attempt the redintegration of vitriol, turpentine, and some other concretes wherein it seemed not unpracticable, he found in it more difficulty than everyone would expect. For the bodies on which such experiments are likeliest to succeed seem to be alum, sea-salt, and vitriol.[+]

And as for alum, he found it a troublesome work to take (as a spagyrist would speak) the principles of it asunder, in regard that it is inconvenient to distil it with a *caput mortuum* (as chemists call any fixed additament), lest that should hinder the desired redintegration of the dissipated parts; and when he distilled it by itself without any such additament, he found that with a moderate heat the alum would scarce part with anything but its phlegm, and if he urged it with a strong fire, he found it would so swell as to endanger the breaking of the retort, or threaten the boiling over into the receiver. (Yet having once been able very warily to abstract as much phlegm and spirit as I conveniently could from a parcel of roche alum, and having poured it back upon that pulverized *caput mortuum* and left the vessel long in a quiet place, I found that the corpuscles of the liquor, having had time after a multitude of occursions to accommodate and reunite themselves to the more fixed parts of the concrete, did by that association (or dissolution) recompose, at the top of the powder, many crystalline grains of finely-figured salt, which increasing with time made me hope that at the length the whole or the greatest part would be reduced into alum, which yet a mischance that robbed me of the glass hindered me to see.)[+]

So likewise of sea-salt, if it be distilled, as it is usual, with thrice its weight of burned clay or beaten brick, it will prove inconvenient in reference to its redintegration; and if it be distilled alone, it is apt to be fluxed by the heat of the fire, and whilst it remains in fusion will scarce yield any spirit at all.[+]

And as for vitriol, though the redintegration of it might seem to be less hopeful than that of the other salts, in regard that it consists not only of a saline but of a metalline body, whence it may be supposed to be of a more intricate and elaborate texture, yet because there needs no *caput mortuum* in the distillation of it, we did, to pursue our author's intimated designs, make two or three attempts upon it, and seemed to miss of our aim rather upon the account of accidental hindrances than of any insuperable difficulty in the thing itself. For once we with a strong fire drew off, from a parcel of common blue vitriol, the phlegm and spirit and some quantity of the heavy oil (as chemists abusively call it). These liquors, as they came over without separation, we divided into several parts, and the remaining very red *caput mortuum* into as many. One of these parcels of liquor we poured overnight upon its correspondent portion of the newly-mentioned red powder. But having left it in a window, and the night proving very bitter, in the morning I found the glass cracked in many places by the violence of the frost, and the liquor seemed to have been soaked up by the powder and to have very much swelled it. This mixture then I took out, and, placing it in an open-mouthed glass in a window, I found after a while divers grains of pure vitriol upon the other matter, and some little swellings, not unlike those we shall presently have occasion to speak of. I took likewise a much larger parcel of the forementioned liquor, and its correspondent proportion of *caput mortuum*, and having leisurely mixed them in a large glass basin, I obtained divers phenomena, that belong not to this place but may be met with where they will more properly fall in. In this basin (which I laid in the window and kept from agitation), I perceived after a while the liquor to acquire a bluish tincture, and after ten or twelve weeks I found the mixture dry (for it seems it was too much exposed to the air), but the surface of it adorned in divers places with grains of vitriol very curiously figured. And besides these, there were store of protuberances, which consisted of abundance of small vitriolate particles, which seemed in the way to a coalition; for having let the basin alone for four or five months longer, the matter appeared crusted over, partly with very elevated saline protuberances, partly with lesser parcels, and partly also with considerably broad cakes of vitriol, some of above half an inch in breadth, and proportionably long: and indeed the whole surface was so oddly diversified, that I cannot count the trouble these trials have put me to mis-spent.[+]

Another time, in a more slender and narrow-mouthed glass, I poured back upon the *caput mortuum* of vitriol the liquors I had by violence of the fire forced from it, so that the liquid part did swim a pretty height above the red calx, and remained awhile limpid and colourless. But the vessel having stood for some time unstopped in a window, the liquor after a while acquired by degrees a very deep vitriolate colour, and not long after there appeared at the bottom and on the top of the calx many fair and exquisitely figured grains of vitriol, which covered the surface of the calx; and the longer the vessel continued in the window, the deeper did this change, made upon the upper part of the powder, seem to penetrate: so that I began to hope that in process of time, almost (if not more than almost) the whole mixture would be reduced to perfect vitriol. But an accident robbed me of my glass before I could see the utmost of the event.

And on this occasion I must not pretermit an odd experiment I lately made, though I dare not undertake to make it again. I elsewhere relate how I digested for divers weeks a quantity of powdered antimony with a greater weight by half of oil of vitriol, and how, having at length committed this mixture to distillation, and thereby obtained besides a little liquor a pretty quantity of combustible antimonial or antimonio-vitriolate sulphur, there remained in the bottom of the retort a somewhat light and very friable *caput mortuum*, all the upper part of which was at least as white as common wood-ashes, and the rest looked like a cinder. And now I must tell you what became of this *caput mortuum*, whereof I there make no further mention. We could not well foresee what could be made of it, but very probable it was that it would afford us some new discovery by being exposed to the fire, in regard of the copious sulphur whereof it seemed to have been deprived, provided it were urged in close vessels where nothing could be lost. Whereupon, committing it to a naked fire in a small glass retort, well coated and accommodated with a receiver, we kept it there many hours, and at length, severing the vessels, we found (which need not be wondered at) no antimonial quicksilver, and much less of sulphur sublimed than we expected: wherefore greedily hastening to the *caput mortuum*, we found it fluxed into a mass, covered with a thin cake of glass, whose fragments being held against the light were not at[45] all coloured, as antimonial glass is wont to be, but were as colourless as common white glass. The lump above mentioned, being broken, was found, somewhat to our wonder, to be perfect black antimony, adorned with long shining streaks, as common antimony is wont to be: only this antimony seemed to have been a little refined by the sequestration of its unnecessary sulphur, which ingredient seems by this experiment, as well as by some other observations of ours, to be more copious in some particular parcels of that mineral than is absolutely requisite to the constitution of antimony – though in our case it *may* be suspected that the reduction of part of the mass to a colourless glass was an effect of the absence of so much of the sulphur, and might *in part* make the remaining mass some amends for it. What we further did with this new or reproduced concrete is not proper to be here told you; only for your satisfaction we have kept a lump of it, that you may with us take notice of what some philosophers would call the mindfulness of nature: which, when a body was deprived of a not inconsiderable portion of its chief ingredient, and had all its other parts dissipated and shuffled and discoloured so as not to be knowable, was able to rally those scattered and disguised parts, and marshal or dispose them into a body of the former consistence, colour, &c., though (which is not here to be overlooked) the contexture of antimony, by reason of the copious shining *stiriae* that ennoble the darker body, be much more elaborate, and therefore more uneasy to be restored, than that of many other concretes.

But among all my trials about the redintegration of bodies, that which seemed to succeed best was made upon turpentine: for having taken some ounces of this, very pure and good, and put it into a glass retort, I distilled so long with a very gentle fire, till I had separated it into a good quantity of very clear liquor and a *caput mortuum* very dry and brittle; then breaking the retort, I powdered the *caput mortuum*, which when it was taken out was exceeding sleek and transparent enough and very red, but being powdered appeared of a pure yellow colour. This powder I carefully mixed with the liquor that had been distilled from it, which immediately dissolved part of it into a deep red balsam; but by further digestion, in a large glass exquisitely stopped, that colour began to grow fainter, though the remaining part of the powder (except a very little, proportionable to so much of the liquor as may be supposed to have been wasted by evaporation and transfusion out of one vessel into another) be perfectly dissolved, and so well reunited to the more fugitive parts of the concrete, that there is scarce any that by the smell, or taste, or consistence, would take it for other than good and laudable turpentine.

AN INTRODUCTION TO THE HISTORY
OF PARTICULAR QUALITIES[1]

CHAPTER I

The past discourse has, I hope, Pyrophilus, given you some tolerable account both of the nature and of the origin of qualities in general. Wherefore it now follows that we proceed to qualities in particular, and consider how far the manner whereby they are produced, and those other phenomena of them that we shall have occasion to take notice of, will accord with and thereby confirm the doctrine I have hitherto proposed, and whether they will not (at least) much better comport with that than with the opinions either of the Peripatetics or the chemists.

I shall not spend time to enquire into all the several significations of the word *quality*, which is used in such various senses as to make it ambiguous enough, since by the subsequent discourse it will sufficiently appear in which of the more usual of those significations we employ that term. But thus much I think it not amiss to intimate in this place, that there are some things that have been looked upon as qualities which ought rather to be looked upon as states of matter, or complexions of particular qualities, as *animal, inanimal*, &c., *health* and *beauty*, which last attribute seems to be made up of *shape, symmetry* or comely proportion, and the *pleasantness of the colours* of the particular parts of the face. And there are some other attributes, namely *size, shape, motion*, and *rest*, that are wont to be reckoned among qualities, which may more conveniently be esteemed the *primary modes* of the parts of matter, since from these simple attributes or primordial affections all the qualities are derived. But this consideration relating to words and names, I shall not insist upon it.

Nor do I think it worth while to enumerate and debate the several partitions that have been made of qualities (of which I have met with divers, and could perchance myself increase the number of them); for though one that were disposed to criticize upon them would not perhaps acquiesce in any of them, but look upon them as being more

arbitrary than grounded upon an attentive consideration of the
nature of the things themselves, yet, because it seems not to me so
easy to make an accurate distribution of qualities till some things
that concern them be better cleared up than yet they are, I shall
content myself for the present to propose to you one of the more
received divisions of physical qualities (for you know I do not
pretend to treat of any other), allowing myself the liberty of making,
where there seems cause, the members of the distribution somewhat
more comprehensive. We will, then, with many of the moderns,
divide physical qualities into *manifest*° and *occult*,° and, reserving the
latter to be treated of apart, we will distribute the former into *1st*,°
2nd° and *3rd*,° to the two last of which we will reserve divers qualities
not wont to be treated of by School writers of physical systems:
which, for distinction's sake, we may without much inconvenience
style some of them the *chemical*° qualities of things, because, as
Aristotle and the schoolmen were not acquainted with them, so they
have been principally introduced and taken notice of by means of
chemical operations and experiments – such as are fumigation,
amalgamation, cupellation, volatilization, precipitation, &c. – by
which operations among other means corporeal things come to
appear volatile or fixed, soluble or insoluble in some menstruums,
amalgamable or unamalgamable, capable or uncapable to
precipitate such bodies or be precipitated by them, and (in a word)
acquire or lose several powers to act on other bodies or dispositions
to be wrought on by them, which (attributes) do as well deserve the
name of *qualities*° as divers other attributes to which it is allowed.
And to these chemical qualities we may add some others, which,
because of the use that physicians, either only, or above other men,
make of them, may be called *medical*,° whereby some bodies taken
into that of a man are deoppilating, others inciding, resolving,
discussing, suppurating, abstersive of noxious adherences, and
thickening the blood and humours, being astringent, anodynous or
appeasing pain, &c. For though *some* of the faculties of medicines –
as those of heating, cooling, drying, attenuating, purging, &c. – may
be conveniently enough referred to the 1st, 2nd or 3rd qualities wont
to be mentioned by naturalists, and *others* are wont to be reckoned
among occult ones, and though these medical qualities are wont to
be treated of by physicians, yet it seems to me that divers of them
ought not to be referred to the qualities to which they are wont to be
so; and the handling of them may be looked upon as a *desideratum* in

natural philosophy and may well enough deserve a distinct place there, since the writers of that science are not wont to treat of them at all, and physicians handle them as physicians, whom it concerns but to know what bodies are endowed with them and what good or ill effects they may have upon human bodies, not as naturalists, whose business it is to enquire into the production and causes of those as well as of other qualities.

CHAPTER II

Before we descend to the mention of any of these particular qualities, I think it very expedient to spend a little time in considering three grand scruples about our and the *Corpuscularian* doctrine touching qualities: which three difficulties, though I remember not to have found them expressly objected by the adversaries of the Corpuscularian philosophy, nor (perhaps only for that reason) to have been purposely solved by the patrons of it, are yet such that, having been suggested to me by considering the nature of the thing, I cannot but fear that they also may occur to and trouble you, since they seem to me of that importance that, unless they be removed, they may very much prejudice the reception of a good part of what I am to deliver about particular qualities.

The first of the above-mentioned objections is grounded upon the received opinion of vulgar and *Aristotelian* philosophers, that diversity of qualities must needs flow from substantial forms, either because it is part of their nature to be the principles of properties and peculiar operations in the bodies they inform, or else because divers of them are such that no mixture of the elements is capable of producing them. | Of the two suppositions whereon this difficulty is founded, we have already showed the former to be unfit to be admitted by what has been said in our examen of substantial and subordinate forms; and therefore it will only remain that we examine also this second supposition, which may therefore deserve the greater consideration because it is much pressed and relied on by the learned Sennertus (and his followers), who improves the argument by this addition, that, as no bare mixture of the elements, so no general *forma mistionis* (such as divers of the moderns have introduced to help out the hypothesis), is sufficient to give an account of divers qualities which he somewhere reckons up.

But (in the first place) whereas the proposers of this difficulty take it for granted that there are four elements from whose various mixtures all other sublunary bodies spring, and are therefore only solicitous to prove that such and such qualities cannot flow from their mixture, I need not much concern myself for their whole discourse, since I admit not that hypothesis of the four elements that is supposed in it; and yet I may be allowed to observe from hence that, by the confession of those modern Peripatetics that urge this argument, those ancient and other Aristotelians were mistaken, who ascribed to the mixtures of the elements effects for which these maintain them to be incompetent.

But since replies of this nature do rather concern the objectors than the objection, I proceed to consider the difficulty itself, not only as it may be proposed by Peripatetics, but by chemists, who, though some of them do not with others of their sect allow of the four elements, do yet agree with the Schools in this, that there is a determinate number of ingredients of compounded bodies from whose mixture and proportion many qualities must be derived, and those that cannot must be resolved to flow from a higher principle, whether it be a substantial form, or something for which chemists have several *names*, though I doubt no settled and intelligible *notion*.

To consider, then, the difficulty itself, I shall for the removal of it present to you four principal considerations.| But before I begin by any of these to answer the objection, I shall readily acknowledge that in some respects, and in some cases, it may not be ill grounded; but I shall add that, in those cases, I look upon it rather as a part of the Corpuscularian doctrine than an objection against it. For when it happens that there is a strict connexion betwixt that modification of matter which is requisite to exhibit *one* phenomenon, and that from which *another* will necessarily follow, in such cases we may not only grant, but teach, that he who by a change of its texture gives a portion of matter the former modification does likewise qualify it by the same change to exhibit the congruous phenomenon, though one would not perchance suspect them to have any such dependence upon one another: as, for instance, strong spirit of distilled vinegar, by virtue of its being an acid spirit, hath the faculty to turn syrup of violets red; but if, by making with this spirit as strong a solution as you can of coral or some such body, you destroy the acidity of the spirit of vinegar, this liquor, as it has quite another taste, so it may and indeed will have another operation than formerly upon syrup of violets. For I remember that, upon a trial I purposely devised to illustrate this matter, I found that the lately-mentioned solution, and some others made with spirit of vinegar, would presently, like an alkalizate or urinous salt, turn syrup of violets from its native blue, not any longer into a red, but into a lovely green; and prosecuting the experiment a little farther, I found that spirit of salt itself, dephlegmed by a fit concrete, though the solution were horribly strong, had yet the same effect on syrup of violets. But because the cases where the above-mentioned connexion of qualities and modifications occur are comparatively but few, I shall here consider them no farther, but proceed to the four particulars I was lately proposing.

And, in the first place, I say that things may acquire by mixture very differing qualities from those of any of the ingredients. | Of this I shall have occasion to give a multitude of instances in the following notes upon particular qualities, and therefore it may now suffice to mention two or three that are the more obvious in the laboratories of chemists: as that sugar of lead is extremely sweet, though the minium and the spirit of vinegar of which it is made be the former of them insipid and the latter sour. And though neither *aqua regis*, nor crude copper, have anything in them of blue, yet the solution of this metal in that liquor is of a deep blue; and sometimes I have had the solution of crude mercury in good *aqua fortis* of a rich green, though it would not long continue so. And of such instances you will, as I was saying, hereafter meet with plenty: so that they are much mistaken who imagine either that no manifest qualities can be produced by mixture except those that reside in the elements, or result immediately from the combinations of the four first qualities. For, not to repeat what variations the mixtures of the most simple ingredients only may produce, it is manifest that nature and art must continually make mixtures of bodies, both of already compounded bodies – as when ashes and sand compose the common coarse glass, and when nature combines sulphur with unripe vitriol, and perhaps other substances, in a marcasite – and also of bodies already decompounded – as native vitriol is made in the bowels of the earth of an aqueous liquor impregnated with an acid salt, and of a cupreous or martial mineral, strictly united both to a combustible sulphureous substance and to another body of a more fixed terrestrial nature. And thus artificers may easily, as trial hath assured me, produce new and fine colours, by skilfully mixing in the flame two pieces of amels (which are already decompounded bodies), of colours more simple or primary than that which results from their colliquation. And this way of so combining bodies not simple or elementary will be acknowledged capable of being made much more fertile in the production of various qualities and phenomena of nature, if you consider how much the variation of the proportion of the ingredients in a mixed body may alter the qualities and operations of it, and that proportion is capable of being varied almost *in infinitum*. Thus much may suffice for our first consideration, especially since divers things by which it may be much confirmed will be met with in the two following chapters.

In the second place, I observe that it is but an ill-grounded hypothesis to suppose that new qualities cannot be introduced into a mixed body, or those that it had before be destroyed, unless by adding or taking away a sensible portion of some one or more of the Aristotelian elements or chemical principles. For there may be many changes as to quality produced in a body without visibly adding or taking away any ingredient, barely by altering the texture or the motion of the minute parts it consists of. For when (for instance) water, hermetically sealed up in a glass, is by the cold of the winter turned into ice, and thereby both loseth its former fluidity and transparency and acquires firmness, brittleness, and oftentimes opacity – all which qualities it loseth again upon a thaw – in this case, I say, I demand what element or hypostatical principle can be proved to get into or out of this sealed glass, and by its intrusion and recess produce these alterations in the included body. And so in that fixed metal, *silver*, what sensible accession or decrement can be proved to be made as to ingredients, when by barely hammering it (which doth but change the situation and texture of the parts) it acquires a brittleness which by ignition, wherein it doth not sensibly lose anything, it may presently be made to exchange for its former malleableness? And the same experiment gives us an instance also that the invisible agitation of the parts may alone suffice to give a body, at least for a while, new qualities: since a thick piece of silver, nimbly hammered, will quickly acquire a considerable degree of heat, whereby it will be enabled to melt some bodies, to dry others, and to exhibit divers phenomena that it could not produce when cold. I might add that spirit of nitre moderately strong, though, when included in a well-stopped vial in the form of a liquor, it will appear diaphanous and without any redness, will yet fill the upper part of the vial with red fumes, if the warm sunbeams or any fit heat (though but externally applied, and though the glass continue close-stopped) do put the nitrous spirits into a somewhat brisker motion than they had or needed whilst in the form of a liquor. I might also demand both what new element or principle is added to a needle, when the bare approach of a vigorous loadstone endows it with those admirable qualities of respecting the poles and (in due circumstances) drawing to it other needles, and what ingredient the steel loses when, by a contrary motion of the loadstone, it is in a minute deprived of its magnetism. And to these I might subjoin divers like questions; but of instances and reflections proper to confirm this second consideration you may meet with so many, partly in another treatise and partly in the ensuing chapters, that it will be needless to multiply them here.+

Wherefore, in the third place, I shall observe that, when we are considering how numerous and various phenomena may be exhibited by mixed bodies, we are not to look upon them precisely in themselves – that is, as they are portions of matter, of such a determinate nature or texture – but as they are parts of a world so constituted as ours is, and consequently as portions of matter which are placed among many other bodies. For being hereby fitted to receive impressions from some of those bodies, and to make impressions upon others of them, they will upon this account be rendered capable of producing, either as principal or auxiliary causes, a much greater number and variety of phenomena than they could exhibit if each of them were placed *in vacuo*, or (if a vacuum be a thing impossible) in a medium that could no way either contribute to or hinder its operations. | This hath been partly proved already in the discourse *Of the Origin of Forms*, and will be farther manifested ere long; and therefore it may suffice that, of the particulars mentioned in those writings, those that are pertinent to this argument be mentally referred hither.

Wherefore having thus dispatched the third consideration, I now proceed to the fourth and last, which is that the four Peripatetic elements and the three chemical principles are so insufficient to give a good account of anything near all the differing phenomena of nature, that we must seek for some more catholic principles; and that those of the Corpuscularian philosophy have a great advantage of the other in being far more fertile and comprehensive than they. I must not here stay to make a full representation of the deficiencies of the Aristotelian hypothesis, having in other tracts said much to that purpose already. But yet our present argument invites me to intimate these two things: the *first*, that such phenomena as the constant and determinate shape and figure of the mountains our telescopes discover (together with their shadows) in the moon, and the strange generation and perishing of the spots of the sun – to omit the differing colour of the planets and divers other qualities of celestial bodies – cannot be ascribed to the four elements or their mixtures, nor to those of the three chemical principles, which are allowed to be confined to the sublunary region; and the *second*, that there are very many phenomena in nature (divers of which I elsewhere[a] take notice of), several whereof neither the Peripatetic nor the chemical doctrine about the elements or the ingredients of bodies will enable a man to give so much as any probable account – such are the eclipses of the sun, the moon, and also the satellites of Jupiter, the proportion of the acceleration of descent observable in heavy bodies, the ebbing and flowing of the sea, a great number of magnetical, musical, statical, dioptrical, catoptrical, and other sorts of phenomena, which haste makes me here leave unmentioned.

And having said thus much about the first part of our proposed consideration, and thereby shown that the vulgar doctrine about the ingredients of bodies falls very short of being able to solve several kinds of nature's phenomena, we may add, in favour of the second part, that it will follow in general that it is fit to look out for some more pregnant and universal principles; and that in particular those of the Corpusculary hypothesis are, as to those two attributes, preferable by far to the vulgar ones, will I hope appear by our answers to the two objections that remain to be examined in the two following chapters, to which that I might the more hasten, I thought fit to insist the less upon the objection hitherto examined, especially because, partly in this and the two next chapters and partly elsewhere, I suppose there is contained a very sufficient reply to that objection. And I confess I should think it strange that the consideration of the various motions and textures of bodies should not serve to solve far more phenomena than the bare knowledge of the number (and even that of the proportions) of their quiescent ingredients: for as local motion is that which enables natural bodies to act upon one another, so the textures of bodies are the main things

---

[a] Principally in *The Sceptical Chemist*.

that both modify the motion of agents and diversify their effects according to the various natures of the patients.

CHAPTER III

I enter now upon the consideration of the second and indeed the grand difficulty objected against the (Corpuscularian) doctrine proposed by me about the *origin of qualities*, viz. that it is incredible that so great a variety of qualities as we actually find to be in natural bodies should spring from principles so few in number as two, and so simple as matter and local motion; whereof the latter is but one of the six kinds of motion reckoned up by Aristotle and his followers, who call it *lation*, and the former, being all of one uniform nature, is according to us diversified only by the effects of local motion. Towards the solving this difficulty, I shall endeavour to show, first, that the other catholic affections of matter are manifestly deducible from local motion; and next, that these principles, being variously associated, are so fruitful that a vast number of qualities and other phenomena of nature may result from them.

The first of these will not take us up much time to make out. For supposing, what is evident, that the (1) *local motion* belonging to some parts of the universal matter does not all tend the same way, but has various determinations in several parts of that matter, it will follow that, by local motion thus circumstanced, matter must be divided into distinct parts, each of which, being finite, must necessarily be of some (2) *bigness* or *size*, and have some determinate (3) *shape* or other. | And since all the parts of the universal matter are not always in motion – some of them being arrested by their mutual implication, or having transferred (as far as our senses inform us) all that they had to other bodies – the consequence will be that some of these portions of the common matter will be in a state of (4) *rest* (taking the word in the popular sense of it). And these are the most primary and simple affections of matter.

But because there are some others that flow naturally from these and are, though not altogether universal, yet very general and pregnant, I shall subjoin those that are the most fertile principles of the qualities of bodies and other phenomena of nature.

Moreover then, not only the greater fragments of matter, but those lesser ones which we therefore call *corpuscles* or *particles*, have certain local respects to other bodies, and to those *situations* which we denominate from the horizon: so that each of these minute fragments may have a particular (5) *posture* or position (as erect, inclining, horizontal, &c.), and, as they respect us men that behold them, there may belong to them a certain (6) *order* or consecution, upon whose score we say one is before or behind another; and many of these fragments, being associated into one mass or body, have a certain manner of existing together which we call (7) *texture*, or, by a word more comprehensive, *modification*. And because there are very few bodies whose constituent parts can, because of the irregularity or difference of their figures and for other reasons, touch one another everywhere so exquisitely as to leave no intervals between them, therefore almost all consistent bodies, and those fluid ones that are made up of grosser parts, will have (8) *pores* in them; and very many bodies having particles which, by their smallness, or their loose adherence to the bigger or more stable parts of the bodies they belong unto, are more easily agitated and separated from the rest by heat and other agents, therefore there will be great store of bodies that will emit those subtle emanations that are commonly called (9) *effluviums*. And as those conventions of the simple corpuscles, that are so fitted to adhere to or be complicated with one another, constitute those durable and uneasily dissoluble clusters of particles that may be called the primary concretions or elements of things, so these themselves may be mingled with one another, and so constitute compounded bodies; and even those resulting bodies may, by being mingled with other compounds, prove the ingredients of decompounded bodies, and so afford a way whereby nature varies matter, which we may call (10) *mixture*, or *composition*° – not that the name is so proper as to the primary concretions of corpuscles, but because it belongs to a multitude of associations, and seems to differ from *texture* (with which it hath so much affinity as perhaps to be reducible to it) in this, that always in mixtures, but not still in textures, there is required a heterogeneity of the component parts. And every distinct portion of matter, whether it be a corpuscle or a primary concretion, or a body of the first or of any other order of mixeds, is to be considered not as if it were placed *in vacuo*, nor as if it had relation only to the neighbouring bodies, but as *being placed in the universe constituted as it is*, amongst an innumerable company of other bodies, whereof some are near it and others very remote, and some are great and some small, some particular and some catholic agents,

and all of them governed as well by (11) *the universal fabric of things*, as
by *the laws of motion* established by the Author of nature in the world.

And now, Pyrophilus, that we have enumerated 11 very general
affections of matter, which with itself make up 12 principles of
variation in bodies, let me on the behalf of the Corpuscularians
apply to the *origin of qualities* a comparison of the old atomists,
employed by Lucretius and others to illustrate the production of an
infinite number of bodies from such simple fragments of matter as
they thought their atoms to be. For since of the 24 letters of the
alphabet, associated several ways as to the number and placing of
the letters, all the words of the several languages in the world may be
made, so, say these naturalists, by variously connecting such and
such numbers of atoms, of such shapes, sizes, and motions, into
masses or concretions, an innumerable multitude of different bodies
may be formed. Wherefore, if to those four affections of matter which
I lately called the most primary and simple, we add the seven other
ways whereby or on whose account it may be altered, that are
though[2] not altogether yet almost as catholic, we shall have *eleven*
principles so fruitful that from their various associations may result a
much vaster multitude of phenomena, and among them of qualities,
than one that does not consider the matter attentively would
imagine. And to invite you to believe this, I shall desire you to take
notice of these three things.

The first is that, supposing these eleven[3] principles were but so
many letters of the alphabet that could be only put together in
differing numbers and in various orders, the combinations and other
associations that might be made of them may be far more numerous
than you yourself will expect, if you are not acquainted with the way
of calculating the number of differing associations that may be made
between eleven[3] things proposed. The best way I know of doing this
is by *algebra*, or symbolical arithmetic, by which it appears that of so
few things so many (α) associations may be made, each of which
will differ from every one of the rest, either in the number of the
things associated or in the order wherein they were placed.

But (which is the second thing to be taken notice of) each of these
eleven[3] producers of phenomena admits of a scarce credible variety.
For not to descend so low as insensible corpuscles (many thousands
of which may be requisite to constitute a grain of mustard seed),
what an innumerable company of different bignesses may we
conceive between the bulk of a mite (a crowd of which is requisite to

weigh one grain) and a mountain, or the body of the sun, which astronomers teach us to be above 100 and threescore times bigger than the whole terrestrial globe. | And so, though (β) figure be one of the most simple modes of matter, yet it is capable, partly in regard of the surface or surfaces of the figured corpuscles (which may consist of triangles, squares, pentagons, &c.) and partly in regard of the shape of the body itself – which may be either flat like a cheese or lozenge, or spherical like a bullet, or elliptical, almost like an egg, or cubical like a die, or cylindrical like a rolling-stone, or pointed like a pyramid or sugar-loaf – figure, I say, though but a simple mode, is, upon these and other scores, capable of so great a multitude of differences, that it is concerning them and their affections that Euclid, Apollonius, Archimedes, Theodosius, Clavius, and later writers than he, have demonstrated so many propositions. And yet all the hitherto-named figures are almost nothing to those irregular shapes such as are to be met with among rubbish, and among hooked and branched particles, &c., that are to be met with among corpuscles and bodies, most of which have no particular appellations, their multitude and their variety having kept men from enumerating them and much more from particularly naming them.

To which let me add that these varieties of figure and shape do also serve to modify the motion and other affections of the corpuscle endowed with them, and of the compounded body whereof it makes a part. | And that the (γ) shape and also size of bodies, whether small or great, may exceedingly diversify their nature and operation, I shall often have occasion to manifest; and therefore I shall now only give you a gross example of it, by inviting you to consider how many differing sorts of tools and instruments, almost each of them fit for many different operations and uses, smiths and other not the noblest sort of tradesmen have been able to form out of pieces of iron, only by making them of differing sizes and giving them differing shapes. For when I have named bodkins, forks, blades, hooks, scissors, anvils, hammers, files, rasps, chisels, gravers, screws, vices, saws, borers, wires, drills, &c. – when (I say) I have named all these, I have left a far greater number unmentioned.

So likewise (δ) motion, which seems so simple a principle, especially in simple bodies, may even in them be very much diversified. For it may be more or less swift, and that in an almost infinite diversity of degrees; it may be simple or compounded, uniform or difform, and the greater celerity may precede or follow.

The body may move in a straight line, or in a circular or in some other curve line, as elliptical, hyperbolical, parabolical, &c., of which geometricians have described several, but of which there may be in all I know not how many more; or else the body's motion may be varied according to the situation or nature of the body it hits against, as that is capable of reflecting it, or refracting it, or both, and that after several manners. The body may also have an undulating motion, and that with smaller or greater waves, or may have a rotation about its own middle parts; or may have both a progressive motion and a rotation, and the one either equal to the other, or swifter than it in almost infinite proportions. As to the determination of motion, the body may move directly upwards or downwards, decliningly or horizontally, east, west, north, or south, &c., according to the situation of the impellent body. And besides these and other modifications of the motion of a simple corpuscle or body, whose phenomena or effects will be also diversified, as I partly noted already, by its bulk and by its figure – besides all these, I say, there will happen a new and great variety of phenomena, when divers corpuscles, though primigenial, and much more if they be compounded, move at once, and so the motion is considered in several bodies. For there will arise new diversifications from the greater or lesser number of the moving corpuscles, from their following one another close or more at a⁴ distance, from the order wherein they follow each other, from the uniformity of their motion or the confusedness of it, from the equality or inequality of their bulk and the similitude or dissimilitude of their figures, from the narrowness or wideness, &c., of the channel or passage in which they move, and the thickness, thinness, pores, and the conditions, of the medium through which they move, from the equal or unequal celerity of their motion and force of their impulse; and the effects of all these are variable by the differing situation and structure of the sensories or other bodies on which these corpuscles beat.

What we have elsewhere said to show that local motion is, next the Author of nature, the principal agent in the production of her phenomena, may, I hope, satisfy you that these diversities in the motion of bodies may produce a strange variety in their nature and qualities. And, as I lately did, so I shall now adumbrate my meaning to you by desiring you to apply to our present purpose what you may familiarly observe in music. For, according as the strings or other instruments of producing sounds do tremble more or less swiftly, they put the air into a vibrating motion more or less brisk, and produce those diversities of sounds which musicians have distinguished into notes, which they have also subdivided, and whereto they have given distinct names. And though the bodies from whence these sounds proceed may be of very differing (ε) natures – as metalline, as wire, gut strings, bells, human voices, wooden pipes, &c. – yet, provided they put the air into the like waving motion, the sound and even the note will be the same, which shows how much that great variety which may be taken notice of in *sounds* is the effect of local motion. And if the sound come from an instrument, as a lute, where not only one string hath its proper sound, but many have among them several degrees of tension and are touched sometimes these, sometimes those, together, whereby more or fewer or none of their vibrations come to be coincident, they will so strike the air as to produce sometimes those pleasing sounds we call *concords*,° and sometimes those harsh ones we call *discords*.°

It would take up too much time to insist upon each of the remaining[5] affections of matter that I lately enumerated and represented to you as exceeding fertile; and by what I elsewhere deliver about pores alone, and the many sorts of phenomena in which they may have an interest, I could add no small confirmation to what has been hitherto discoursed, if the inserting of it here would not enormously increase the bulk of this paper: which I rather decline doing, because what has been already said of those we have now, though but very briefly, treated of may, I hope, be sufficient to persuade you that such principles as these are capable of being made far more pregnant than one would expect so few principles should be. And this persuasion will be much facilitated if we consider how great a variety may be produced, not only by the diversifications that each single principle (upon the score of the attributes that may belong to it) is capable of, but much more by the several (ζ) combinations that may be made of them, especially considering withal that our external and internal senses are so constituted that each, or almost each, of those diversifications or modifications may produce a distinct impression on the organ, and a correspondent perception in the discerning faculty, many of which perceptions, especially if distinguished by proper names, belong to the list of particular qualities.

CHAPTER IV

The third and last difficulty that now remains to be considered may be thus proposed: that whereas, according to the Corpuscularian hypothesis, not only one or two qualities, but all of them, proceed from the bigness and shape and contexture of the minute parts of matter, it is consonant to their principles that, if two bodies agree in one quality, and so in the structure on which that quality depends, they ought to agree in other qualities also, since those do likewise depend upon the structure wherein they do agree; and consequently it will be scarce possible to conceive that two such bodies should be endowed with so many differing qualities as experience shows they may.

To illustrate this objection by an example, it is pretended that the whiteness of froth proceeds from the multitude and hemispherical figure of the bubbles it is made up of. And if this or any other mechanical fabric or contexture be the cause of whiteness, how comes it to pass that some white bodies are inodorous and insipid, as the calx of hartshorn; others both strongly scented and strongly tasted, as the volatile salt of hartshorn or of blood; some dissoluble in water, as salt of tartar; others indissoluble in that liquor, as calcined hartshorn, &c.; some fixed in the fire, as the bodies last named; others fugitive, as powdered sal-ammoniac; some incombustible, as salt of tartar; others very inflammable, as camphor – to which examples a greater variety of white bodies might be added, if it were necessary?

This, I confess, is a considerable difficulty may puzzle more than a novice in the Corpuscularian philosophy; wherefore, to do somewhat in order to the clearing of it, I shall recommend to you the 4 following considerations:

1. And first I shall consider that, in the pores of visible and stable bodies, there may be often lodged invisible and heterogeneous corpuscles, to which a particular quality that belongs not to the body as such is to be referred. Thus we see in a perfumed glove that in the pores of the leather odoriferous particles are harboured which are of quite another nature than the leather itself, and wholly adventitious to it, and yet endue it with the fragrancy for which it is prized. A like example is afforded us in raspberry wine made with

claret. For the pleasing smell is imparted to the wine by the corpuscles of the berries dispersed *per minima* through the whole body of it.

2. The second thing that I consider is this, that oftentimes corpuscles of very differing natures, if they be but fitted to convene, or to be put together after certain manners which yet require no radical change to be made in their essential structures, but only a certain juxtaposition or peculiar kind of composition – such bodies, I say, may notwithstanding their essential differences exhibit the same quality. For invisible changes made in the minute and perhaps undiscernible parts of a stable body may suffice to produce such alterations in its texture as may give it new qualities, and consequently differing from those of other bodies of the same kind or denomination; and therefore, though there remains as much of the former structure as is necessary to make it retain its denomination, yet it may admit of alterations sufficient to produce new qualities.+

Thus when a bar of iron has been violently hammered, though it continues iron still, and is not visibly altered in its texture, yet the insensible parts may have been put into so vehement an agitation as may make the bar too hot to be held in one's hand. And so if you hammer a long and thin piece of silver, though the change of texture will not be visible, it will acquire a springiness that it had not before; and if you leave this hammered piece of silver awhile upon the glowing coals, and after let it cool, though your eye will perchance as little perceive that the fire has altered its texture, as it did before that the hammer had, yet you will find the elasticity destroyed. | If on the surface of a body there arise or be protuberant a multitude of sharp and stiff parts, placed thick or close together, let the body be iron, silver, or wood, or of what matter you please, these exstant and rigid parts will suffice to make all these bodies to exhibit the same quality of asperity or roughness. | And if all the exstant parts of a (physical) superficies be so depressed to a level with the rest that there is a coequation, if I may so speak, made of all the superficial parts of a body, this is sufficient to deprive it of former roughness, and give it that contrary quality we call *smoothness*.° And if this smoothness be considerably exquisite, and happen to the surface of an opacous body of a close and solid contexture, and fit to reflect the incident rays of light and other bodies unperturbed, this is enough to make it specular, whether the body be steel, or silver, or brass, or marble, or flint, or quicksilver, &c. | And so, as I noted in the last chapter on another occasion, if a body be so framed and stretched as being duly moved by another body to put the air into an undulating motion brisk enough to be heard by us, we call that *sonorous*, whether it be a metalline bell, or gut strings, or wires, &c. Nay, if waving motions whereinto the air is put by such differing bodies be alike, these bodies will not only in general give a sound, but will yield that particular degree of sound that men call the same *note*.

For here it is to be considered that, besides that peculiar and essential modification which constitutes a body and distinguishes it from all other that are not of the same species, there may be certain other attributes that we call *extra-essential*, which may be common to that body with many others, and upon which may depend those more external affections of the matter which may suffice to give it this or that relation to other bodies, divers of which relations we style *qualities*.° | Of this I shall give you an evident example in the production of heat. For provided there be a sufficient and confused agitation made in the insensible parts of a body, whether it be iron, or brass, or silver, or wood, or stone, that vehement agitation, without destroying the nature of the body that admits it, will fit it for such an operation upon our sense of feeling, and upon bodies easy to be melted (as butter, wax, &c.), as we call *heat*.° | And so, in the instance named in the objection about whiteness, it is accidental to that quality that the corpuscles it proceeds from should be little hemispheres. For though it happen to be so in water agitated into froth, yet in water frozen to ice, and beaten very small, the corpuscles may be of all manner of shapes, and yet the powder be white. And it being sufficient to the producing of whiteness that the incident light be reflected copiously every way and untroubled by the reflecting body, it matters not whether that body be water, or white wine, or some other clear liquor, turned into froth; or ice, or glass, or crystal, or clarified rosin, &c., beaten into powder: since, without dissolving the essential texture of these formerly diaphanous bodies, it suffices that there be a comminution into grains numerous and small enough, by the multitude of their surfaces, and those of the air (or other fluid) that gets between them, to hinder the passage of the beams of light, and reflect them every way, as well copiously as unperturbed.

Perhaps it may not be impertinent to add to this that there may be other catholic affections of corpuscles, besides the shape or structure of them, by virtue whereof aggregates even of such as are (as to sense) homogeneous may exhibit differing qualities: as, for instance, they may have some when they are in a brisk motion, and others when they are but in a languid one or at rest. As saltpetre, when its parts are sufficiently agitated by the fire in a crucible, is not only fluid but transparent almost like water, whereas when it cools again it becomes a hard and white body, and butter that is opacous in its most usual state may be diaphanous when it is melted, so I shall hereafter have occasion to show you that a great quantity of beaten alabaster, which usually retains the form of a moveless heap of white powder, by being after a due manner exposed to heat obtains (and that without being brought to fusion) many of the principal qualities of a fluid body. And if with good spirit of nitre, or *aqua fortis*, you fill a glass half full, it will (unless it be extraordinarily dephlegmed) exhibit no redness nor approaching colour in the vessel; but if you warm it a little, or cast into it a bit of iron or of silver, that it may put the liquor into a commotion, then the nitrous spirits, divesting the form of a liquor and ascending in that of fumes, will make all the upper part of the glass look of a deep yellow or a red.

3. The third thing I would recommend to your consideration is to reflect on what I proposed in the last foregoing section, where I told you that, in reference to the production of qualities, a body is not to be considered barely in itself, but as it is placed in and is a portion of the universe. But of this subject I have said so much in the newly-mentioned discourse, and in that which you are there referred to, that I shall now only put you in mind that divers of the particulars to be met with in those discourses are applicable to our present purpose.

4. To all this let me add in the last place that, as to that part of the grand objection that we are clearing, which urges the difficulty of explicating upon the Corpuscular principles how, for example, the same body whose structure makes it shaped so as to be fit to exhibit whiteness should likewise have divers other qualities that seem to have no affinity with whiteness – this scruple, I say, we may, by what we have already discoursed, be assisted to remove, especially if we subjoin another consideration to it. For if corpuscles, without losing that texture which is essential to them, may (as we have showed they may) have their shape or their surfaces or their situation changed, and may also admit of alterations (especially as these corpuscles make up an aggregate or *congeries*) as to motion or rest, as to these or those degrees or other circumstances of motion, as to laxity and

density of parts, and divers other affections, why should we not think it possible that a single (though not indivisible) corpuscle, and much more an aggregate of corpuscles, may by some of these or the like changes – which, as I was saying, destroy not the essential texture – be fitted to produce divers other qualities, besides these that necessarily flow from it? Especially considering (which is that I have now to add) that, the qualities commonly called *sensible*° and many others too being according to our opinion but relative attributes, one of these now-mentioned alterations, though but mechanical, may endow the body it happens to with new relations both to the organs of sense and also to some other bodies, and consequently may endow it with additional qualities.

If from good Venice or other turpentine you gently evaporate or abstract about a third part of its whole weight, you may obtain a fine transparent and almost reddish colophony. If you beat this very small, it will lose its colour and transparency and will afford you an opacous and very white powder. If you expose this to a moderate heat, it will quickly and without violence both regain its colour and transparency, and acquire fluidity; and if, whilst it is thus melted, you put the end of a quill or reed a little beneath the surface and blow skilfully into it, you may obtain bubbles adorned with very various and vivid colours. If, when it has lost its fluidity, but whilst it is yet pretty warm, you take it into your hands, you will find that it has in that state a viscosity by virtue of which you may draw it out into threads as you may paste, but as soon as it grows quite cold it becomes exceeding brittle; and if, whilst it is yet warm, you give it the shape of a triangular prism, and make it of a convenient bulk, it will exhibit variety of colours almost like a triangular glass. Whilst this colophony is cold, and its parts are not put into a due motion, straws and other light bodies may be held unmoved close to it; but if by rubbing it a little you put the parts into a convenient agitation, though perhaps without sensibly warming the colophony, it displays an electrical quality, and readily draws to it the hairs, straws, &c., that it would not move before. All or most of these things you may also perform, if I mistake not, with clarified rosin, though I am not sure it will do so well.

To this I shall add one instance more, which may let you see how the same body, which the chemists themselves will tell you is simple and homogeneous, may, by virtue of its shape and other mechanical affections (for it is a factitious body, and that is made by the destruction of a natural one), have such differing respects to different sensories, and to the pores, &c., of divers other bodies, as to display several very differing qualities. The example I speak of is afforded me by the distillation of putrefied urine. For though such urine have already lost its first texture before it come to be distilled, yet when it has undergone 2 or 3 distillations to dephlegm it, the spirits of it swimming in a phlegmatic vehicle have a pungent saltness upon the tongue, and a very strong and to most persons an offensive smell in the nostrils; and when they are freed from the water, they are wont to appear white to the eye; and to very tender parts, as to those that are excoriated, or to the *conjunctiva*, they feel exceeding sharp and seem to burn, almost like a caustic, not to say like fire, insomuch that I have seen them presently make blisters upon the tongue itself, that was not raw or sore before they touched it. The same saline particles invisibly flying up to the eyes prick them and make them water, and invading the nose often cause that great commotion in the head and other parts of the body that we call sneezing. The same corpuscles, if they are much smelt to by a woman in hysterical fits, do very often suddenly relieve her, and so may be reckoned among the specific remedies of that odd and manifold disease – which is not the only one in which they are considerable medicines, as we have elsewhere declared. The same corpuscles taken into human bodies have the qualities that in other medicines we call diaphoretic and diuretic. The same particles being put upon filings of brass produce a fine blue, whereas upon the blue or purple juices of many plants they presently produce a green. Being put to work upon copper, whether crude or calcined, they do readily dissolve it, as corrosive menstruums are wont to do other metals; and yet the same corpuscles, being blended in a due proportion with the acid salts of such menstruums, have the virtue to destroy their corrosiveness, and, if they be put into solutions made with such menstruums, they have a power, excepting in very few cases, to precipitate the bodies therein dissolved. I might here add, Pyrophilus, how the same particles applied to several other bodies, to which they have differing relations, have such distinct operations on them as may entitle these saline spirits to other qualities. But to enumerate them in this place were tedious, especially having already named so many qualities residing in this spirituous salt, which I therefore the rather pitched upon because, being a factitious body and made out of a putrefied one, and so simple as to be a chemical salt (which, you know, spagyrists make one of the three principles of compounded bodies), I suppose you will make the less scruple to admit that it works by virtue of its mechanical affections. Of which to persuade you the more, I shall add that, if you compound this urinous salt with the saline particles of common salt (which is also a factitious thing, and confessed by chemists to be a simple principle of the concrete that yields it), these two being mingled in a due proportion and suffered leisurely to combine will associate themselves into corpuscles, wherein the urinous salt loses most of the qualities I have been ascribing to it, and with the acid spirit composes, as I have often tried, a body little differing from sal-ammoniac, which great change can be ascribed to nothing so probably as to that of the shape and motion (not here to add the size) of the urinous salt, which changes the one and loses a great part of the other by combining with the acid spirits. And to confirm that both these do happen, I have several times slowly exhaled the *superfluous*, but not near the *whole*, liquor from a mixture made in a due proportion of the spirit of urine and that of salt, and found that, answerably to my conjecture, there remained in the bottom a salt not only far more sluggish than the fugitive one of urine, but whose visible shape was quite differing from that of the volatile crystals of urine, this compounded salt being generally figured either like combs or like feathers.

If after all this we do (either add or) inculcate that the extra-essential changes that may be made in the shape, contexture, and motion, &c., of bodies that agree in their essential modifications, may not only qualify them to work themselves immediately after a differing manner upon differing sensories, and upon other bodies also whose pores, &c., are differently constituted, but may dispose them to receive other impressions than before, or receive wonted ones after another manner from the more catholic agents of nature – if, I say, we recommend this also to your consideration, what has been delivered in the whole discourse will, I hope, let you see that the scruple proposed at the beginning of it is not so perplexing a one to our philosophy as perhaps you then imagined it.

The three difficulties considered partly in this, and partly in the two foregoing sections, I was the more inclined to take notice of in this place (for in divers other passages of my writings you will meet with things that are applicable to the past discourse and should be referred thither), partly because the scruples themselves are of great moment and for aught I know have not been discussed by others, and partly because, these difficulties relating in some sort to the Corpuscularian hypothesis in the general, the clearing of them may both serve to confirm several of these things that have above been written about the origin of forms and qualities (to which it might therefore have been joined), and will be conducive to a clearer understanding and explicating divers of the particulars that I am about to deliver, and perhaps several other phenomena of nature.

MS NOTES ON A GOOD AND
AN EXCELLENT HYPOTHESIS[1]

The Requisites of a *Good Hypothesis* are
1. That it be Intelligible.
2. That it Contain nothing Impossible or manifestly False.
3. That it Suppose not any thing tht is either Unintelligible, Impossible or Absurd.
4. That it be Consistent with it self.
5. That it be[2] fit & Sufficient to Explicate the *Phaenomena*, especially the Chief.
6. That it be at lest Consistent with the rest of the *Phaenomena* it particularly relates to, & do not Contradict any other known Phaenomena of Nature, or manifest Physical Truth.

The Qualities & Conditions of an *Excellent Hypothesis* are
1. That it be not Precarious, but have sufficient Grounds in the nature of the Thing it self, or at lest be well recommended by some Auxiliary Proofs
2. That it be the Simplest of all the Good ones we are able to frame, at lest Containing nothing tht is Superfluous or Impertinent.
3. That it be the only Hypothesis tht Can explicate the *Phaenomena*, or at lest tht does explicate them so well.
4. That it enable a skilfull Naturalist to Foretell Future *Phaenomena*, by their Congruity or Incongruity to it: and especially the Events of such Expts as are aptly devisd to Examine it; as Things tht ought or ought not to be Consequent to it.

OF THE IMPERFECTION OF THE
CHEMISTS' DOCTRINE OF QUALITIES

CHAPTER I

Since a great part of those learned men, especially physicians, who have discerned the defects of the vulgar philosophy, but are not yet come to understand and relish the *Corpuscularian*, have slid into the doctrine of the chemists, and since the spagyrists are wont to pretend to make out all the qualities of bodies from the predominancy of some one of their three *hypostatical principles*, I suppose it may both keep my opinion from appearing too presumptuous, and (which is far more considerable) may make way for the fairer reception of the *Mechanical* hypothesis about qualities, if I here intimate (though but briefly and in general) some of those defects that I have observed in chemists' explications of qualities.

And I might begin with taking notice of the *obscurity* of those principles, which is no small defect in notions whose proper office it should be to conduce to the illustration of others. For how can that facilitate the understanding of an obscure quality or phenomenon, which is itself scarcely intelligible, or at least needs almost as much explanation as the thing it is designed and pretended to explicate? Now a man need not be very conversant in the writings of chemists to observe in how lax, indefinite, and almost arbitrary, senses they employ the terms of *salt*, *sulphur* and *mercury*, of which I could never find that they were agreed upon any certain definitions or settled notions – not only differing authors, but not unfrequently one and the same, and perhaps in the same book, employing them in very differing senses. But I will not give the chemists any rise to pretend that the chief fault that I find with their hypothesis is but verbal, though that itself may not a little blemish any hypothesis, one of the first of whose requisites ought to be *clearness*; and therefore I shall now advance and take notice of defects that are manifestly of another kind.

And first, the doctrine that all their theory is grounded on seems to me *inevident* and undemonstrated, not to say precarious. It is somewhat strange to me that neither the spagyrists themselves, nor yet their adversaries, should have taken notice that chemists have rather supposed, than evinced, that the analysis of bodies by fire, or even that at least some *analysis*, is the only instrument of investigating what ingredients mixed bodies are made up of: since in divers cases that may be discovered by composition as well as by resolution, as it may appear that vitriol consists of metalline parts (whether martial, or venereal, or both), associated by coagulation with acid ones – one may, I say, discover this as well by making true vitriol with spirit (improperly called *oil°*) of sulphur, or that of salt, as by distilling or resolving vitriol by the fire.| But I will not here enlarge on this subject, nor yet will I trouble you with what I have largely discoursed in *The Sceptical Chemist*, to call in question the grounds on which chemists assert that all mixed bodies are compounded of *salt, sulphur*, and *mercury*. For it may suffice me now to tell you that, whatsoever they may be able to obtain from other bodies, it does not appear by experience – which is the grand, if not the only, argument they rely on – that all mixed bodies that have qualities consist of their *tria prima*, since they have not been able, that we know, truly and without new compositions, to resolve into those three either *gold*, or *silver*, or *crystal*, or *Venetian talc*, or some other bodies that I elsewhere name; and yet these bodies are endowed with divers *qualities*, as the two former with fusibleness and malleability, and all of them with weight and fixity: so that, in these and the like bodies, whence chemists have not made it yet appear that their salt, sulphur and mercury can be truly and adequately separated, it will scarce be other than precarious to derive the malleableness, colour, and other qualities of such bodies from those principles.

Under this head I consider also that a great part of the chemical doctrine of qualities is bottomed on, or supposes, besides their newly-questioned analysis by fire, some other things which, as far as I know, have not yet been well proved, and I question whether they ever will be.

One of their main suppositions is that this or that quality must have its πρῶτον δεκτικόν – as Sennertus, the learnedest champion of this opinion, calls it – or some particular material principle, to the participation of which, as of the primary, native and genuine subject, all other bodies must owe it. But upon this point having purposely discoursed elsewhere, I shall now only observe that, not to mention local motion and figure, I think it will be hard to show what is the πρῶτον δεκτικόν of gravity, volatility, heat, sonorousness, transparency, and opacity, which are qualities to be indifferently met with in bodies whether simple or mixed.

And whereas the spagyrists are wont to argue that, because this or that quality is not to be derived truly from this or that particular principle – as *salt*, for instance, and *mercury* – therefore it must needs be derivable from the third – as *sulphur* – this way of arguing involves a farther supposition than that newly examined. For it implies that every quality in a compounded body must arise from some one of the *tria prima*, whereas experience assures us that bodies may, by composition, obtain qualities that were not to be found in any of the separate ingredients: as we see in painting that, though blue and yellow be neither of them green, yet their mixture will be so; and though no single sound will make an octave or *diapason*, yet two sounds whose proportion is double will have an eighth; and tin and copper, melted and mingled together in a due proportion, will make a bell-metal far more sonorous than either of them was before. It is obvious enough for chemists themselves to observe that, though lead be an insipid body, and spirit of vinegar a very sharp one, yet *saccharum saturni*, that is compounded out of these two, has a sweetness that makes it not ill deserve its name.

But this ill-grounded supposition of the chemists is extended farther in a usual topic of theirs, according to which they conclude that I know not how many qualities, as well manifest as occult, must be explicated by their *tria prima*, because they are not explicable by the four elements of the *Peripatetics*: to make which argumentation valid, it must be proved (which I fear it will never be) that there are no other ways by which those qualities may be explicated, but by a determinate number of material principles, whether four or three; besides that, till they have shown that such qualities may be intelligibly explicated by *their* principles, the objection will lie as strong for the Aristotelians against them as for them against the Aristotelians.

CHAPTER II

Next I consider that there are divers qualities, even in mixed bodies, wherein it does not appear that the use of the chemical doctrine is *necessary*: as, for instance, when pure *gold* is by heat only brought to fusion, and consequently to the state of fluidity, and upon the remission of that heat grows a solid and consistent body again, what addition or expulsion or change of any of the *tria prima* does appear to be the cause of this change of consistence – which is easy to be accounted for according to the *Mechanical* way, by the vehement agitation that the fire makes of the minute parts of the gold to bring it to fusion, and the cohesion of those parts, by virtue of their gravity and fitness to adhere to one another, when that agitation ceases? When *Venice glass* is, merely by being beaten to powder, deprived of its transparency and turned into a body opacous and white, what need or use of the *tria prima* have we in the explication of this phenomenon; or of that other which occurs when, by barely melting down this white and opacous body, it is deprived of its opacity and colour, and becomes diaphanous? And of this sort of instances you will meet with divers in the following notes about particular qualities; for which reason I shall forbear the mention of them here.

CHAPTER III

I observe, too, that the spagyrical doctrine of qualities is *insufficient* and too narrow to reach to all the phenomena, or even to all the notable ones, that ought to be explicable by them. And this insufficiency I find to be twofold. For *first*, there are divers qualities of which chemists will not so much as attempt to give us explications; and of other particular qualities the explications, such as they are that they give us, are often very deficient and unsatisfactory, and do not sometimes so much as take notice of divers considerable phenomena that belong to the qualities whereof they pretend to give an account: of which you will meet with divers instances in the ensuing notes. And therefore I shall only (to declare my meaning the better) invite you to observe with me that, though *gold* be the body they affect to be most conversant with, yet it will be very hard to show how the specific weight of gold can be deduced from any or all of the three principles, since *mercury* itself, that is of bodies known to us the heaviest next to gold, is so much lighter than gold that, whereas I have usually found mercury to be to an equal weight of water somewhat, though little, less than fourteen to one, I find *pure* gold to be about nineteen times as heavy as so much water: which will make it very difficult, not to say impossible, for them to explain how gold should, barely by participating of mercury, which is a body much lighter than itself, obtain that great specific gravity we find it to have; for the two other hypostatical principles, we know, are far lighter than mercury. And I think it would much puzzle the chemists to give us any examples of a compounded body that is specifically heavier than the heaviest of the ingredients that it is made up of. And this is the *first* kind of insufficiency I was taking notice of in the chemical doctrine of qualities.

The *other* is that there are several bodies which the most learned among themselves confess not to consist of their *tria prima*, and yet are endowed with qualities which, consequently, are not in those subjects to be explicated by the *tria prima* which are granted not to be found in them. Thus *elementary water*, though never so pure (as distilled rain-water), has fluidity and coldness and humidity and transparency and volatility, without having any of the *tria prima*. And the purest *earth*, as ashes carefully freed from the fixed salt, has gravity and consistence and dryness and colour and fixity, without owing them either to salt, sulphur, or mercury; not to mention that there are celestial bodies which do not appear, nor are wont to be pretended, to consist of the *tria prima*, that yet are endowed with qualities: as the *sun* has light and, as many philosophers think, heat and colour, and the *moon* has a determinate consistence and figuration (as appears by her mountains), and astronomers observe that the higher planets and even the fixed stars appear to be differingly coloured. But I shall not multiply instances of this kind, because what I have said may not only serve for my present purpose, but bring a great confirmation to what I lately said when I noted that the chemical principles were in many cases *not necessary* to explicate qualities: for since in earth, water, &c., such diffused qualities as gravity, fixedness, colour, transparency, and fluidity, must be acknowledged not to be derived from the *tria prima*, it is plain that portions of matter may be endowed with such qualities by other causes and agents than salt, sulphur, and mercury. And then why should we deny that also in compounded bodies those qualities may be (sometimes at least) produced by the same or the like causes – as we see that the reduction of a diaphanous solid to powder produces whiteness, whether the comminution happens to rock-crystal, or to Venice glass, or to ice, the first of which is acknowledged to be a natural and perfectly mixed body, the second a factitious and not only mixed but decompounded body, and the last, for aught appears, an elementary body, or at most very slightly and imperfectly mixed? And so by mingling air in small portions with a diaphanous liquor, as we do when we beat such a liquor into foam, a whiteness is produced, as well in pure water, which is acknowledged to be a simple body, as in white wine, which is reckoned among perfectly mixed bodies.

CHAPTER IV

I further observe that the chemists' explications do not reach *deep*° and *far*° enough. For *first*, most of them are not sufficiently distinct and full so as to come home to the particular phenomena, nor oftentimes so much as to all the grand ones that belong to the history of the qualities they pretend to explicate. You will readily believe that a chemist will not easily make out by his salt, sulphur, and mercury, why a loadstone capped with steel may be made to take up a great deal more iron – sometimes more than eight or ten times as much – than if it be immediately applied to the iron; or why, if one end of the magnetic needle is disposed to be attracted by the north pole, for instance, of the loadstone, the other pole of the loadstone will not attract it but drive it away; or why a bar or rod of iron, being heated red-hot and cooled perpendicularly, will with its lower end drive away the flower-de-luce, or the north end of a mariner's needle, which the upper end of the same bar or rod will not repel but draw to it. In short, of above threescore properties or notable phenomena of magnetic bodies that some writers have reckoned up, I do not remember that any three have been by chemists so much as attempted to be solved by their three principles. And even in those qualities in whose explications these principles may more probably than elsewhere pretend to have a place, the spagyrists' accounts are wont to fall so short of being distinct and particular enough, that they use to leave divers considerable phenomena untouched, and do but very lamely or slightly explicate the more obvious or familiar. And I have so good an opinion of divers of the embracers of the spagyrical theory of qualities (among whom I have met with very learned and worthy men) that I think that if, a quality being proposed to them, they were at the same time presented with a good catalogue of the phenomena, that they may take in the history of it as it were with one view, they would plainly perceive that there are more particulars to be accounted for than at first they were aware of, and divers of them such as may quite discourage considering men from taking upon them to explain them all by the *tria prima*, and oblige them to have recourse to more catholic and comprehensive principles. I know not whether I may not add on this occasion that methinks a chemist who, by the help of his *tria prima*, takes upon him to interpret that Book of Nature of which the qualities of bodies make a great part, acts at but a little better rate than he that, seeing a great book written in a cipher whereof he were acquainted but with three letters, should undertake to decipher the whole piece. For though it is like he would in many words find one of the letters of his short key, and in divers words two of them, and perhaps in some all three, yet, besides that in most of the words wherein the known letter or letters may be met with they may be so blended with other unknown letters as to keep him from deciphering a good part of those very words, it is more than probable that a great part of the book would consist of words wherein none of his three letters were to be found.

CHAPTER V

And this is the *first* account on which I observe that the chemical theory of qualities does not reach far enough; but there is *another* branch of its deficiency. For even when the explications seem to come home to the phenomena, they are not primary and, if I may so speak, *fontal* enough. To make this appear, I shall at present employ but these two considerations. The first is that those substances themselves that chemists call their *principles*° are each of them endowed with several qualities. Thus *salt* is a consistent, not a fluid, body; it has its weight; it is dissoluble in water, is either diaphanous or opacous, fixed or volatile, sapid or insipid (I speak thus disjunctively because chemists are not all agreed about these things, and it concerns not my argument which of the disputable qualities be resolved upon). And *sulphur*, according to *them*, is a body fusible, inflammable, &c.; and according to experience, is consistent, heavy, &c. So that it is by the help of more primary and general principles that we must explicate some of those qualities which, being found in bodies supposed to be perfectly similar or homogeneous, cannot be pretended to be derived in one of them from the other. And to say that it is the nature of a principle to have this or that quality – as, for instance, of sulphur to be fusible – and therefore we are not to exact a reason why it is so, though I could say much by way of answer, I shall now only observe that this argument is grounded but upon a supposition, and will be of no force if, from the primary affections of bodies, one may deduce any good Mechanical explication of fusibility in the general, without necessarily supposing such a primigenial sulphur as the chemists fancy, or deriving it from thence in other bodies. And indeed, since not only saltpetre, sea-salt, vitriol and alum, but salt of tartar and the volatile salt of urine, are all of them fusible, I do not well see how chemists can derive the fusibleness even of salts obtained by their own *analysis* (such as salt of tartar and of urine) from the participation of the sulphureous ingredient: especially since, if such an attempt should be made, it would overthrow the hypothesis of three simple bodies whereof they will have all mixed ones to be compounded, and still it would remain to be explicated upon what account the principle that is said to endow the other with such a quality comes to be endowed therewith itself. For it is plain that a mass of sulphur is not an atomical or adamantine body, but consists of a multitude of corpuscles of determinate figures, and connected after a determinate manner: so that it may be reasonably demanded why such a convention of particles, rather than many another that does not, constitutes a fusible body.

CHAPTER VI

And this leads me to a further consideration, which makes me look upon the chemists' explications as not deep and radical enough; and it is this, that when they tell us, for instance, that the fusibleness of bodies proceeds from sulphur, in case they say true they do but tell us *what* material ingredient it is that, being mingled with and dispersed through the other parts of a body, makes it apt to melt: but this does not intelligibly declare *what it is* that makes a portion of matter fusible, and *how* the sulphureous ingredient introduces that disposition into the rest of the mass wherewith it is commixed or united. And yet it is such explications as these that an inquisitive naturalist chiefly looks after, and which I therefore call *philosophical.* And to show that there may be more fontal explications, I shall only observe that, not to wander from our present instance, sulphur itself is fusible; and therefore, as I lately intimated, fusibility, which is not the quality of one atom or particle, but of an aggregate of particles, ought itself to be accounted for in that principle, before the fusibleness of all other bodies be derived from it. And it will in the following notes appear that in *sulphur* itself that quality may be probably deduced from the convention of corpuscles of determinate shapes and sizes, contexed or connected after a convenient manner. And if either nature, or art, or chance, should bring together particles endowed with the like mechanical affections, and associate them after the like manner, the resulting body would be fusible, though the component particles had never been parts of the chemists' primordial sulphur; and such particles so convening might perhaps have made sulphur itself, though before there had been no such body in the world.+

And what I say to those chemists that make the sulphureous ingredient the cause of fusibility may easily, *mutatis mutandis*, be applied to *their* hypothesis, that rather ascribe that quality to the mercurial or the saline principle, and consequently cannot give a rational account of the fusibility of sulphur. And therefore, though I readily allow (as I shall have afterwards occasion to declare) that sulphur or another of the *tria prima* may be met with, and even abound, in several bodies endowed with the quality that is attributed to their participation of that principle, yet, that this may be no certain sign that the proposed quality must flow from that ingredient, you may perhaps be assisted to discern by this illustration, that, if tin be duly mixed with copper or gold, or, as I have tried, with silver or iron, it will make them very brittle; and it is also an ingredient of divers other bodies that are likewise brittle, as blue, green, white, and otherwise coloured, amels, which are usually made of calcined tin (which the tradesmen call *putty*), colliquated with the ingredients of crystal-glass and some small portion of mineral pigment. But though in all the above-named brittle bodies tin be a considerable ingredient, yet it were very unadvised to affirm that brittleness in general proceeds from tin. For, provided the solid parts of consistent bodies touch one another but according to small portions of their surfaces, and be not implicated by their contexture, the metalline or other composition may be brittle though there be no tin at all in it. And in effect, the materials of glass being brought to fusion will compose a brittle body as well when there is no putty colliquated with them as when there is. Calcined lead by the action of the fire may be melted into a brittle mass, and even into transparent glass, without the help of tin or any other additament. And I need not add that there are a multitude of other bodies that cannot be pretended to owe their brittleness to any participation of tin, of which they have no need if the matter they consist of wants not the requisite mechanical dispositions.

And here I shall venture to add that the way employed by the chemists, as well as the Peripatetics, of accounting for things by the ingredients – whether elements, principles, or other bodies – that they suppose them to consist of, will often frustrate the naturalist's expectation of events, which may frequently prove differing from what he promised himself upon the consideration of the qualities of each ingredient. For the ensuing notes contain divers instances, wherein there emerges a new quality differing from, or even contrary to, any that is conspicuous in the ingredients: as two transparent bodies may make an opacous mixture; a yellow body and a blue, one that is green; two malleable bodies, a brittle one; two actually cold bodies, a hot one; two fluid bodies, a consistent one, &c. And as this way of judging by material principles hinders the foreknowledge of events from being certain, so it much more hinders the assignation of causes from being satisfactory: so that perhaps some would not think it very rash to say that those who judge of all mixed bodies as apothecaries do of medicines, barely by the qualities and proportions of the ingredients (such as among the Aristotelians are the four elements, and among the chemists the *tria prima*), do as if one should pretend to give an account of the phenomena and operations of clocks and watches and their diversities by this, that some are made of brass wheels, some of iron, some have plain ungilt wheels, others of wheels overlaid with gold, some furnished with gut strings, others with little chains, &c., and that therefore the qualities and predominancies of these metals that make parts of the watch ought to have ascribed to them what indeed flows from their coordination and contrivance.

CHAPTER VII

The *last* defect I observe in the chemical doctrine of qualities is that in many cases it *agrees not well*° with the phenomena of nature, and that by one or both of these ways. First, there are divers changes of qualities wherein one may well expect that a chemical principle should have a great stroke, and yet it does not at all appear to have so. He that considers what great operations divers of the hermetics ascribe to this or that hypostatical principle, and how many qualities according to them must from it be derived, can scarce do other than expect that a great change as to those qualities happening in a mixed body should at least be accompanied with some notable action *of*, or alteration *in*, the principle. And yet I have met with many instances wherein qualities are produced, or abolished, or very much altered, without any manifest introduction, expulsion, or considerable change, of the principle whereon *that* quality is said to depend, or perhaps of either of the two *others*: as when a piece of fine silver, that, having been nealed in the fire and suffered to cool leisurely, is very flexible, is made stiff and hard to bend, barely by a few strokes of a hammer; and a string of a lute acquires or loses a sympathy, as they call it, with another string of the same or another instrument, barely by being either stretched so as to make a unison with it, or screwed up or let down beyond or beneath that degree of tension.

To multiply instances of this kind would be to anticipate those you will hereafter meet with in their due places. And therefore I shall pass on from the first sort of phenomena that favour not the chemical hypothesis about qualities, to the other, which consists of those wherein either that does not happen which according to their hypothesis ought to happen, or the contrary happens to what according to their hypothesis may justly be expected. Of this you will meet with instances hereafter; I shall now trouble you but with one, the better to declare my meaning. It is not unknown to those chemists that work much in silver and in copper that the former will endure ignition and become red-hot in the fire, before it will be brought to fusion, and the latter is yet far more difficult to be melted down than the other; yet if you separately dissolve those two metals in *aqua fortis*, and by evaporation reduce them to crystals, these will be brought to fusion in a very little time, and with a very moderate heat, without breaking the glasses that contain them. If you ask a vulgar chemist the cause of this facility of fusion, he will probably tell you without scruple that it is from the saline parts of the *aqua fortis*, which, being embodied in the metals and of a very fusible nature, impart that easiness of fusion to the metals they are mixed with. According to which plausible explication one might well expect that, if the saline corpuscles were exquisitely mingled with tin, they would make it far more fusible than of itself it is: and yet, as I have elsewhere noted, when I put tin into a convenient quantity of *aqua fortis*, the metal, being corroded, subsided as is usual in the form of whites of eggs, which being well dried, the tin was so far from being grown more fusible by the addition of the saline particles of the menstruum that, whereas it is known that simple tin will melt long before it come to be red-hot, this prepared tin would endure for a good while not only a thorough ignition, but the blast of a pair of double bellows (which we usually employed to melt silver and copper itself), without being at all brought to fusion. And as for those spagyrists that admit, as most of them are granted to do, that all kinds of metals may be turned into gold by a very small proportion of what they call the philosopher's *elixir*, one may I think show them, from their own concessions, that divers qualities may be changed even in such constant bodies as metals, without the addition of any considerable proportion of the simple ingredients to which they are wont to ascribe those qualities, provided the agent (as an efficient rather than as a material cause) be able to make a great change in the mechanical affections of the parts whereof the metal it acts on is made up. Thus if we suppose a pound of silver, a pound of lead, and a pound of iron, to be transmuted into gold, each by a grain of the powder of projection, this tinging powder as a material cause is inconsiderable, by reason of the smallness of its bulk, and as an efficient cause it works differing and even contrary effects, according to the disposition wherein it finds the metal to be transmuted, and the changes it produces in the constituent texture of it. Thus it brings quicksilver to be fixed, which it was not before, and deprives it of the fluidity which it had before; it brings silver to be indissolvable in *aqua fortis*, which readily dissolved it before, and dissoluble in *aqua regis*, which before would not touch it; and, which is very considerable to our present purpose, whereas it makes iron much more fusible than mars, it makes lead much less fusible than whilst it retained its pristine form: since saturn melts ere it come to ignition, which gold requires to bring it to fusion. But this is proposed only as an argument *ad hominem*, till the truth of the transmutation of metals into gold by way of projection be sufficiently proved, and the circumstances and phenomena of it particularly declared.

I must not forget to take notice that some learned modern chemists would be thought to explicate divers of the changes that happen to bodies in point of odours, colours, &c., by saying that in such alterations the sulphur or other hypostatical principle is *introverted* or *extraverted*, or, as others speak, *inverted*. But, I confess, to me these seem to be rather new terms than real explications. For, to omit divers of the arguments mentioned in this present treatise that may be applied to this way of solving the phenomena of qualities, one may justly object that the supposed extraversion or introversion of sulphur can by no means reach to give an account of so great a variety of odours, colours, and other qualities as may be found in the changed portions of matter we are speaking of. And, which is more, what they call by these and the like names cannot be done without local motion transposing the particles of the matter, and consequently producing in it a change of texture, which is the very thing we would infer; and which being supposed, we may grant sulphur to be oftentimes actually present in the altered bodies, without allowing it to be always necessary to produce the alterations in them, since corpuscles so conditioned and contexed would perform such effects, whether sulphur as such did, or did not, make up the subject-matter of the change.

And now I shall conclude, and partly recapitulate, what has been delivered in this and the two foregoing chapters, with this summary consideration, that the chemists' salt, sulphur and mercury themselves are not the first and most simple principles of bodies, but rather primary concretions of corpuscles or particles more simple than they, as being endowed only with the first or most radical (if I may so speak) and most catholic affections of simple bodies, namely bulk, shape, and motion or rest, by the different conventions or coalitions of which minutest portions of matter are made those differing concretions that chemists name *salt*,° *sulphur*,° and *mercury*.° And to this doctrine it will be consonant that several effects of this or that spagyrical principle need not be derived from salt, for instance, or sulphur, as such, but may be explained by the help of some of those corpuscles that I have lately called more *simple*° and *radical*;° and such explications, being more simple and mechanical, may be thought upon that score more fundamental and satisfactory.

CHAPTER VIII

I know it may be objected in favour of the chemists that, as their hypostatical principles – salt, sulphur, and mercury – are but three, so the Corpuscularian principles are but very few, and the chief of them, *bulk*, *size*, and *motion*, are but three neither: so that it appears not why the chemical principles should be more barren than the Mechanical. To which allegation I answer that, besides that these last-named principles are more numerous, as taking in the posture, order and situation, the rest and, above all, the almost infinitely diversifiable contextures, of the small parts, and the thence-resulting structures of particular bodies and fabric of the world – besides this, I say, each of the three Mechanical principles specified in the objection, though but one in name, is equivalent to many in effect: as *figure*, for instance, comprehends not only triangles, squares, rhombuses, rhomboids, trapezions, and a multitude of polygons whether ordinate or irregular, but, besides cubes, prisms, cones, spheres, cylinders, pyramids, and other solids of known denominations, a scarce numerable multitude of hooked, branched, eel-like, screw-like, and other irregular bodies, whereof though these and some others have distinct appellations, yet the greatest part are nameless. So that it need be no wonder that I should make the Mechanical principles so much more fertile, that is, applicable to the production and explication of a far greater number of phenomena, than the chemical, which, whilst they are considered but as similar bodies that are ingredients of mixed and compounded ones, are chiefly variable but by the greater or lesser quantity that is employed by nature or art to make up the mixed body. And painters observe that black and white, though mixed in differing proportions, will still make but lighter and darker greys. And if it be said that these ingredients, by the texture resulting from their mixtures, may acquire qualities that neither of them had before, I shall answer that to allege this is in effect to confess that they must take in the

Mechanical principles (for to them belongs the texture or structure of bodies) to assist the *chemical* ones. And on this occasion, to borrow an illustration from our unpublished *Dialogue of the Requisites of a Good Hypothesis*, I shall add that a chemist that should pretend that, because his three principles are as many as those of the Corpuscularians, they are as sufficient as these to give an account of the Book of Nature – methinks, I say, he would do like a man that should pretend that with four and twenty words he would make up a language as well as others can with the four and twenty letters of the alphabet, because he had as many words already formed as they had of bare letters: not considering that, instead of the small number of variations that can be made of his words by prepositions and terminations, the letters of the alphabet being variously combined, placed, and reiterated, can be easily made to compose not only his four and twenty words with their variations, but as many others as a whole language contains.

CHAPTER IX

Notwithstanding all that I have been obliged to say to the disadvantage of the chemical principles in reference to the explication of qualities, I would not be thought to grant that the *Peripatetics* have reason to triumph, as if their four elements afforded a better theory of qualities. For if I had, together with leisure enough to perform such a task, any obligation to undertake it, I presume it would not be difficult to show that the Aristotelian doctrine about particular qualities is liable to some of the same objections with the chemical, and to some others no less considerable; and that, to derive all the phenomena their doctrine ought to solve from *substantial forms* and *real qualities elementary* is to impose on us a theory more barren and precarious than that of the spagyrists.

That to derive the particular qualities of bodies from those substantial forms whence the Schools would have them to flow is but an insufficient and unfit way of accounting for them, may appear by this, that *substantial forms* themselves are things whose existence many learned philosophers deny, whose theory many of them think incomprehensible, and the most candid and judicious of the Peripatetics themselves confess it to be very abstruse, so that from such doubtful and obscure principles we can hardly expect clear explications of the nature and phenomena of qualities – not to urge that the Aristotelian definitions, both of qualities in general, and of divers of the more familiar qualities in particular, as heat, cold, moisture, diaphaneity, &c., are far enough from being clear and well framed, as we elsewhere have occasion to show.

Another thing which makes the scholastic doctrine of qualities unsatisfactory is that it seldom so much as attempts to teach the manner how the qualities themselves and their effects or operations are produced. Of this you may elsewhere find an instance given in the quality that is wont to be first in the list, viz. that of *heat*, which, though it may intelligibly and probably be explicated by the Corpuscular hypothesis, yet in the Peripatetic account that is given of it is both too questionable and too superficial to give much content to a rational enquirer. And indeed, to say that a *substantial form* (as that of the *fire*) acts by a quality (called *heat*°) whose nature it is to produce such an effect (as to soften wax or harden clay) seems to be no other in substance than to say that it produces such an effect by some power it has to produce it. But what that power is, and how it operates, is that which, though we most desire to know, we are left to seek. But to prosecute the imperfections of the *Peripatetic hypothesis* were to entrench upon another discourse, where they are more fully laid open. And therefore I shall now but lightly glance upon a couple of imperfections that more particularly relate to the doctrine of qualities.

And first, I do not think it a convincing argument that is wont to be employed by the *Aristotelians* for their *elements*, as well as by the *chemists* for their *principles*, that, because this or that quality, which they ascribe to an element or a principle, is found in this or that body, which they call *mixed*,° therefore it must owe that quality to the participation of that principle or element. For the same texture of parts, or other modification of matter, may produce the like quality in the more simple and the more compounded body, and they may both separately derive it from the same cause, and not one from the participation of the other. So water and earth and metals and stones, &c., are heavy upon the account of the common cause of gravity, and not because the rest partake of the earth: as may appear in elementary water, which is as simple a body as it, and yet is heavy. So water and oil and exactly-dephlegmed spirit of wine and mercury – and also metals and glass of antimony, and minium or calcined lead, whilst these three are in fusion – are fluid, being made so by the variously determined motions of their minute parts and other causes of fluidity, and not by the participation of water: since the arid calces of lead and antimony are not like to have retained in the fire so volatile a liquor as water, and since fluidity is a quality that mercury enjoys in a more durable manner than water itself; for that metalline liquor, as also spirit of wine well rectified, will not be brought to freeze with the highest degree of cold of our sharpest winters, though a far less degree of cold would make water cease to be fluid and turn it into ice.

To this I shall only add, in the second place, that it is not unpleasant to see how arbitrarily the Peripatetics derive the qualities of bodies from their four elements, as if, to give an instance in the lately-named quality, *liquidity*, you show them exactly-dephlegmed spirit of wine and ask them whence it has its great fluidness, they will tell you 'from water', which yet is far less fluid than it, and this spirit of wine itself is much less so than the flame into which the spirit of wine is easily resoluble. But if you ask whence it becomes totally inflammable, they must tell you 'from the fire'; and yet the whole body, at least as far as sense can discover, is fluid, and the whole body becomes flame (and then is most fluid of all), so that fire and water, as contrary as they make them, must both be by vast odds predominant in the same body. This spirit of wine also being a liquor, whose least parts that are sensible are actually heavy and compose a liquor which is seven or eight hundred times as heavy as air of the same bulk, which yet experience shows not to be devoid of weight, must be supposed to abound with earthy particles; and yet this spirituous liquor may in a trice become flame, which they would have to be the lightest body in the world.

But to enlarge on this subject would be to forget that the design of this tract engages me to deal not with the *Peripatetic* school, but the *spagyrical*: to which I shall therefore return, and give you this advertisement about it, that what I have hitherto objected is meant against the more common and received doctrine about the material principles of bodies reputed mixed, as it is wont by vulgar chemists to be applied to the rendering an account of the qualities of substances corporeal; and therefore I pretend not that the past objections should conclude against other chemical theories than that which I was concerned to question. And if *adept* philosophers (supposing there be such), or any other more than ordinarily intelligent spagyrists, shall propose any particular hypotheses differing from those that I have questioned, as their doctrine and reasons are not yet known to me, so I pretend not that the past arguments should conclude against them; and am willing to think that persons advantaged with such peculiar opportunities to dive into the mysteries of nature will be able to give us, if they shall please, a far better account of the qualities of bodies than what is wont to be proposed by the generality of chemists.

Thus, dear Pyrophilus, I have laid before you some of the chief imperfections I have observed in the vulgar chemists' doctrine of qualities, and consequently I have given you some of the chief reasons that hinder me from acquiescing in it. And as my objections are not taken from the scholastical subtleties nor the doubtful speculations of the Peripatetics or other adversaries of the hermetic philosophy, but from the nature of things and from chemical experiments themselves, so I hope, if any of your spagyrical friends have a mind to convince me, he will attempt to do it by the most proper way, which is by actually giving us clear and particular explications, at least of the grand phenomena of qualities: which if he shall do, he will find me very ready to acquiesce in a truth that comes ushered in and endeared by so acceptable and useful a thing as a philosophical theory of qualities.

ABOUT THE EXCELLENCY AND GROUNDS
OF THE MECHANICAL HYPOTHESIS[1]

The importance of the question you propose would oblige me to refer you to the *Dialogue about a Good Hypothesis*, and some other papers of that kind, where you may find my thoughts about the advantages of the *Mechanical* hypothesis somewhat amply set down and discoursed of. But since your desires confine me to deliver in few words, not what I believe resolvedly, but what I think may be probably said for the preference or the pre-eminence of the *Corpuscular* philosophy above *Aristotle's* or that of the *chemists*, you must be content to receive from me, without any preamble, or exact method, or ample discourses, or any other thing that may cost many words, a succinct mention of some of the chief advantages of the hypothesis we incline to. And I the rather comply on this occasion with your curiosity, because I have often observed you to be alarmed and disquieted, when you hear of any book that pretends to uphold or repair the decaying philosophy of the Schools, or some bold chemist that arrogates to those of his sect the title of *philosophers*° and pretends to build wholly upon experience, to which he would have all other naturalists thought strangers. That therefore you may not be so tempted to despond, by the confidence or reputation of those writers that do some of them applaud, and others censure, what I fear they do not understand (as when the Peripatetics cry up *substantial forms*, and the chemists *mechanical explications* of nature's phenomena),[2] I will propose some considerations that, I hope, will not only keep you kind to the philosophy you have embraced, but perhaps (by some considerations which you have not yet met with) make you think it probable that the new attempts you hear of from time to time will not overthrow the Corpuscularian philosophy, but either be foiled by it or found reconcilable to it.

But when I speak of the *Corpuscular* or *Mechanical* philosophy, I am far from meaning, with the Epicureans, that *atoms*, meeting together by chance in an infinite *vacuum*, are able of themselves to produce the world and all its phenomena; nor, with some modern philosophers, that, supposing God to have put into the whole mass of matter such an invariable quantity of motion, he needed do no more to make the world, the material parts being able by their own unguided motions to cast themselves into such a system (as we call by that name). But I plead only for such a philosophy as reaches but to things purely corporeal, and, distinguishing between the first *original of things* and the subsequent *course of nature*, teaches concerning the *former*, not only that God gave motion to matter, but that in the beginning he so guided the various motions of the parts of it as to contrive them into the world he designed they should compose (furnished with the *seminal* principles and structures or models of living creatures), and established those *rules of motion*, and that order amongst things corporeal, which we are wont to call the *laws of nature*. And having told this as to the *former*, it may be allowed as to the *latter* to teach that, the universe being once framed by God, and the laws of motion being settled and all upheld by his incessant concourse and general providence, the phenomena of the world thus constituted are physically produced by the mechanical affections of the parts of matter, and what they operate upon one another according to mechanical laws. And now, having shown what kind of *Corpuscular* philosophy it is that I speak of, I proceed to the particulars that I thought the most proper to recommend it.

I. The first thing that I shall mention to this purpose is the *intelligibleness*° or *clearness*° of Mechanical principles and explications.+

I need not tell you that among the *Peripatetics* the disputes are many and intricate about *matter, privation, substantial forms* and their *eduction*, &c. And the *chemists* are sufficiently puzzled (as I have elsewhere shown) to give such definitions and accounts of their hypostatical principles as are reconcilable to one another, and even to some obvious phenomena. And much more dark and intricate are their doctrines about the *archeus, astral beings, gas, blas*, and other odd notions, which perhaps have in part occasioned the darkness and ambiguity of their expressions, that could not be very clear when their conceptions were far from being so. And if the principles of the Aristotelians and spagyrists are thus obscure, it is not to be expected the explications that are made by the help only of such principles should be clear. And indeed many of them are either so general and slight, or otherwise so unsatisfactory, that, granting their principles, it is very hard to understand or admit their applications of them to particular phenomena. And even in some of the more ingenious and subtle of the Peripatetic discourses upon their superficial and narrow theories, methinks the authors have better played the part of *painters* than *philosophers*, and have only had the skill, like drawers of landscapes, to make men fancy they see castles and towns, and other structures that appear solid and magnificent and to reach to a large extent, when the whole piece is superficial, and made up of colours and art, and comprised within a frame perhaps scarce a yard long. But to come now to the *Corpuscular* philosophy, men do so easily understand one another's meaning, when they talk of *local motion, rest, bigness, shape, order, situation,* and *contexture* of material substances, and these principles do afford such clear accounts of those things that are rightly deduced from them only, that even those Peripatetics or chemists that maintain other principles acquiesce in the explications made by these, when they can be had, and seek not any further – though perhaps the effect be so admirable as would make it pass for that of a hidden form or occult quality. Those very Aristotelians that believe the celestial bodies to be moved by intelligences have no recourse to any peculiar agency of theirs to account for *eclipses*. And we laugh at those East Indians that to this day go out in multitudes with some instruments that may relieve the distressed luminary, whose loss of light they fancy to proceed from some fainting fit out of which it must be roused. For no intelligent man, whether chemist or Peripatetic, flies to his peculiar principles, after he is informed that the moon is eclipsed by the interposition of the earth betwixt her and it, and the sun by that of the moon betwixt him and the earth. And when we see the image of a man cast into the air by a concave spherical looking-glass, though most men are amazed at it, and some suspect it to be no less than an effect of witchcraft, yet he that is skilled enough in *catoptrics* will, without consulting Aristotle or Paracelsus, or flying to hypostatical principles and substantial forms, be satisfied that the phenomenon is produced by the beams of light reflected, and thereby made convergent, according to optical and consequently mathematical laws.

But I must not now repeat what I elsewhere say, to show that the Corpuscular principles have been declined by philosophers of different sects, not because they think not our explications clear – if not much more so than their own – but because they imagine that the applications of them can be made but to few things, and consequently are insufficient.

II. In the next place, I observe that there cannot be *fewer* principles than the two grand ones of Mechanical philosophy – *matter* and *motion*. For matter alone, unless it be moved, is altogether unactive; and whilst all the parts of a body continue in one state without any motion at all, that body will not exercise any action nor suffer any alteration itself, though it may perhaps modify the action of other bodies that move against it.

III. Nor can we conceive any principles more *primary* than matter and motion. For either both of them were immediately created by God, or (to add that for their sakes that would have matter to be unproduced), if *matter* be eternal, *motion* must either be produced by some immaterial supernatural agent, or it must immediately flow by way of emanation from the nature of the matter it appertains to.

IV. Neither can there be any physical principles more *simple* than matter and motion, neither of them being resoluble into any things whereof it may be truly, or so much as tolerably, said to be compounded.

V. The next thing I shall name to recommend the Corpuscular principles[3] is their great *comprehensiveness*.°+

I consider, then, that the genuine and necessary effect of the sufficiently strong motion of one part of matter against another is either to drive it on in its entire bulk, or else to break or divide it into particles of determinate *motion, figure, size, posture, rest, order* or *texture*. The two first of these, for instance, are each of them capable of numerous varieties. For the *figure* of a portion of matter may either be one of the five regular figures treated of by geometricians, or some determinate species of solid figures, as that of a *cone, cylinder*, &c., or irregular, though not perhaps anonymous, as the grains of sand, hoops, feathers, branches, forks, files, &c. And as the *figure*, so the *motion* of one of these particles may be exceedingly diversified, not only by the determination to this or that part of the world, but by several other things – as particularly by the almost infinitely varying degrees of celerity, by the manner of its progression with or without rotation and other modifying circumstances, and more yet by the line wherein it moves, as (besides straight) circular, elliptical, parabolical, hyperbolical, spiral, and I know not how many others. For, as later geometricians have shown that those crooked lines may be compounded of several motions (that is, traced by a body whose motion is mixed of, and results from, two or more simpler motions), so how many more curves may, or rather may not, be made by new compositions and decompositions of motion is no easy task to determine.

Now, since a *single* particle of matter, by virtue of two only of the mechanical affections that belong to it, be diversifiable so many ways, how vast a number of variations may we suppose capable of being produced by the compositions and decompositions of *myriads* of single invisible corpuscles that may be contained and contexed in one small body, and each of them be imbued with more than two or three of the fertile catholic principles above mentioned? Especially since the aggregate of those corpuscles may be farther diversified by the *texture* resulting from their convention into a body, which, as so made up, has its own bigness and shape and pores (perhaps very many and various), and has also many capacities of acting and suffering upon the score of the place it holds among other bodies in a world constituted as ours is: so that, when I consider the almost innumerable diversifications that compositions and decompositions may make of a small number, not perhaps exceeding twenty, of distinct things, I am apt to look upon those who think the Mechanical principles may serve indeed to give an account of the phenomena of this or that particular part of natural philosophy, as *statics, hydrostatics*, the *theory of the planetary motions*, &c., but can never be applied to all the phenomena of things corporeal – I am apt, I say, to look upon those, otherwise learned, men as I would do upon him that should affirm that, by putting together the letters of the *alphabet*, one may indeed make up all the words to be found in one book, as in Euclid or Virgil, or in one language, as Latin or English, but that they can by no means suffice to supply words to all the books of a great library, much less to all the languages in the world.

And whereas there is another sort of philosophers that, observing the great efficacy of the bigness and shape and situation and motion and connexion in engines, are willing to allow that those Mechanical principles may have a great stroke in the operations of bodies of a sensible bulk and manifest mechanism, and therefore may be usefully employed in accounting for the effects and phenomena of such bodies, they[4] yet will not admit that these principles can be applied to the hidden transactions that pass among the minute particles of bodies, and therefore think it necessary to refer these to what they call *nature, substantial forms, real qualities*, and the like unmechanical principles and agents.

But this is not necessary. For both the mechanical affections of matter are to be found, and the laws of motion take place, not only in the great masses and the middle-sized lumps, but in the smallest fragments of matter; and a lesser portion of it, being as well a body as a greater, must, as necessarily as it, have its determinate bulk and figure. And he that looks upon sand in a good microscope will easily perceive that each minute grain of it has as well its own size and shape as a rock or mountain. And when we let fall a great stone and a pebble from the top of a high building, we find not but that the latter as well as the former moves conformably to the laws of acceleration in heavy bodies descending. And the rules of motion are observed not only in cannon bullets, but in small shot; and the one strikes down a bird according to the same laws that the other batters down a wall. And though *nature* (or rather its divine Author) be wont to work with much finer materials, and employ more curious contrivances, than *art* (whence the structure even of the rarest watch is incomparably inferior to that of a human body), yet an artist himself, according to the quantity of the matter he employs, the exigency of the design he undertakes, and the bigness and shape of the instruments he makes use of, is able to make pieces of work of the same nature or kind of extremely differing bulk, where yet the like, though not equal, art and contrivance, and oftentimes motion too, may be observed – as a smith, who, with a hammer and other large instruments, can out of masses of iron forge great bars or wedges, and make those strong and heavy chains that were employed to load malefactors and even to secure streets and gates, may with lesser instruments make smaller nails and filings almost as minute as dust, and may yet, with finer tools, make links of a strange slenderness and lightness, insomuch that good authors tell us of a chain of divers links that was fastened to a flea and could be moved by it; and, if I misremember not, I saw something like this, besides other instances, that I beheld with pleasure, of the littleness that art can give to such pieces of work as are usually made of a considerable bigness. And therefore to say that, though in natural bodies whose bulk is manifest and their structure visible the Mechanical principles may be usefully admitted, they[5] are not to be extended to such portions of matter whose parts and texture are invisible, may perhaps look to some as if a man should allow that the laws of mechanism may take place in a town clock, but cannot in a pocket-watch, or (to give you an instance mixed of natural and artificial) as if, because the terraqueous globe is a vast magnetical body of seven or eight thousand miles in diameter, one should affirm that magnetical laws are not to be expected to be of force in a spherical piece of loadstone that is not perhaps an inch long; and yet experience shows us that, notwithstanding the inestimable disproportion betwixt these two globes, the *terrella*, as well as the *earth*, hath its poles, equator, and meridians, and in divers other magnetical properties emulates the terrestrial globe.

They that, to solve the phenomena of nature, have recourse to agents which, though they involve no self-repugnancy in their very notions, as many of the judicious think *substantial forms* and *real qualities* to do, yet are such that we conceive not how they operate to bring effects to pass – these, I say, when they tell us of such indeterminate agents as the *soul of the world*, the *universal spirit*, the *plastic power*, and the like, though they may in certain cases tell us some things, yet they tell us nothing that will satisfy the curiosity of an inquisitive person, who seeks not so much to know what is the *general* agent that produces a phenomenon, as *by what means*, and *after what manner*, the phenomenon is produced. The famous Sennertus and some other learned physicians tell us of diseases which proceed from incantation: but sure it is but a very slight account that a sober physician, that comes to visit a patient reported to be bewitched, receives of the strange symptoms he meets with and would have an account of, if he be coldly answered that it is a witch or the devil that produces them; and he will never sit down with so short an account if he can by any means reduce those extravagant symptoms to any more known and stated diseases, as *epilepsies, convulsions, hysterical fits*, &c., and, if he cannot, he will confess his knowledge of this distemper to come far short of what might be expected and attained in other diseases, wherein he thinks himself bound to search into the nature of the morbific matter, and will not be satisfied till he can, probably at least, deduce from that, and the structure of a human body, and other concurring physical causes, the phenomena of the malady. And it would be but little satisfaction to one that desires to understand the causes of what occurs to observation in a watch, and how it comes to point at and strike the hours, to be told that it was such a watchmaker that so contrived it; or to him that would know the true cause of an *echo* to be answered that it is a man, a vault, or a wood, that makes it.

And now at length I come to consider that which I observe the most to alienate other sects from the Mechanical philosophy, namely, that they think it pretends to have principles so universal, and so mathematical, that no other physical hypothesis can comport with it, or be tolerated by it.

But this I look upon as an easy, indeed, but an important mistake, because by this very thing, that the Mechanical principles are so universal and therefore applicable to so many things, they are rather fitted to *include*, than necessitated to *exclude*, any other hypothesis that is founded in nature, as far as it is so. And such hypotheses, if prudently considered by a skilful and moderate person who is rather disposed to unite sects than multiply them, will be found, as far as they have truth in them, to be either legitimately (though perhaps not immediately) deducible from the Mechanical principles, or fairly reconcilable to them. For such hypotheses will probably attempt to account for the phenomena of nature either by the help of a determinate number of material ingredients, such as the *tria prima* of the chemists, by participation whereof other bodies obtain their qualities, or else by introducing some general agents, as the Platonic *soul of the world* or the *universal spirit* asserted by some spagyrists, or by both these ways together.

Now to dispatch *first* those that I named in the second place, I consider that the chief thing that inquisitive naturalists should look after in the explicating of difficult phenomena is not so much what the *agent* is or does, as what changes are made in the *patient* to bring it to exhibit the phenomena that are proposed, and by what means, and after what manner, those changes are effected: so that, the *Mechanical* philosopher being satisfied that one part of matter can act upon another but by virtue of local motion or the effects and consequences of local motion, he considers that as, if the proposed agent be not intelligible and physical, it can never physically *explain* the phenomena, so, if it be intelligible and physical, it will be reducible to *matter* and some or other of those only catholic affections of matter already often mentioned. And the indefinite divisibility of matter, the wonderful efficacy of motion, and the almost infinite variety of coalitions and structures that may be made of minute and insensible corpuscles, being duly weighed, I see not why a philosopher should think it impossible to make out, by their help, the mechanical possibility of any corporeal agent, how subtle or diffused or active soever it be, that can be solidly proved to be really existent in nature, by what name soever it be called or disguised.

And though the *Cartesians* be Mechanical philosophers, yet according to them their *materia subtilis*, which the very name declares to be a corporeal substance, is, for aught I know, little (if it be at all) less diffused through the universe, or less active in it, than the universal spirit of some spagyrists, not to say the *anima mundi* of the Platonists. But this upon the bye; after which I proceed, and shall venture to add that, whatever be the physical agent, whether it be inanimate or living, purely corporeal or united to an intellectual substance, the above-mentioned changes, that are wrought in the body that is made to exhibit the phenomena, may be effected by the same or the like means, or after the same or the like manner – as, for instance, if corn be reduced to meal, the materials and shape of the millstones, and their peculiar motion and adaptation, will be much of the same kind; and (though they should not, yet) to be sure the grains of corn will suffer a various contrition and comminution in their passage to the form of meal, whether the corn be ground by a water-mill or a windmill, or a horse-mill, or a hand-mill: that is, by a mill whose stones are turned by inanimate, by brute, or by rational, agents. And if an angel himself should work a real change in the nature of a body, it is scarce conceivable to us men how he could do it without the assistance of local motion, since, if nothing were displaced or otherwise moved than before (the like happening also to all external bodies to which it related), it is hardly conceivable how it should be in itself other than just what it was before.

But to come now to the other sort of hypotheses formerly mentioned, if the *chemists* or others that would deduce a complete natural philosophy from *salt*, *sulphur*, and *mercury*, or any other set number of ingredients of things, would well consider what they undertake, they might easily discover that the material parts of bodies, as such, can reach but to a small part of the phenomena of nature, whilst these ingredients are considered but as quiescent things, and therefore they would find themselves necessitated to suppose them to be active; and that things purely corporeal cannot be, but by means of local motion, and the effects that may result from that, accompanying variously shaped, sized, and aggregated parts of matter: so that the chemists and other materialists (if I may so call them) must (as indeed they are wont to do) leave the greatest part of the phenomena of the universe unexplicated by the help of the ingredients (be they fewer or more than three) of bodies, without taking in the mechanical and more comprehensive affections of matter, especially local motion. I willingly grant that salt, sulphur, and mercury, or some substances analogous to them, are to be obtained by the action of the fire from a very great many dissipable bodies here below; nor would I deny that, in explicating divers of the phenomena of such bodies, it may be of use to a skilful naturalist to know and consider that this or that ingredient, as sulphur for instance, does abound in the body proposed: whence it may be probably argued that the qualities that usually accompany that principle, when predominant, may be also upon its score found in the body that so plentifully partakes of it. But not to mention, what I have elsewhere shown, that there are many phenomena to whose explication this knowledge will contribute very little or nothing at all, I shall only here observe that, though chemical explications be sometimes the most obvious and ready, yet they are not the most fundamental and satisfactory: for the chemical ingredient itself, whether sulphur or any other, must owe its nature and other qualities to the union of insensible particles in a convenient size, shape, motion or rest, and contexture, all which are but mechanical affections of convening corpuscles. And this may be illustrated by what happens in artificial fireworks. For though, in most of those many differing sorts that are made, either for the use of war or for recreation, gunpowder be a main ingredient, and divers of the phenomena may be derived from the greater or lesser measure wherein the compositions partake of it, yet, besides that there may be fireworks made without gunpowder (as appears by those made of old by the Greeks and Romans), gunpowder itself owes its aptness to be fired and exploded to the mechanical contexture of more simple portions of matter – *nitre, charcoal,* and *sulphur* – and sulphur itself, though it be by many chemists mistaken for a hypostatical principle, owes its inflammability to the convention of yet more simple and primary corpuscles: since chemists confess that it has an inflammable ingredient, and experience shows that it very much abounds with an acid and uninflammable salt and is not quite devoid of terrestreity. I know it may be here alleged that the productions of chemical analyses are simple bodies and, upon that account, irresoluble. But that divers substances, which chemists are pleased to call the *salts* or *sulphurs* or *mercuries* of the bodies that afforded them, are not simple and homogeneous, has elsewhere been sufficiently proved. Nor is their not being easily dissipable or resoluble a clear proof of their not being made up of more primitive portions of matter; for compounded and even decompounded bodies may be as difficultly resoluble as most of those that chemists obtain by what they call their *analysis* by the fire: witness common green glass, which is far more durable and irresoluble than many of those that pass for hypostatical substances. And we see that some *amels* will be several times even vitrified in the fire, without losing their nature or oftentimes so much as their colour; and yet amel is manifestly not only a compounded but a decompounded body, consisting of salt, and powder of pebbles or sand, and calcined tin, and, if the amel be not white, usually of some tinging metal or mineral. But how indestructible soever the chemical principles be supposed, divers of the operations ascribed to them will never be well made out without the help of local motion (and that diversified too), without which we can little better give an account of the phenomena of many bodies by knowing what ingredients compose them, than we can explain the operations of a watch by knowing of how many and of what metals the balance, the wheels, the chain, and other parts, are made; or than we can derive the operations of a windmill from the bare knowledge that it is made up of wood and stone and canvas and iron.+

And here let me add that it would not at all overthrow the Corpuscularian hypothesis though, either by more exquisite purifications or by some other operations than the usual analysis of the fire, it should be made appear that the material principles or elements of mixed bodies should not be the *tria prima* of the vulgar chemists, but either substances of another nature, or else fewer or more in number – as would be if that were true, which some spagyrists affirm (but I could never find), that from all sorts of mixed bodies, five, and but five, differing similar substances can be separated; or as if it were true that the Helmontians had such a resolving menstruum as the *alkahest* of their master, by which he affirms that he could reduce stones into salt of the same weight with the mineral, and bring both that salt and all other kind of mixed and tangible bodies into insipid water. For whatever be the number or qualities of the chemical principles, if they be really existent in nature, it may very possibly be shown that they may be made up of insensible corpuscles of determinate bulks and shapes; and by the various coalitions and contextures of such corpuscles, *not only* three or five *but* many more material ingredients may be composed or made to result. But though the alkahestical reductions newly mentioned should be admitted, yet the Mechanical principles might well be accommodated even to them. For the solidity, taste, &c., of salt may be fairly accounted for by the stiffness, sharpness, and other mechanical affections, of the minute particles whereof salts consist; and if, by a farther action of the alkahest, the salt or any other solid body be reduced into insipid water, this also may be explicated by the same principles, supposing a further comminution of the parts, and such an attrition as wears off the edges and points that enabled them to strike briskly the organ of taste: for as to fluidity and firmness, those mainly depend upon two of our grand principles, *motion* and *rest*. And I have elsewhere shown by several proofs that the agitation or rest, and the looser contact or closer cohesion, of the particles is able to make the same portion of matter at one time a firm and at another time a fluid body: so that, though the further sagacity and industry of chemists (which I would by no means discourage) should be able to obtain from mixed bodies homogeneous substances differing, in number or nature or both, from their vulgar salt, sulphur, and mercury, yet the Corpuscular philosophy is so *general* and *fertile* as to be fairly reconcilable to such a discovery, and also so *useful* that these new material principles will, as well as the old *tria prima*, stand in need of the more catholic principles of the Corpuscularians, especially local motion. And indeed, whatever elements or ingredients men have (that I know of) pitched upon, yet, if they take not in the mechanical affections of matter, their principles have been so deficient that I have usually observed that the materialists, without at all excepting the chemists, do not only, as I was saying, leave many things unexplained, to which their narrow principles will not extend; but, even in the particulars they presume to give an account of, they either content themselves to assign such common and indefinite causes as are too general to signify much towards an inquisitive man's satisfaction, or, if they venture to give particular causes, they assign precarious or false ones, and liable to be easily disproved by circumstances or instances whereto their doctrine will not agree, as I have often elsewhere had occasion to show. And yet the chemists need not be frighted from acknowledging the prerogative of the Mechanical philosophy, since that may be reconcilable with the truth of their own principles, as far as these agree with the phenomena they are applied to. For these more confined hypotheses may be subordinated to those more general and fertile principles, and there can be no ingredient assigned that has a real existence in nature, that may not be derived, either immediately or by a row of decompositions, from the universal matter, modified by its mechanical affections. For if, with the same bricks, diversly put together and ranged, several walls, houses, furnaces, and other structures, as vaults, bridges, pyramids, &c., may be built, merely by a various contrivement of parts of the same kind, how much more may great variety of ingredients be produced by – or, according to the institution of nature, result from – the various coalitions and contextures of corpuscles, that need not be supposed, like bricks, all of the same or near the same size and shape, but may have amongst them, both of the one and the other, as great a variety as need be wished for, and indeed a greater than can easily be so much as imagined? And the primary and minute concretions that belong to these ingredients may, without opposition from the Mechanical philosophy, be supposed to have their particles so minute and strongly coherent, that nature of herself does scarce ever tear them asunder: as we see that *mercury* and *gold* may be successively made to put on a multitude of disguises, and yet so retain their nature as to be reducible to their pristine forms. And you know I lately told you that common glass and good amels, though both of them but factitious bodies, and not only mixed but decompounded concretions, have yet their component parts so strictly united, by the skill of illiterate tradesmen, as to maintain their union in the vitrifying violence of the fire. Nor do we find that common glass will be wrought upon by *aqua fortis* or *aqua regis*, though the former of them will dissolve *mercury*, and the latter *gold*.

From the foregoing discourse it may (probably at least) result that if, besides rational souls, there are any immaterial substances (such as the heavenly intelligences and the substantial forms of the Aristotelians) that regularly are to be numbered among natural agents, their way of working being unknown to us, they can but help to constitute and effect things, but will very little help us to conceive *how* things are effected: so that, by whatever principles natural things be *constituted*, it is by the Mechanical principles that their phenomena must be clearly *explicated*. As, for instance, though we should grant the Aristotelians that the planets are made of a quintessential matter, and moved by angels or immaterial intelligences, yet to explain the stations, progressions and retrogradations, and other phenomena, of the planets, we must have recourse either to eccentrics, epicycles, &c., or to motions made in elliptical or other peculiar lines; and, in a word, to theories wherein the motion and figure, situation, and other mathematical or mechanical affections, of bodies are mainly employed. But if the principles proposed be corporeal things, they will be then fairly reducible or reconcilable to the Mechanical principles, these being so general and pregnant that among things corporeal there is nothing *real* (and I meddle not with *chimerical* beings, such as some of Paracelsus's) that may not be derived from, or be brought to a subordination to, such comprehensive principles. And when the chemists shall show that mixed bodies owe their qualities to the predominancy of this or that of their three grand ingredients, the *Corpuscularians* will show that the very qualities of this or that ingredient flow from its peculiar texture and the mechanical affections of the corpuscles it is made up of. And to affirm that, because the furnaces of chemists afford a great number of uncommon productions and phenomena, there are bodies or operations amongst things purely corporeal that cannot be derived from, or reconciled to, the comprehensive and pregnant principles of the Mechanical philosophy, is as if, because there are a great number and variety of anthems, hymns, pavans, threnodies, courantes, gavottes, branles, sarabands, jigs, and other (grave and sprightly) tunes, to be met with in the books and practices of musicians, one should maintain that there are in them a great many tunes, or at least notes, that have no dependence on the scale of music; or as if, because, besides rhombuses, rhomboids, trapeziums, squares, pentagons, chiliagons, myriagons, and innumerable other polygons, regular and irregular, one should presume to affirm that there are among them some rectilinear figures that are not reducible to triangles, or have affections that will overthrow what Euclid has taught of *triangles* and *polygons*.

To what has been said I shall add but one thing more: that as, according to what I formerly intimated, Mechanical principles and explications are for their clearness preferred, even by materialists themselves, to others, in the cases where they can be had, so – the sagacity and industry of modern naturalists and mathematicians having happily applied them to several of those difficult phenomena (in *hydrostatics*, the practical part of *optics*, *gunnery*, &c.) that before were or might be referred to occult qualities – it is probable that, when this philosophy is deeplier searched into and farther improved, it will be found applicable to the solution of more and more of the phenomena of nature. And on this occasion let me observe that it is not always necessary, though it be always desirable, that he that propounds a hypothesis in astronomy, chemistry, anatomy, or other part of physics, be able *a priori* to prove his hypothesis to be true, or demonstratively to show that the other hypotheses proposed about the same subject must be false. For as, if I mistake not, Plato said that the world was God's epistle written to mankind – and might have added, consonantly to another saying of his,[a] it was written in mathematical letters – so, in the physical explications of the parts and system of the world, methinks there is somewhat like what happens when men conjecturally frame several keys to enable us to understand a letter written in ciphers. For though one man by his sagacity have found out the right key, it will be very difficult for him either to prove, otherwise than by trial, that this or that word is not such as it is guessed to be by others according to their keys, or to evince *a priori* that theirs are to be rejected and his to be preferred; yet if, due trial being made, the key he proposes shall be found so agreeable to the characters of the letter as to enable one to understand them and make a coherent sense of them, its suitableness to what it should decipher is, without either confutations or extraneous positive proofs, sufficient to make it be accepted as the right key of that cipher. And so in physical hypotheses there are some that, without noise or falling foul upon others, peaceably obtain discerning men's approbation only by their fitness to solve the phenomena for which they were devised, without crossing any known observation or law of nature. And therefore, if the Mechanical philosophy go on to explicate things corporeal at the rate it has of late years proceeded at, it is scarce to be doubted but that, in time, unprejudiced persons will think it sufficiently recommended by its consistency with itself, and its applicableness to so many phenomena of nature.

A Recapitulation

Perceiving, upon a review of the foregoing paper, that the difficulty and importance of the subject has seduced me to spend many more words about it than I at first designed, it will not now be amiss to

---

[a] 'ὁ Θεὸς ἀεὶ γεωμετρεῖ.'

give you this short summary of what came into my mind, to recommend to you the *Mechanical philosophy* and obviate your fears of seeing it supplanted; having first premised, once for all, that presupposing the Creation and general providence of God, I pretend to treat but of things *corporeal*, and do abstract in this paper from *immaterial beings* (which otherwise I very willingly admit) and all agents and operations miraculous or supernatural.

I. Of the principles of things corporeal, none can be more *few*, without being insufficient, or more *primary*, than *matter* and *motion*.

II. The natural and genuine effect of variously determined *motion* in portions of *matter* is to divide it into parts of differing sizes and shapes, and to put them into different motions; and the consequences that flow from these, in a world framed as ours is, are, as to the separate fragments, posture, order, and situation; and, as to the conventions of many of them, peculiar compositions and contextures.

III. The parts of matter endowed with these catholic affections are by various associations reduced to natural bodies of several kinds, according to the plenty of the matter, and the various compositions and decompositions of the principles, which all suppose the common matter they diversify; and these several kinds of bodies, by virtue of their motion, rest, and other mechanical affections, which fit them to act on and suffer from one another, become endowed with several kinds of qualities (whereof some are called *manifest*° and some *occult*°), and those that act upon the peculiarly framed organs of sense, whose perceptions by the animadversive faculty of the soul are sensations.

IV. These principles – *matter*, *motion* (to which *rest* is related), *bigness*, *shape*, *posture*, *order*, *texture* – being so *simple*,° *clear*° and *comprehensive*, are applicable to all the real phenomena of nature, which seem not explicable by any other not consistent with ours. For if recourse be had to an immaterial principle or agent, it may be such a one as is not intelligible; and however it will not enable us to *explain* the phenomena, because its *way* of working upon things material would probably be more difficult to be physically made out than a Mechanical account of the phenomena. And notwithstanding the immateriality of a *created* agent, we cannot conceive how it should produce changes in a body without the help of Mechanical principles, especially *local motion*; and accordingly, we find not that the reasonable soul in man is able to produce what changes it pleases in the body, but is confined to such as it may produce by determining or guiding the motions of the spirits, and other parts of the body subservient to voluntary motion.

V. And if the agents or active principles resorted to be not immaterial, but of a corporeal nature, they must *either* in effect be the same with the corporeal principles above-named; *or*, because of the great universality and simplicity of ours, the new ones proposed must be less general than *they*, and consequently capable of being subordinated or reduced to *ours*, which by various compositions may afford matter to several hypotheses, and by several coalitions afford minute concretions exceedingly numerous and durable, and consequently fit to become the elementary ingredients of more compounded bodies, being in most trials similar and, as it were, the radical parts, which may after several manners be diversified: as, in Latin, the themes are by prepositions, terminations, &c., and in Hebrew, the roots by the heemantic letters. So that the fear that so much of a *new* physical hypothesis as is *true* will overthrow, or make useless, the Mechanical principles, is as if one should fear that there will be a language proposed that is discordant from, or not reducible to, the letters of the alphabet.

AN ESSAY[1]
CONTAINING A REQUISITE DIGRESSION,
CONCERNING THOSE THAT WOULD
EXCLUDE THE DEITY FROM
INTERMEDDLING WITH MATTER

I ignore not that not only Leucippus, Epicurus, and other *atomists* of old, but of late some persons for the most part adorers of *Aristotle's* writings, have pretended to be able to explicate the first *beginning of things*, and the world's *phenomena*, without taking in or acknowledging any divine Author of it. And therefore, though we may elsewhere, by the assistance of that Author, have an opportunity to give you an account of our unsatisfiedness with the attempts made by some bold wits in favour of such pretensions, yet, since the main truth we plead for in this discourse is so nearly concerned in what hath been taught by those that would keep God from being thought to have any share in the production of the universe, I can scarce forbear (as unwilling as I am to digress) to represent to you on the present occasion a few considerations, which may assist you, if not to lessen the arrogance of such persons, at least to keep yourself from thinking their evidence as great as their confidence is wont to be. Now of the philosophers we speak of, some being atomists, and others not, it will be requisite to say something to each of the two sorts; and because we not long since, in an illustrious company where you, Pyrophilus, are not unknown, met with one of them who avowedly grounded his opinions on the Aristotelian or vulgar physiology, we shall first recommend to you two or three considerations concerning such arrogant Peripatetics (for I speak not of that sect in general, of which I know there are divers excellent men).

First, then, you will in many passages of the following essays find that divers things that have been very magisterially taught and confidently believed among the followers of Aristotle are errors or mistakes, and that, as several even of the obvious phenomena of nature do contradict the common Peripatetic doctrine, so divers at least of those that are more abstruse are not explicable by it; and as confidently as these his followers talk of the expounding the very riddles of nature, yet I remember that he himself somewhere (for I cannot call to mind the place) did not scruple to confess that *as the eyes of owls are to the splendour of the day, so are those of our minds even to things obvious and manifest.*

I shall next take notice that philosophers who scorn to ascribe anything to God do often deceive themselves in thinking they have sufficiently satisfied our enquiries, when they have given us the nearest and most immediate causes of some things; whereas oftentimes the assignment of those causes is but the manifesting that such and such effects may be deduced from the more catholic affections of things, though these be not unfrequently as abstruse as the phenomena explicated by them, as having only their effects more obvious, not their nature better understood: as when, for instance, an account is demanded of that strange supposed sympathy betwixt quicksilver and gold, in that we find that, whereas all other bodies swim upon quicksilver, it will readily swallow up gold and hide it in its bosom. This pretended sympathy the naturalist may explicate by saying that, gold being the only body heavier than quicksilver of the same bulk, the known laws of the *hydrostatics* make it necessary that gold should sink in it and all lighter bodies swim on it; but though the cause of this effect be thus plausibly assigned, by deducing it from so known and obvious an affection of bodies as gravity, which every man is apt to think he sufficiently understands, yet will not this put a satisfactory period to a severe enquirer's curiosity, who will perchance be apt to allege that, though the effects of gravity indeed be very obvious, yet the cause and nature of it are as obscure as those of almost any phenomenon it can be brought to explicate, and that therefore he that desires no further account desists too soon from his enquiries, and acquiesces long before he comes to his journey's end.[a] And indeed, the investigation of the true nature and adequate cause of gravity is a task of that difficulty that, in spite of aught I have hitherto seen or read, I must yet retain great doubts whether they have been clearly and solidly made out by any man. And sure, Pyrophilus, there are divers effects in nature, of which, though the immediate cause may be plausibly assigned, yet if we further enquire into the causes of those causes, and desist not from ascending in the scale of causes till we are arrived at the top of it, we shall perhaps find the more catholic and primary causes of things to

---

[a] 'Physiologo qui veritatem contemplatur ultimarum causarum cognitio non finis est, sed initium ad primas supremasque causas proficiscendi.' – Plutarch, *De Primo Frigido*, cap. 8. 'τὸ πρῶτον αἴτιον ἐν τῇ εὑρήσει ἔσχατον.' – Aristotle, *Ethica Nicomachea*, lib. III, cap. 3.

be either certain primitive, general, and fixed laws of nature (or rules of action and passion among the parcels of the universal matter); or else the shape, size, motion, and other primary affections of the smallest parts of matter, and of their first coalitions or clusters, especially those endowed with seminal faculties or properties; or (to dispatch) the admirable conspiring of the several parts of the universe to the production of particular effects – of all which it will be difficult to give a satisfactory account without acknowledging an intelligent Author or Disposer of things.

And the better to clear so weighty a truth, let us further consider on this occasion that not only Aristotle and those that, misled by his authority, maintain the eternity of the world, but very many other philosophers and physicians, who ascribe so much to nature that they will not be reduced to acknowledge an Author of it, are wont very much to delude both themselves and others in the account they presume to give us, as satisfactory, of the causes or reasons of very many effects. I will not instance in the magnetic properties of things, nor any of those numerous abstrusities of nature which it is well known that the Aristotelians are wont to refer to 'sympathy', 'antipathy', or 'occult qualities', and strive to put men off with empty names, whereby they do not so much lessen our ignorance as betray their own. But I shall instance in those more obvious phenomena of which they suppose they have given us very satisfactory accounts. If you ask one of those I speak of whence it comes to pass that, if a man put one end of a long reed into a vessel full of water and suck at the other end, his mouth will be immediately filled with that liquor, he will readily tell you that, the suction drawing the air out of the cavity of the reed, the water must necessarily succeed in the place deserted by the air, to prevent a vacuity abhorred by nature. If you likewise ask such a man why, to women about a certain age, their *purgationes menstruae* do commonly supervene, he will think he has sufficiently answered you when he has told you that about that age, beginning to be ripe for procreation, nature has wisely provided that their superfluous blood should be sent to the uterine vessels, partly to disburden the mass of blood of a useless load, and partly to contribute matter, or at least afford nourishment, in case of conception. But though these solutions are wont to be acquiesced in by such as those that give them, yet I see not how they can satisfy a rigid reasoner. For – not now to mention what may be objected against them out of some modern mechanical and anatomical observations – let us a little consider that to say that the ascent of the water in the first problem proceeds from nature's detestation of a vacuity supposes that there is a kind of *anima mundi*, furnished with various passions, which watchfully provides for the safety of the universe; or that a brute and inanimate creature, as water, not only has a power to move its heavy body upwards, contrary (to speak in their language) to the tendency of its particular nature, but knows both that air has been sucked out of the reed and that, unless it succeed the attracted air, there will follow a vacuum, and that this water is withal so generous as, by ascending, to act contrary to its particular inclination for the general good of the universe, like a noble patriot that sacrifices his private interests to the public ones of his country.

But to show men by an easy experiment how little attraction is performed to avoid a vacuum, I have sometimes done thus: I have taken a slender pipe of glass, of about four foot long, and, putting one of the open ends of it into a vessel full of quicksilver, I have sucked as strongly as I could at the other, and caused one to watch the ascent of the quicksilver and mark where it was at the highest, and I found not that at one suck I could raise it up much above a foot; and having caused a couple of strong men, one after another, to suck at the same end of the same pipe, I found not that either of them could draw it up much higher. Nor did it appear that by repeated suctions, though the upper end of the pipe were each time stopped to hinder the relapse of the quicksilver, it could at all be raised above the seven and twenty digits at which it used to subsist in the Torricellian experiment *de vacuo*; whereas the same end of that tube being put into a small vessel of water, I could at one suck make the water swiftly ascend through the perpendicularly held tube into my mouth: which argues that the ascension of liquors upon suction rather depends upon the pressure of the air against the sucker's chest,[3] and their respective measures of gravity and lightness compared to that pressure, than it proceeds from such an abhorrency of a vacuum as is presumed.

And so likewise, in the other question proposed, it is implied that there is in a female body something that knows the rule of physicians that of a *plethora* the cure is the convenient evacuation of blood; and that this intelligent faculty is wise enough also to propose to itself the double end, above mentioned, in this evacuation, and therefore will not provide a quantity of blood great enough to require an excretion, nor begin it till the female be come to an age wherein it is possible for both the ends to be obtained; and that also this presiding nature is so charitable as, that mankind might not fail, it will make the female subject to such monthly superfluities of blood, from which experience informs us that a whole set of diseases peculiar to that sex does frequently proceed. And in a word, there is a multitude of problems, especially such as belong to the use of the parts of a human body, and to the causes and cures of the diseases incident thereunto, in whose explication those we write of content themselves to tell us that nature does such and such a thing because it was fit for her so to do; but they endeavour not to make intelligible to us what they mean by this *nature*,° and how mere and consequently brute bodies can act according to laws, and for determinate ends, without any knowledge either of the one or of the other. Let them, therefore, till they have made out their hypothesis more intelligibly, either cease to ascribe to irrational creatures such actions as in men are apparently the productions of reason and choice, and sometimes even of industry and virtue; or else let them with us acknowledge that such actions, of creatures in themselves irrational, are performed under the superintendence and guidance of a wise and intelligent Author of things.+

But that you may not mistake me, Pyrophilus, it will be requisite for me to acquaint you in two or three words with some of my present thoughts concerning this subject. That there are some actions so peculiar to man, upon the account of his intellect and will, that they cannot be satisfactorily explicated after the manner of the actings of mere corporeal agents, I am very much inclined to believe; and whether or no there may be some actions of some other animals, which cannot well be mechanically explicated, I have not here leisure or opportunity to examine. But for (most of) the other phenomena of nature, methinks we may without absurdity conceive that God, of whom in the scripture it is affirmed *that all his works are known to him from the beginning*,[b] having resolved before the Creation to make such a world as this of ours, did divide (at least if he did not create it incoherent) that matter which he had provided into an innumerable multitude of very variously figured corpuscles, and both connected those particles into such textures or particular bodies, and placed them in such situations, and put them into such

[b] *Acts* xv. 18.

motions, that, by the assistance of his ordinary preserving concourse, the phenomena which he intended should appear in the universe must as orderly follow, and be exhibited by the bodies necessarily acting according to those impressions or laws, though they understand them not at all: as if each of those creatures had a design of self-preservation, and were furnished with knowledge and industry to prosecute it, and as if there were diffused through the universe an intelligent being, watchful over the public good of it, and careful to administer all things wisely for the good of the particular parts of it, but so far forth as is consistent with the good of the whole and the preservation of the primitive and catholic laws established by the supreme cause. As, in the formerly-mentioned clock of Strasbourg, the several pieces making up that curious engine are so framed and adapted, and are put into such a motion, that though the numerous wheels and other parts of it move several ways, and that without anything either of knowledge or design, yet each performs its part in order to the various ends for which it was contrived, as regularly and uniformly as if it knew and were concerned to do its duty; and the various motions of the wheels and other parts concur to exhibit the phenomena designed by the artificer in the engine, as exactly as if they were animated by a common principle which makes them knowingly conspire to do so, and might to a rude Indian seem to be more intelligent than Cunradus Dasypodius himself, that published a description of it wherein he tells the world that he contrived it, who could not tell the hours and measure time so accurately as his clock. And according to this notion, if you be pleased to bear it in your memory, Pyrophilus, you may easily apprehend in what sense I use many common phrases, which custom hath so authorized that we can scarce write of physiological subjects without employing either them or frequent and tedious circumlocutions in their stead. Thus when I say that a stone 'endeavours' to descend towards the centre of the earth, or that, being put into a vessel of water, it 'affects' the lowest place, I mean not[4] that such a mathematical point as the centre of the earth hath power to attract all heavy bodies, the least of which, it being a point, it cannot harbour; or that a stone does really aim at that unknown and unattainable centre: but that, as we say that a man 'strives' or 'endeavours' to go to any place, at which he would quickly arrive, if he were not forcibly hindered by somebody that holds him fast where he is and will not let him go, so a stone may be said to 'strive to descend', when, either by the magnetical steams of the earth, or the pressure of some subtle matter incumbent on it, or by whatever else may be the cause of gravity, the stone is so determined to tend downwards that, if all impediments interposed by the neighbouring bodies were removed, it would certainly and directly fall to the ground; or being put into a vessel with water, or any other liquor much less heavy than itself (for on quicksilver, which is heavier, stones will swim), the same gravity will make it subside to the bottom of the vessel and consequently thrust away its bulk of water, which, though heavy in itself, yet because it is less ponderous than the stone, seems to be light. And so in our late instance in the clock, if it be said that the hand that points at the hours 'affects a circular motion', because it constantly moves round the centre of the dial-plate, it is evident that the inanimate piece of metal affects not that motion more than any other, but only that the impression it receives from the wheels, and the adaptation of the rest of the engine, determine it to move after that manner. And although, if a man should with his finger stop that index from proceeding in its course, it may be said in some sense that it 'strives' or 'endeavours' to prosecute its former circular motion, yet that will signify no more than that, by virtue of the contrivance of the engine, the index is so impelled that, if the obstacle put by the finger of him that stops it were taken away, the index would move onwards from that part of the circle where it was stopped towards the mark of the next hour. Nor do I by this, Pyrophilus, deny that it may in a right sense be said, as it is wont to be in the Schools, that *opus naturae est opus intelligentiae*; neither do I reject such common expressions as *Nature always affects and intends that which is best* and *Nature doth nothing in vain*. For since I must, according to the above-mentioned notion, refer many of the actions of irrational creatures to a most wise Disposer of things, it can scarce seem strange to me that, in those particulars in which the Author intended, and[5] it was requisite, that irrational creatures should operate so and so for their own preservation, or the propagation of their species, or the public good of the universe, their actions, being ordered by a reason transcending ours, should not only oftentimes resemble the actings of reason in us, but sometimes even surpass them: as in effect we see that silkworms and spiders can, without being taught, spin much more curiously their balls and webs than our best spinsters could, and that several birds can build and fasten their nests more artificially than many a man, or perhaps

any man, could frame and fasten such little and elaborate buildings.
And the industries of foxes, bees, and divers other beasts, are such
that it is not much to be wondered at that those creatures should
have reason ascribed to them by divers learned men, who yet,
perhaps, would be less confident, if they considered how much may
be said for the immortality of all rational souls; and that the subtle
actings of these beasts are determined to some few particulars
requisite for their own preservation or that of their species, whereas
on all other occasions they seem to betray their want of reason, and
by their voice and gestures seem to express nothing but the natural
passions, and not any rational or logical conceptions. And therefore,
as when (to resume our former comparison) I see in a curious clock
how orderly every wheel and other part performs its own motions,
and with what seeming unanimity they conspire to show the hour
and accomplish the other designs of the artificer, I do not imagine
that any of the wheels, &c., or the engine itself, is endowed with
reason, but commend that of the workman who framed it so
artificially, so, when I contemplate the actions of those several
creatures that make up the world, I do not conclude the inanimate
pieces, at least, that it is made up of, or the vast engine itself, to act
with reason or design, but admire and praise the most wise Author
who, by his admirable contrivance, can so regularly produce effects
to which so great a number of successive and conspiring causes are
required.

And thus much, Pyrophilus, having been represented concerning
those that, rejecting from the production and preservation of things
all but nature, yet embrace the principles of the vulgar philosophy,
you will perhaps think it more than enough, but object that what is
not to be expected from the barren principles of the Schools may yet
be performed by those atomical ones which we ourselves have,
within not very many pages, seemed to acknowledge ingenious. And
I know, indeed, that the modern admirers of Epicurus confidently
enough pretend that he and his expositors have already, without
being beholding to a Deity, clearly made out at least the origin of the
world and of the principal bodies it is made up of. But I confess I am
so far from being convinced of this that I have been confirmed,
rather than unsettled, in my opinion of the difficulty of making out
the original of the world, and of the creatures, especially the living
ones, that compose it, by considering the accounts which are given
us of the nativity (if I may so speak) of the universe and of animals

by those great deniers of Creation and Providence, Epicurus and his paraphrast Lucretius: whose having shown themselves (as I freely confess they have) very subtle philosophers in explicating divers mysteries of nature, ought not so much to recommend to us their impious errors about the original of things, as to let us see the necessity of ascribing it to an intelligent cause. This, then, is the account of this matter which is given us by Epicurus himself, in that Epistle of his to Herodotus which we find in Diogenes Laertius: '*Quod ad meteora attinet, existimari non oportet aut motum aut conversionem aut eclipsin aut ortum occasumve aut alia huiuscemodi ideo fieri, quod sit praefectus aliquis qui sic disponat, disposueritve, ac simul beatitudinem immortalitatemque possideat.*'[c] And having interposed some lines to prove that the providence of God is not consistent with his felicity, he adds: '*Quare opinandum est tum cum mundus procreatus est factos fuisse eos circumplexus convolventium se atomorum, ut nata fuerit haec necessitas qua circuitus tales obierint.*'[d] And elsewhere in the same Epistle: '*Infiniti,*' says he, '*sunt mundi, alii similes isti, alii vero dissimiles. Quippe atomi cum sint infinitae, ut non multo ante demonstratum est per infinitatem spatiorum, et alibi aliae, ac procul ab hoc ad fabrefactionem mundorum infinitorum varie concurrunt.*'[e] And lest this Epicurean explication of the world's original should seem to owe all its unsatisfactoriness to its obscure brevity, we shall not scruple to give you that elegant paraphrase and exposition of it which Lucretius has delivered in his 5th Book *De Rerum Natura*:

> *Sed quibus ille modis coniectus materiai*
> *Fundarit coelum ac terram pontique profunda*
> *Solis lunai cursus ex ordine ponam.*
> *Nam certe neque consiliis*[6] *primordia rerum*
> *Ordine se quaeque atque sagaci mente locarunt,*

---

[c] 'As to the meteors, you ought not to believe that there is either motion, or change, or eclipse, or the rise or setting of them, because of any superior president which doth or hath so disposed of it and himself possesses all the while happiness and immortal life.'

[d] 'Wherefore you must think that, when the world was made, those implications and foldings of atoms happened, which caused this necessity, that these bodies should pass through these motions.'

[e] 'There are infinite worlds, some like this, some unlike it; for, since atoms are infinite (as I newly showed from the infiniteness of the spaces), some in one, others in other distant parts of these spaces far from us, variously concur to the making of infinite worlds.'

> *Nec quos quaeque darent motus pepigere profecto;*
> *Sed quia multa modis multis primordia rerum*
> *Ex infinito iam tempore percita plagis*
> *Ponderibusque suis consuerunt concita ferri*
> *Omnimodisque coire atque omnia pertentare*
> *Quaecunque inter se possent congressa creare:*
> *Propterea fit ut magnum volgata per aevum*
> *Omnigenos coetus et motus experiundo*
> *Tandem conveniant ea quae coniuncta repente*
> *Magnarum rerum fiant exordia saepe*
> *Terrai maris et coeli generisque animantum*[f]

The hypothesis expressed in these verses (which please our author so well that he has almost the same lines in several other places of his poem) he prosecutes and applies to some particular parts of the universe in the same 5th Book. But whilst he thus refuseth to allow God an interest in the world's production, his hypothesis requires that we should allow him several things which he doth assume, not prove: as (1)[7] that matter is eternal. (2) That from eternity it was actually divided, and that into such insensibly small parts as may deserve the name of *atoms*;° whereas it may be supposed that matter, though eternal, was at first one coherent mass, it belonging to matter to be divisible, but not so of necessity to be actually divided. (3) That the number of these atoms is really infinite. (4) That these atoms have an *inane infinitum* (as the Epicureans speak) to move in. (5) That

---

[f] 'But how at first, when matter thus was whirled,
Heaven, earth, and sea, the high and lower world,
The sun and moon and all were made, I'll show.
For sure the first rude atoms never knew
By sage intelligence and counsel grave
To appoint the places that all beings have;
Nor will I think that all the motions here
Ordered at first by fixed agreements were,
But the elements, that long had beat about,
Been buffeted now in, now carried out,
Screwed into every hole, and tried to take
With any thing in any place to make
Somewhat at last, after much time and coil,
Motions and meetings, and a world of toil,
Made up this junto. And thus being joined,
And thus in kind embraces firmly twined
And linked together, they alone did frame
Heaven, earth, and sea, and the creatures in the same.'

these atoms are endowed with an almost infinite variety of determinate figures, some being round, others cubical, others hooked, others conical, &c.; whereas – not to mention beforehand what we may elsewhere object besides against this assumption – he shows not why nor how this atom came to be spherical rather than conical, and another hooked rather than pyramidal. But these assumptions I insist not on, because of two others much more considerable, which our author is fain to take for granted in his hypothesis. For (6) he supposes his eternal atoms to have from eternity been their own movers; whereas it is plain that motion is no way necessary to the essence of matter, which seems to consist principally in extension: for matter is no less matter when it rests than when it is in motion, and we daily see many parcels of matter pass from the state of motion to that of rest, and from this to that, communicating their motion to matter that lay still before, and thereby losing it themselves. Nor has any man, that I know, satisfactorily made out how matter can move itself. And indeed, in the bodies which we here below converse withal, we scarce find that anything is moved but by something else; and even in these motions of animals that seem spontaneous, the will or appetite doth not produce the motion of the animal, but guide and determine that of the spirits which by the nerves move the muscles, and so the whole body, as may appear by the weariness and unwieldiness of animals when by much motion the spirits are spent. And accordingly I find that Anaxagoras, though he believed, as Aristotle did after him, that matter was eternal, yet he discerned that, the notion of matter not necessarily including motion, there was a necessity of taking in a *mens*, as he styles God, to set this sluggish matter a-moving. And I remember Aristotle himself, in one place of his *Metaphysics*, disputing against some of the ancienter philosophers, asks: '*Quonamque modo movebuntur si nulla erit actu causa? non enim ipsa materia seipsam movebit,* ἀλλὰ τεκτονικὴ *rerum opifex virtus.*'[g] But though elsewhere I have met with passages of his near of kin to this, yet he seems not to express his opinion uniformly and clearly enough to engage me to define it or make a weapon of it; and therefore I shall rather proceed to take notice that, according to the Epicurean hypothesis, not only

---

[g] Aristotle, *Metaphysics*, lib. XII, cap. 6: 'How shall things be moved if there be no actual cause? For matter cannot move itself, but requires to be moved by a *tectonic* thing, creating power.'

the motion but the determination of that motion is supposed. For Epicurus will have his atoms move downwards, and that not in parallel lines – lest they should never meet to constitute the world – but according to lines somewhat inclining towards one another; so that there must be not only motion, but gravity, in atoms, before there be any *centrum gravium*[8] for them to move towards, and they must move rather downwards than upwards or sideways, and in such lines as nothing is produced capable of confining them to: which are assumptions so bold and precarious that I find some even of his admirers to be ashamed of them, which will save me the labour of arguing against them, and allow me to take notice (7) that this Epicurean doctrine supposes that, a sufficient number of atoms and their motion downwards being granted, there will need nothing but their fortuitous concourse in their fall, to give a being to all those bodies that make up the world. Indeed, that the various coalitions of atoms, or at least small particles of matter, might have constituted the world, had not been perhaps a very absurd opinion for a philosopher if he had, as reason requires, supposed that the great mass of lazy matter was created by God at the beginning, and by him put into a swift and various motion, whereby it was actually divided into small parts of several sizes and figures, whose motion and crossings of each other were so guided by God as to constitute, by their occursions and coalitions, the great inanimate parts of the universe, and the seminal principles of animated concretions. And therefore I wonder not much that the Milesian Thales (the first of the Grecian philosophers (as Cicero informs us) that enquired into these matters) should hold that opinion which Tully expresses in these words: '*aquam dixit esse initium rerum, Deum autem eam mentem, quae ex aqua cuncta finxerat*';[h] and that of Anaxagoras the same author should give us this account: '*omnium rerum descriptionem et modum mentis infinitae vi ac ratione designari et confici voluit*'.[i] For though these great men exceedingly erred in thinking it necessary that God should be provided of a pre-existent, and by him not created, matter to make the world of, yet at least they discerned and acknowledged the necessity of a wise and powerful agent to dispose and fashion this rude matter, and contrive it into so goodly a structure as we behold,

[h] Cicero, *De Natura Deorum*, lib. I, cap. 10: 'He said water was the principle of all things, but God was that intelligence that made all things out of water.'

[i] Id., cap. 11: 'The delineation and manner of all things he thought to be designed and made by the power and reason of infinite intelligence.'

without imagining with Epicurus that chance should turn a chaos into a world. And really it is much more unlikely that so many admirable creatures that constitute this one exquisite and stupendous fabric of the world should be made by the casual confluence of falling atoms, jostling or knocking one another in the immense vacuity, than that in a printer's working-house a multitude of small letters, being thrown upon the ground, should fall disposed into such an order as clearly to exhibit the history of the Creation of the world described in the 3 or 4 first chapters of *Genesis*, of which history it may be doubted whether chance may ever be able to dispose the fallen letters into the words of one line.+

I ignore not that sometimes odd figures, and almost pictures, may be met with, and may seem casually produced, in stones and divers other inanimate bodies; and I am so far from denying this, that I may elsewhere have opportunity to show you that I have been no careless observer of such varieties. | But first, even in divers minerals, as we may see in nitre, crystal, and several others, the figures that are admired are not unquestionably produced by chance, but perhaps by something analogous to seminal principles, as may appear by their uniform regularity in the same sort of concretions, and by the practice of some of the skilfullest of the saltpetre men, who, when they have drawn as much nitre as they can out of the nitrous earth, cast not the earth away, but preserve it in heaps for six or seven years, at the end of which time they find it impregnated with new saltpetre, produced chiefly by the seminal principle of nitre implanted in that earth. To prove that metalline bodies were not all made at the beginning of the world, but have some of them a power, though slowly, to propagate their nature when they meet with a disposed matter, you may find many notable testimonies and relations in a little book of *Physico-chemical Questions* written by Jo. Conradus Gerhardus, a German doctor, and most of them recited (together with some of his own) by the learned Sennertus. But lest you should suspect the narratives of these authors, as somewhat partial to their fellow chemists' opinions, I shall here annex that memorable relation which I find recorded by Linschoten and Garcias ab Horto, a pair of unsuspected writers in this case, concerning diamonds, whereby it may appear that the seminal principles of those precious stones, as of plants, are lodged in the bowels of the mine they grow in. 'Diamonds,' says the first (in that chapter of his Travels where he treats of those jewels), 'are digged

like gold out of mines; where they digged one year the length of a
man into the ground, within three or four years after there are found
diamonds again in the same place, which grow there. Sometimes
they find diamonds of 400 or 800 grains.'[9] '*Adamantes*,' says the
latter, '*qui altissime in terrae visceribus multisque annis perfici debebant, in
summo fere solo generantur et duorum aut trium annorum spatio perficiuntur.
Nam si in ipsa fodina hoc anno ad cubiti altitudinem fodias, adamantes
reperies. Post biennium, rursus illic excavato, ibidem invenies adamantes.*'[j]+

And next, how inconsiderable, alas, are these supposed
productions of chance, in comparison of the elaborate contrivances
of nature in animals: since in the body of man, for instance, of so
many hundred parts it is made up of, there is scarce any that can be
either left out, or made otherwise than as it is, or placed elsewhere
than where it is, without an apparent detriment to that curious
engine, some of whose parts, as the eye and the valves of the veins,
would be so unfit for anything else, and are so fitted for the uses that
are made of them, that it is so far from being likely that such skilful
contrivances should be made by any being not intelligent, that they
require a more than ordinary intelligence to comprehend how
skilfully they are made.| As for the account that Lucretius, out of
Epicurus, gives us of the first production of men, in I know not what
wombs adhering to the ground, and which much more becomes him
as a poet than as a philosopher, I shall not here waste time to
manifest its unlikeliness, that witty father Lactantius having already
done that copiously for me.[k][10] And indeed it seems so pure a fiction
that, were it not that the hypothesis he took upon him to maintain
could scarce afford him any less extravagant account of the original
of animals, the unsuitableness of this *romance* to those excellent
notions with which he has enriched divers other parts of his works
would make me apt to suspect that, when he writ this part of his
poem, he was in one of the fits of that frenzy, which some even of his
admirers suppose him to have been put into by a philtre given him
by his either wife or mistress Lucilia, in the intervals of which they
say that he writ his books.

[j] D. Garcias ab Horto, *Aromatum et Simplicium Aliquot Medicamentorum apud Indos
Nascentium Historia*, lib. I, cap. 47: 'Diamonds, which ought to be brought to perfection
in the deepest bowels of the earth and in a long tract of time, are generated almost at
the top of the ground, and in three or four years' space made perfect. For if you dig
this year but the depth of a cubit, you will find diamonds; and after two years dig
there, you will find diamonds again.'

[k] Lactantius, *Divinae Institutiones*, lib. II, cap. 11.

And here let us further consider that, as confidently as many atomists and other naturalists presume to know the true and genuine causes of the things they attempt to explicate, yet very often the utmost they can attain to in their explications is that the explicated phenomena *may*° be produced after such a manner as they deliver, but not that they really *are*° so. For, as an artificer can set all the wheels of a clock a-going as well with springs as with weights, and may with violence discharge a bullet out of the barrel of a gun not only by means of gunpowder but of compressed air and even of a spring, so the same effects may be produced by divers causes different from one another; and it will oftentimes be very difficult, if not impossible, for our dim reasons to discern surely which of those several ways whereby it is possible for nature to produce the same phenomena she has really made use of to exhibit them. And sure, he that in a skilful watchmaker's shop shall observe how many several ways watches and clocks may be contrived, and yet all of them show the same things, and shall consider how apt an ordinary man, that had never seen the inside but of one sort of watches, would be to think that all these are contrived after the same manner as that whose fabric he has already taken notice of – such a person, I say, will scarce be backward to think that so admirable an engineer as nature, by many pieces of her workmanship, appears to be, can by very various and differing contrivances perform the same things; and that it is a very easy mistake for men to conclude that, because an effect may be produced by such determinate causes, it must be so, or actually is so. And as confident as those we speak of use to be of knowing the true and adequate causes of things, yet Epicurus himself, as appears by ancient testimony and by his own writings, was more modest, not only contenting himself on many occasions to propose several possible ways whereby a phenomenon may be accounted for, but sometimes seeming to dislike the so pitching upon any one explication as to exclude and reject all others; and some modern philosophers that much favour his doctrine do likewise imitate his example, in pretending to assign not precisely the true, but possible, causes of the phenomenon they endeavour to explain. And I remember that Aristotle himself (whatever confidence he sometimes seems to express) does in his first Book of *Meteors* ingenuously confess that, concerning many of nature's phenomena, he thinks it sufficient that they *may*° be so performed as he explicates them. But granting that we did never so certainly know, in the general, that these phenomena of nature must proceed from the magnitudes, figures, motions, and thence-resulting qualities, of atoms, yet we may be very much to seek as to the particular causes of this or that particular effect or event. For it is one thing to be able to show it possible for such and such effects to proceed from the various magnitudes, shapes, motions, and concretions, of atoms; and another thing to be able to declare what precise and determinate figures, sizes, and motions, of atoms will suffice to make out the proposed phenomena, without incongruity to any others to be met with in nature: as it is one thing for a man ignorant of the mechanics to make it plausible that the motions of the famed clock at Strasbourg are performed by the means of certain wheels, springs, and weights, &c., and another to be able to describe distinctly the magnitude, figures, proportions, motions, and (in short) the whole contrivance, either of that admirable engine, or some other capable to perform the same things.

Nay, a lover of disputing would proceed farther, and question that way of reasoning which even the eminentest atomists are wont to employ to demonstrate that they explicate things aright.| For the grand argument by which they use to confirm the truth of their explications is that either the phenomenon must be explicated after the manner by them specified, or else it cannot at all be explicated intelligibly. In what sense we disallow not, but rather approve, this kind of ratiocination, we may elsewhere tell you. But that which is in this place more fit to be represented is that this way of arguing seems not in our present case so cogent as they that are wont to employ it think it to be: for besides that it is bold to affirm, and hard to prove, that what they cannot yet explicate by their principles cannot possibly be explicated by any other men, or any other philosophy – besides this, I say, that which they would reduce their adversaries to as an absurdity seems not to deserve that name. For supposing the argument to be conclusive, that either the proposed explication must be allowed or men can give none at all that is intelligible, I see not what absurdity it were to admit of the consequence: for who has demonstrated to us that men must be able to explicate all nature's phenomena, especially since divers of them are so abstruse that even the learnedest atomists scruple not to acknowledge their being unable to give an account of them? And how will it be proved that the omniscient God, or that admirable contriver nature, can exhibit phenomena by no ways but such as are explicable by the dim reason of man? I say *explicable,*° rather than *intelligible,*° because there may be things which, though we might understand well enough if God or some more intelligent being than our own did make it his work to inform us of them, yet we should never of ourselves find out those truths: as an ordinary watchmaker may be able to understand the curiousest contrivance of the skilfullest artificer, if this man take care to explain his engine to him, but would never have understood it if he had not been taught; whereas to explicate the nature and causes of the phenomena we are speaking of, we must not only be able to understand, but to investigate them.

And whereas it is peremptorily insisted on by some Epicureans, who thereby pretend to demonstrate the excellency and certainty of their explications, that, according to them, nature is declared to produce things in the way that is most facile and agreeable to our reason, it may be replied that what we are to enquire after is how things have been, or are really, produced, not whether or no the manner of their production be such as may the most easily be understood by us. For if all things were, as those we reason withal maintain, casually produced, there is no reason to imagine that chance considered what manner of their production would be the most easily intelligible to us. And if God be allowed to be, as indeed he is, the Author of the universe, how will it appear that he, whose knowledge infinitely transcends ours, and who may be supposed to operate according to the dictates of his own immense wisdom, should in his creating of things have respect to the measure and ease of human understandings, and not rather, if of any, of angelical intellects? So that whether it be to God or to chance that we ascribe the production of things, that way may often be fittest or likeliest for nature to work by, which is not easiest for us to understand.

And as for the way of arguing so often employed (especially against the truth we now contend for) and so much relied on by many modern philosophers, namely, that they cannot clearly conceive such or such a thing proposed, and therefore think it fit to be rejected, I shall readily agree with them in the not being forward to assent to anything, especially in philosophy, that cannot well be conceived by knowing and considering men. But there is so much difference among men as to their faculty of framing distinct notions of things; and through men's partiality or laziness, many a particular person is so much more apt than these men seem to be aware of to think, or at least to pretend, that he cannot conceive what he has no mind to assent to, that a man had need be wary how he rejects opinions that are impugned only by this way of ratiocination, by which, I hope, it will not be expected that we should be more prevailed with than that sect of philosophers that employs it most. And among those that resolve the phenomena of nature into the mechanical powers of things, or the various figures, sizes, and motions, of the parts of matter, I meet with some, as the Epicureans, who tell us they cannot frame a notion of an incorporeal substance or spirit, nor conceive how, if the soul were such, it could act upon the body; and yet others, that seem no less speculative, seriously and solemnly profess that they can conceive a clear and distinct notion of a spirit – which they believe the human soul, that regulates at least, if not produces, divers motions of the body, to be – denying on the other side that it can be clearly conceived either that anything that is only material can think, or that there can possibly be any vacuum (that is, place without any body) in the universe, both which the Epicureans profess themselves not only to conceive as possible, but to believe as true.

And thus much, Pyrophilus, it may suffice to have said in relation to those who would reject God from having anything to do, either in the production or government of the world, upon this ground, that they, if you will believe them, can explicate the original and phenomena of it without him; but it is not all, nor the greatest part of, the favourers of the atomical philosophy that presume so much of themselves and derogate so much from God. To say therefore something to the more moderate and judicious of that persuasion, we will candidly propose on their behalf the most plausible objection we can foresee against the truth we have been all this while pleading for. They may then thus argue against us that, though the atomists cannot sufficiently demonstrate from what natural causes every particular effect proceeds, and satisfactorily explicate after what determinate manner each particular phenomenon is produced, yet it may suffice to take away the necessity of having recourse to a Deity, that they can make out in general that all the things that appear in the world may, and must, be performed by merely corporeal agents; or, if you please, that all nature's phenomena may be produced by the parcels of the great mass of universal matter, variously shaped, connected, and moved: as a man that sees a screwed gun shot off, though he may not be able to describe the number, bigness, shape, and coaptation, of all the pieces of the lock, stock, and barrel, yet he may readily conceive that the effects of the gun, how wonderful soever they may seem, may be performed by certain pieces of steel or iron, and some parcels of wood, of gunpowder, and of lead, all fashioned and put together according to the exigency of the engine, and will not doubt but that they are produced by the power of some such mechanical contrivance of things purely corporeal, without the assistance of spiritual or supernatural agents.

In answer to this objection, I must first profess to you that I make a great doubt whether there be not some phenomena in nature which the atomists cannot satisfactorily explain by any figuration, motion, or connexion, of material particles whatsoever: for some faculties and operations of the reasonable soul in man are of so peculiar and transcendent a kind that, as I have not yet found them solidly explicated by corporeal principles, so I expect not to see them in haste made out by such. And if a spiritual substance be admitted to enter the composition of a man and to act by and upon his body, besides that one of the chief and fundamental doctrines of the Epicureans (namely, that there is nothing in the universe but *corpus* and *inane*) will thereby be subverted, it will appear that an incorporeal and intelligent being may work upon matter: which would argue at least a possibility that there may be a spiritual Deity, and that he may intermeddle with and have an influence upon the operations of things corporeal. But to insist no longer on this, let us give a further and direct answer to the proposed objection, by representing that, although, as things are now established in the world, an atomist were able to explain the phenomena we meet with by supposing the parts of matter to be of such sizes, and such shapes, and to be moved after such a manner, as is agreeable to the nature of the particular phenomenon to be thereby exhibited, yet it would not thence necessarily follow that, at the first production of the world, there was no need of a most powerful and intelligent Being, to dispose that *chaos* or confused heap of numberless atoms into the world, to establish the universal and conspiring harmony of things, and especially to connect those atoms into those various seminal contextures upon which most of the more abstruse operations and elaborate productions of nature appear to depend. For many things may be performed by matter variously figured and moved, which yet would never be performed by it if it had been still left to itself, without being, at first at least, fashioned after such a manner and put into such a motion by an intelligent agent: as the quill that a philosopher writes with, being dipped in ink, and then moved after such and such a manner upon white paper, all which are corporeal things or their motions, may very well trace an excellent and rational discourse, but the quill would never have been moved after the requisite manner upon the paper had not its motion been guided and regulated by the understanding of the writer. Or rather, yet once more to resume our former example of the Strasbourg clock, though a skilful artist, admitted to examine and consider it both without and within, may very well discern that such wheels, springs, weights, and other pieces of which the engine consists, being set together in such a coaptation, are sufficient to produce such and such motions and such other effects as that clock is celebrated for, yet, the more he discerns the aptness and sufficiency of the parts to produce the effects emergent from them, the less he will be apt to suspect that so curious an engine was produced by any casual concurrence of the parts it consists of, and not rather by the skill of an intelligent and ingenious contriver; or that the wheels and other parts were of this or that size, or this or that determinate shape, for any other reason than because it pleased the artificer to make them so: though the reason that moved the artificer to employ such figures and quantities sooner than others may well be supposed to have been that the nature of his design made him think them very proper and commodious for its accomplishment, if not better than any other suited to the several exigencies of it.

If an Epicurean should be told that a man, after having been for some days really dead, became alive again, I think it will not be doubted but that he would reject such a relation as impossible, and therefore too manifestly false to be believed by any man in his wits. And yet, according to his principles, the man, as well soul as body, consisted only of divers particles of the universal matter, by various motions brought together, and disposed after a certain manner; and consequently he must ground his persuasion that it is impossible to redintegrate the engine once spoiled by death upon this, that as chance cannot with the least probability be presumed to have produced such a strange effect, so, according to him, there can be no cause assigned knowing and powerful enough to rally and bring together again the disbanded and scattered parcels of matter (or substitute other equivalent ones) that, together with the remaining carcass, composed the dead man, so to reunite them to the rest, and lastly so to place and put into motion both the one and the other, as were requisite to make a living man once more result from them. I know that this example reaches not all the circumstances of the controversy we have been debating; but yet, if I mistake not, it will serve the turn for which I propose it. For, not now to insist upon this inference from it, that a considering man may confidently reject a thing that is not absolutely impossible, provided it be highly incredible – not to insist on this, I say, the thing I aim at in the mention of it is only to show that such things may possibly be effected by matter and motion as no wise man will believe to have been produced by a bare agitation of the particles of matter, not guided by the superintendency of a powerful and knowing Director.

Now that the atoms or particles of matter of which the world consists made no agreement with each other to convene and settle in the manner requisite to constitute the universe, Lucretius does not so properly confess, as affirm, in that fore-cited passage, where he judiciously tells us that

> *certe neque consiliis primordia rerum*
> *Ordine se quaeque atque sagaci mente locarunt,*
> *Nec quos quaeque darent motus pepigere profecto.* |

And the thing itself is manifest enough, from the nature of atoms confessedly inanimate and devoid of understanding:| so that, although we should grant, Pyrophilus, the possible emergency of the innumerable effects we admire in the world from the various properties and coalitions of atoms, yet still you see the formerly-mentioned difficulty (touching the resulting of all things from matter left to itself) would recur. And it would as well be incredible that an innumerable multitude of insensible particles, as that a lesser number of bigger parcels of matter, should either conspire to constitute or fortuitously jostle themselves into so admirable and harmonious a fabric as the universe, or as the body of man; and consequently it is not credible that they should constitute either, unless as their motions were (at least, in order to their seminal contextures and primary coalitions) regulated and guided by an intelligent contriver and orderer of things. And I should so little think it a disparagement to have but so much said of any hypothesis of mine, that I suppose I may affirm it without offending either the most sober or the generality of the atomical philosophers, to whom, and to their doctrine, my writings will manifest me to be no otherwise affected than I ought.

A FREE ENQUIRY INTO THE VULGARLY
RECEIVED NOTION OF NATURE

SECTION II

A considering person may well be tempted to suspect that men have generally had but imperfect and confused notions concerning *nature*, if he but observes that they apply that *name* to several things, and those too such as have some of them very little dependence on, or connexion with, such others. And I remember that in Aristotle's *Metaphysics* I met with a whole chapter expressly written to enumerate the various acceptions of the Greek word φύσις, commonly rendered *nature*, of which, if I mistake not, he there reckons up six. In English also we have not fewer, but rather more numerous, significations of that term. For sometimes we use the word *nature* for that *Author of nature* whom the schoolmen, harshly enough, call *natura naturans*, as when it is said that *nature* hath made man partly corporeal and partly immaterial. Sometimes we mean by the *nature* of a thing the *essence*, or that which the schoolmen scruple not to call the *quiddity* of a thing, namely, the *attribute* or *attributes* on whose score it is what it is, whether the thing be corporeal or not, as when we attempt to define the *nature* of an *angel*, or of a *triangle*, or of a *fluid* body, as such. Sometimes we confound that which a man has by *nature* with what accrues to him by birth, as when we say that such a man is noble *by nature*,° or such a child *naturally*° forward, or sickly, or frightful. Sometimes we take *nature* for an internal principle of motion, as when we say that a stone let fall in the air is by *nature* carried towards the centre of the earth, and, on the contrary, that fire or flame does *naturally*° move upwards towards heaven.| Sometimes we understand by *nature* the established course of things, as when we say that *nature* makes the night succeed the day, *nature* hath made respiration necessary to the life of men.| Sometimes we take *nature* for an aggregate of powers belonging to a body, especially a living one, as when physicians say that *nature* is strong or weak or spent, or that in such or such diseases *nature* left to herself will do the cure. Sometimes we take *nature* for the universe, or system of the corporeal works of God, as when it is said of a phoenix, or a chimera, that there is no such thing *in nature*, i.e. in the world. And sometimes too, and that most commonly, we would express by the word *nature* a semi-deity or other strange kind of being, such as this discourse examines the notion of.[+]

And besides these more absolute acceptions, if I may so call them, of the word *nature*, it has divers others (more relative), as *nature* is wont to be set in opposition or contradistinction to other things, as when we say of a stone when it falls downwards that it does it by a *natural motion*, but that if it be thrown upwards its motion that way is *violent*.[°] So chemists distinguish vitriol into *natural* and *factitious*,[1] or made by art, i.e. by the intervention of human power or skill; so it is said that water, kept suspended in a sucking pump, is not in its *natural* place, as that is which is stagnant in the well. We say also that wicked men are still in the state of *nature*, but the regenerate in a state of *grace*; that cures wrought by medicines are *natural* operations, but the miraculous ones wrought by Christ and his apostles were *supernatural*.[°] Nor are these the only forms of speech that a more diligent collector than I think it necessary I should here be might instance in to manifest the ambiguity of the word *nature*, by the many and various things it is applied to signify, though some of those already mentioned should be judged too near to be coincident. Among Latin writers I found the acceptions of the word *nature* to be so many that I remember one author reckons up no less than fourteen or fifteen. From all which it is not difficult to gather how easy it is for the generality of men, without excepting those that write of *natural* things, to impose upon others and themselves in the use of a word so apt to be misemployed.

On this occasion I can scarce forbear to tell you that I have often looked upon it as an unhappy thing, and prejudicial both to philosophy and physic, that the word *nature* hath been so frequently and yet so unskilfully employed, both in books and in discourse, by all sorts of men, learned and illiterate. For the very great ambiguity of this term, and the promiscuous use men are wont to make of it without sufficiently attending to its different significations, makes many of the expressions wherein they employ it (and think they do it well and truly) to be either not intelligible or not proper or not true: which observation, though it be not heeded, may with the help of a little attention be easily verified, especially because the term *nature* is so often used that you shall scarce meet with any man who, if he have occasion to discourse anything long of either natural or medicinal subjects, would not find himself at a great loss, if he were prohibited the use of the word *nature* and of those phrases whereof it makes the principal part. And I confess I could heartily wish that philosophers and other learned men (whom the rest in time would follow) would, by common (though perhaps tacit) consent, introduce some more significant and less ambiguous terms and expressions in the room of the too licentiously abused word *nature* and the forms of speech that depend on it, or would at least decline the use of it as much as conveniently they can; and where they think they must employ it, would add a word or two to declare in what clear and determinate sense they use it. For without somewhat of this kind be done, men will very hardly avoid being led into divers mistakes, both of things and of one another; and such wranglings about words and names will be (if not continually multiplied) still kept on foot, as are wont to be managed with much heat, though little use, and no necessity.

And here I must take leave to complain, in my own excuse, of the scarce superable difficulty of the task that the design of a *free enquiry* puts me upon. For it is far more difficult than anyone that hath not tried (and I do not know that any man hath) would imagine, to discourse long of the corporeal works of God, and especially of the *operations* and *phenomena* that are attributed to *nature*, and yet decline making oftentimes use of that term, or forms of speech whereof it is a main part, without much more frequent and perhaps tedious circumlocutions than I am willing to trouble you with. And therefore I hope you will easily excuse me if, partly to shun these and to avoid using often the same words too near one another, and partly out of unwillingness to employ vulgar terms likely to occasion or countenance vulgar errors, I have several times been fain to use paraphrases or other expressions less short than those commonly received, and sometimes, for one or other of these reasons or out of inadvertence, missed of avoiding the terms used by those that admit and applaud the vulgar notion of nature: whom I must here advertise you that, partly because they do so and partly for brevity's sake, I shall hereafter many times call *naturists*, which appellation I rather choose than that of *naturalists*, because many, even of the learned among them, as logicians, orators, lawyers, arithmeticians, &c., are not physiologers.

But if on this occasion you should be very urgent to know what course I would think expedient, if I were to propose any, for the avoiding the inconvenient use of so ambiguous a word as *nature*, I should *first* put you in mind that, having but very lately declared that I thought it very difficult, in physiological discourses especially, to decline the frequent use[2] of that term, you are not to expect from me the satisfaction you may desire in an answer. And *then* I would add that yet my unwillingness to be altogether silent, when you require me to say somewhat, makes me content to try whether the mischief complained of may not be in some measure either obviated or lessened, by looking back upon the (eight) various significations that were not long since delivered of the word *nature*, and by endeavouring to express them in other terms or forms of speech.

1. Instead then of the word *nature* taken in the first sense [for *natura naturans*], we may make use of the term it is put to signify, namely *God*, wholly discarding an expression which, besides that it is harsh and needless and in use only among the schoolmen, seems not to me very suitable to the profound reverence we owe the divine majesty, since it seems to make the *Creator* differ too little by far from a *created* (not to say an *imaginary*) being.

2. Instead of *nature* in the second sense [for *that on whose account a thing is what it is, and is so called*], we may employ the word *essence*, which is of great affinity to it, if not of an adequate import. And sometimes also we may make use of the word *quiddity*, which, though a somewhat barbarous term, is yet frequently employed and well enough understood in the Schools, and – which is more considerable – is very comprehensive, and yet free enough from ambiguity.

3. What is meant by the word *nature* taken in the third sense of it [for *what belongs to a living creature at its nativity or accrues to it by its birth*] may be expressed sometimes by saying that a man or other animal is *born* so, and sometimes by saying that a thing has been *generated* such, and sometimes also that it is thus or thus qualified by its *original temperament and constitution*.

4. Instead of the word *nature* taken in the fourth acception [for *an internal principle of local motion*], we may say sometimes that this or that body *moves, as it were*, or else that it *seems to move, spontaneously* (or *of its own accord*), upwards, downwards, &c., or that it is put into this or that motion or determined to this or that action by the concourse of such or such (proper) causes.

5. For *nature* in the fifth signification [for *the established course of*

things corporeal], it is easy to substitute what it denotes, *the established order*, or *the settled course of things*.

6. Instead of *nature* in the sixth sense of the word [for *an aggregate of the powers belonging to a body, especially a living one*], we may employ the *constitution*, *temperament*, or the *mechanism*, or the *complex of the essential properties or qualities*, and sometimes the *condition*,° the *structure*,° or the *texture*° of that body. And if we speak of the greater portions of the world, we may make use of one or other of these terms, *fabric of the world*, *system of the universe*, *cosmical mechanism*, or the like.

7. Where men are wont to employ the word *nature* in the seventh sense [for *the universe*, or *the system of the corporeal works of God*], it is easy and as short to make use of the word *world* or *universe*; and, instead of *the phenomena of nature*, to substitute *the phenomena of the universe* or *of the world*.

8. And as for the word *nature* taken in the eighth and last of the forementioned acceptions [for either (as some pagans styled her) *a goddess*, or a kind of *semi-deity*], the best way is not to employ it in that sense at all; or at least as seldom as may be, and that for divers reasons which may in due place be met with in several parts of this essay.

But though the foregoing diversity of terms and phrases may be much increased, yet I confess it makes but a part of the remedy I propose against the future mischiefs of the confused acception of the word *nature* and the phrases grounded on it. For besides the synonymous words and more literal interpretations lately proposed, a dextrous writer may oftentimes be able to give such a form (or, as the modern Frenchmen speak, such a *tour*) to his many-ways variable expressions as to avoid the necessity of making use of the word *nature*, or sometimes so much as of those shorter terms that have been lately substituted in its place. And to all this I must add that, though one or two of the eight forementioned terms or phrases, as *quiddity* and *cosmical mechanism*, be barbarous or ungenteel, and some other expressions be less short than the word *nature*, yet it is more the interest of philosophy to tolerate a harsh term that has been long received in the Schools in a determinate sense, and bear with some paraphrastical expressions, than not to avoid an ambiguity that is liable to such great inconveniences as have been lately, or may be hereafter, represented.

There are, I know, some learned men who (perhaps being startled to find nature usually spoken of so much like a kind of *goddess*) will have the *nature* of every thing to be only the *law* that it receives from the Creator, and according to which it acts on all occasions. And this opinion seems much of kin to, if not the same with, that of the famous Helmont, who, justly rejecting the Aristotelian tenent of the contrariety or hostility of the elements, will have every body, without any such respect, to act that which it is commanded to act. And indeed this opinion about nature, though neither clear nor comprehensive enough, seems capable of a fair construction. And there is oftentimes some resemblance between the orderly and regular motions of inanimate bodies and the actions of agents that, in what they do, act conformably to laws. And even I sometimes scruple not to speak of the *laws*° of motion and rest that God has established among things corporeal, and now and then (for brevity's sake or out of custom) to call them, as men are wont to do, the *laws of nature*, having in due place declared in what sense I understand and employ these expressions.

But to speak strictly (as becomes philosophers in so weighty a matter), to say that the *nature* of this or that body is but the *law of God prescribed to it* is but an improper and figurative expression. For, besides that this gives us but a very defective *idea* of *nature*, since it omits the general fabric of the world and the contrivances of particular bodies, which yet are as well necessary as local motion itself to the production of particular *effects* and *phenomena* – besides this, I say, and other imperfections of this *notion of nature* that I shall not here insist on, I must freely observe that, to speak properly, a *law* being but a *notional rule of acting according to the declared will of a superior*, it is plain that nothing but an intellectual being can be properly capable of receiving and acting by a *law*. For if it does not understand, it cannot know what the will of the *legislator* is; nor can it have any intention to accomplish it, nor can it act with regard to it, or know when it does, in acting, either conform to it or deviate from it. And *it is intelligible to me* that God should at the beginning impress determinate motions upon the parts of matter, and guide them as he thought requisite for the primordial constitution of things, and that, ever since, he should by his ordinary and general concourse maintain those powers which he gave the parts of matter to transmit their motion thus and thus to one another. But *I cannot conceive* how a body devoid of understanding and sense, truly so called, can moderate and determine its own motions, especially so as to make them conformable to laws that it has no knowledge or apprehension of. And that inanimate bodies, how strictly soever called *natural*, do properly act by laws, cannot be evinced by their sometimes acting regularly and, as men think, in order to determinate ends, since in artificial things we see many motions very orderly performed, and with a manifest tendency to particular and predesigned ends: as in a watch the motions of the spring, wheels, and other parts, are so contemperated and regulated that the hand upon the dial moves with a great uniformity, and seems to moderate its motion so as not to arrive at the points that denote the time of the day either a minute sooner, or a minute later, than it should do to declare the hour. And when a man shoots an arrow at a mark, so as to hit it, though the arrow moves towards the mark as it would if it could and did design to strike it, yet none will say that this arrow moves by a law, but by an external though well-directed impulse.

SECTION IV

Having shown that the definition given of *nature* by Aristotle himself, as great a *logician* as he was, has not been able to satisfy so much as his interpreters and disciples what his own idea of nature was, it would be to little purpose to trouble you and myself with enquiring into the definitions and disputes of other Peripatetics about so obscure and perplexed a subject, especially since it is not my business in this tract solicitously to examine what *Aristotle* thought nature to be, but what is to be thought of the *vulgarly received notion* of nature. And though of this the Schools have been the chief propagators, for which reason it was fit to take notice of their master Aristotle's definition, yet the best way I know to investigate the commonly received opinion of nature is to consider what *effata* or *axioms* do pass for current about her, and what titles and epithets are unanimously given her, both by philosophers and other writers, and by the generality of men that have occasion to discourse of her and her actings.

Of these axioms and epithets, the principal seem to be these that follow.

> *Natura est sapientissima, adeoque opus naturae est opus intelligentiae.*
> *Natura nihil facit frustra.*[a]

---

[a] Aristotle, *De Coelo*, lib. II, cap. 11.

Natura fine suo nunquam excidit.
Natura semper facit quod optimum est.[b]
Natura semper agit per vias brevissimas.
Natura neque redundat in superfluis, neque deficit in necessariis.
Omnis natura est conservatrix sui.
Natura est morborum medicatrix.
Natura semper invigilat conservationi universi.
Natura vacuum horret.

From all these particulars put together, it may appear that the *vulgar notion of nature* may be conveniently enough expressed by some such description as this: | *nature* is a most wise being, that *does nothing* in vain; *does not* miss of her ends; *does always* that which (of the things she can do) is best to be done; and this she *does* by *the most direct* or *compendious ways, neither* employing any things superfluous, *nor* being wanting in things necessary; she teaches and inclines every one of her works to preserve itself. And, as in the *microcosm* (*man*) it is she that is the curer of diseases, so in the *macrocosm* (*the world*), for the conservation of the universe, she abhors a vacuum, making particular bodies act contrary to their own inclinations and interests to prevent it, for the public good.

What I think of the particulars that make up this panegyrical description of nature will (God permitting) be told you in due place, my present work being only to make you the clearest representation I can of what men generally (if they understand themselves) *do*, or with congruity to the axioms they admit and use *ought* to, conceive nature to be.

It is not unlike that you may expect or wish that on this occasion I should propose some definition or description of nature as my own. But declining (at least at present) to say anything dogmatically about this matter, I know not whether I may not on this occasion confess to you that I have sometimes been so paradoxical, or (if you please) so extravagant, as to entertain as a serious doubt what I formerly intimated, viz. *whether nature be a thing or a name* – I mean, whether it be a *real* existent being, or a *notional* entity, somewhat of kin to those fictitious terms that men have devised that they might compendiously express several things together by one name. As

---

[b] Aristotle, *De Coelo*, lib. II, cap. 5; *De Generatione & Corruptione*, lib. II, cap. 10, sect. 22.

when, for instance, we speak of the *concocting faculty* ascribed to animals, those that consider and are careful to understand what they say do not mean I know not what entity, that is distinct from the human body, as it is an engine curiously contrived and made up of stable and fluid parts; but, observing an actuating power and fitness in the teeth, tongue, spittle, fibres and membranes of the gullet and stomach, together with the natural heat, the ferment, or else the menstruum, and some other agents, by their co-operation to cook or dress the aliments and change them into chyle – observing these things, I say, they thought it convenient, for brevity's sake, to express the *complex* of those causes and the *train of their actions* by the summary appellation of *concocting faculty*.

Whilst I was indulging myself in this kind of ravings, it came into my mind that the naturists might demand of me how, without admitting their notion, I could give any tolerable account of those most useful forms of speech which men employ when they say that *nature does this* or *that*, or that *such a thing is done by nature*, or *according to nature*, or else *happens against nature*. And this question I thought the more worth answering, because these phrases are so very frequently used by men of all sorts, as well learned as illiterate, that this custom hath made them be thought not only very convenient, but necessary, insomuch that I look upon it as none of the least things that has procured so general a reception to the *vulgar notion of nature*, that these ready and commodious forms of speech suppose the truth of it.

It may, therefore, in this place be pertinent to add that such phrases as that *nature*, or *faculty*, or *suction*, *doth this or that* are not the only ones wherein I observe that men ascribe to a *notional* thing that which indeed is performed by *real* agents: as when we say that the *law* 'punishes' murder with death, that it 'protects' the innocent, 'releases' a debtor out of prison when he has satisfied his creditors (and the ministers of justice), on which or the like occasions we may justly say that it is plain that the *law*, which being in itself a dead letter is but a *notional* rule, cannot in a physical sense be said to perform these things; but they are really performed by judges, officers, executioners, and other men, acting according to that rule. Thus when we say that *custom does this or that*, we ought to mean only that such things are done by proper agents, acting with conformity to what is usual (or customary) on such occasions. And to give you a yet more apposite instance, do but consider how many events are wont to be ascribed to *fortune* or *chance*; and yet *fortune* is in reality no physical cause of anything (for which reason probably it is that ancienter naturalists than Aristotle, as himself intimates, take no notice of it when they treat of *natural* causes), and only denotes that those effects that are ascribed to it were produced by their true and proper agents without intending to produce them: as, when a man shoots at a deer and the arrow, lightly glancing upon the beast, wounds some man that lay beyond him unseen by the archer, it is plain that the arrow is a physical agent that acts by virtue of its fabric and motion in both these effects, and yet men will say that the slight hurt it gave the deer was brought to pass according to the course of *nature*, because the archer designed to shoot the beast, but the mortal wound it gave the man happened by *chance*, because the archer intended not to shoot him or any man else. And whereas divers of the old atomical philosophers, pretending (without good reason, as well as against piety) to give an account of the origin of things without recourse to a Deity, did sometimes affirm the world to have been made by *nature*, and sometimes by *fortune* – promiscuously employing those terms – they did it (if I guess aright) because they thought neither of them to denote any true and proper *physical cause*, but rather certain *conceptions* that we men have of the manner of acting of true and proper agents. And therefore, when the Epicureans taught the world to have been made by *chance*, it is probable that they did not look upon *chance* as a true and architectonic cause of the system of the world, but believed all things to have been made by the *atoms*, considered as their conventions and concretions into the sun, stars, earth, and other bodies, were made without any design of constituting those bodies.

Whilst this vein of framing paradoxes yet continued, I ventured to proceed so far as to question whether one may not infer, from what hath been said, that the chief advantage a philosopher receives from what men call *nature* be not that it affords them on divers occasions a compendious way of expressing themselves: since (thought I), to consider things otherwise than in a popular way, when a man tells me that *nature does such a thing*, he does not really help me to understand or to explicate how it is done. For it seems manifest enough that whatsoever is done in the world, at least wherein the rational soul intervenes not, is really effected by corporeal causes and agents, acting in a world so framed as ours is, according to the laws of motion settled by the omniscient Author of things.

When a man knows the contrivance of a *watch* or *clock*, by viewing the several pieces of it and seeing how, when they are duly put together, the spring or weight sets one of the wheels a-work, and by that another, till by a fit consecution of the motions of these and other parts at length the index comes to point at the right hour of the day, the man if he be wise will be well enough satisfied with this knowledge of the cause of the proposed effect, without troubling himself to examine whether a notional philosopher will call the time-measuring instrument an *ens per se*, or an *ens per accidens*, and whether it performs its operations by virtue of an internal principle such as the spring of it ought to be, or of an external one such as one may think the appended weight. And as he that cannot, by the mechanical affections of the parts of the universal matter, explicate a phenomenon, will not be much helped to understand how the effect is produced by being told that *nature* did it, so, if he can explain it mechanically, he has no more need to think, or (unless for brevity's sake) to say, that *nature* brought it to pass, than he that observes the motions of a clock has to say that it is not the *engine*, but it is *art*, that shows the hour; whereas, without considering that general and uninstructive name, he sufficiently understands how the parts that make up the engine are determined, by their construction and the *series* of their motions, to produce the effect that is brought to pass.

When the lower end of a reed being dipped, for instance, in milk or water, he that holds it does cover the upper end with his lips and fetches his breath, and hereupon the liquor flows into his mouth, we are told that *nature* raiseth it to prevent a vacuum, and this way of raising it is called *suction*; but when this is said, the word *nature* does but furnish us with a short term to express a concourse of several causes, and so does in other cases but what the word *suction* does in this. For neither the one nor the other helps us to conceive how this seemingly spontaneous ascension of a heavy liquor is effected: which they that know that the outward air is a heavy fluid, and gravitates, or presses more upon the *other parts* of the liquor than the air contained in the reed (which is rarefied by the dilatation of the sucker's thorax) does upon the *included part* of the surface, will readily apprehend that the smaller pressure will be surmounted by the greater, and consequently yield to the ascension of the liquor, which is by the prevalent external pressure impelled up into the pipe, and so into the mouth (as I, among others, have elsewhere fully made out). So that according to this doctrine, without recurring to nature's care to prevent a vacuum, one that had never heard of the

Peripatetic notions of *nature* or of *suction* might very well understand the mentioned phenomenon. And if afterwards he should be made acquainted with the received opinions and forms of speech used on this occasion, he would think that so to ascribe the effect to *nature* is needless if not also erroneous, and that the common theory of *suction* can afford him nothing but a compendious term to express at once the concourse of the agents that make the water ascend.

How far I think these extravagant reasonings may be admitted, you will be enabled to discern by what you will hereafter meet with, relating to the same subjects, in the VII Section of this discourse. And therefore, returning now to the rise of this digression – namely, that it is not unlike you may expect I should, after the vulgar notion of nature that I lately mentioned without acquiescing in it, substitute some definition or description of nature as mine – I hope you will be pleased to remember that the design of this paper was to *examine* the vulgar notion of nature, not *propose* a new one of my own. And indeed the ambiguity of the word is so great, and it is even by learned men usually employed to signify such different things, that, without enumerating and distinguishing its various acceptions, it were very unsafe to give a definition of it, if not impossible to deliver one that would not be liable to censure. I shall not therefore presume to define a thing of which there is yet no settled and stated notion agreed on among men. And yet that I may, as far as I dare, comply with your curiosity, I shall tell you that, if I were to propose a notion as less unfit than any I have met with to pass for the *principal notion* of *nature*, with regard to which many axioms and expressions relating to that word may be not inconveniently understood, I should distinguish between the *universal* and the *particular nature* of things. And of *universal nature* the notion I would offer should be some such as this: that *nature is the aggregate of the bodies that make up the world, framed as it is, considered as a principle by virtue whereof they act and suffer according to the laws of motion prescribed by the Author of things.* Which description may be thus paraphrased: that *nature* in general is *the result of the universal matter, or corporeal substance of the universe, considered as it is contrived into the present structure and constitution of the world, whereby all the bodies that compose it are enabled to act upon, and fitted to suffer from, one another, according to the settled laws of motion.* I expect that this description will appear *prolix* and require to be heedfully perused, but the intricateness and importance of the subject hindered me from making it shorter, and made me choose rather to presume upon your attention than not endeavour to express myself intelligibly and warily about a subject of such moment. And this will make way for the other (*subordinate*) notion that is to attend the former description, since the *particular nature* of an *individual body* consists in the *general* nature, *applied to a distinct portion of the universe*; or rather, supposing it to be placed as it is in a world framed by God like ours, it consists in *a convention of the mechanical affections* (such as bigness, figure, order, situation, contexture, and local motion) *of its parts* (whether sensible or insensible) *convenient and sufficient to constitute* in *or to entitle* to *its particular species or denominations the particular body they make up, as the concourse of all these is considered as the principle of motion, rest, and changes in that body*.

If you will have me give to these two notions more compendious expressions, now that, by what hath been said, I presume you apprehend my meaning, I shall express what I called *general nature* by *cosmical mechanism*; that is, a comprisal of all the mechanical affections (figure, size, motion, &c.) that belong to the matter of the great system of the universe. And to denote the *nature* of this or that particular body, I shall style it the *private*,° the *particular*,° or (if you please) the *individual*° *mechanism* of that body – or, for brevity's sake, barely the *mechanism* of it; that is, the *essential modification*, if I may so speak, by which I mean the comprisal of all its mechanical affections convened in the particular body, considered as it is determinately placed in a world so constituted as ours is.

It is like you will think it strange that in this description I should make the *present fabric of the universe* a part, as it were, of the notion I frame of nature, though the generality of philosophers, as well as other men, speak of her as a plastic principle of all the mundane bodies, as if they were her effects; and therefore they usually call them the *works of nature*, and the changes that are observed in them the *phenomena of nature*. But for my part, I confess I see no need to acknowledge any architectonic being, besides God, antecedent to the first formation of the world. | The Peripatetics, whose school either devised or mainly propagated the received notion of nature, conceiving (not only matter, but) the world to be eternal, might look upon it as the *province*, but could not as the *work*, of nature, which in their hypothesis is its *guardian*, without having been its *architect*. | The Epicureans themselves, that would refer all things that are done in the world to nature, cannot, according to their principles, make what they now call *nature* to have been antecedent to the first formation of our present world. For according to their hypothesis, whilst their numberless *atoms* wildly roved in their infinite *vacuity*, they had nothing belonging to them but *bigness, figure* and *motion*, and it was by the coalition or convention of these atoms that the world had its beginning. So that, according to them, it was not *nature* but *chance* that framed the world: though afterwards this original fabric of things does, by virtue of its structure and the innate and unlosable motive power of atoms, continue things in the same state for the main; and this course, though casually fallen into and continued without design, is that which, according to their hypothesis, ought to pass for *nature*.

And as mere reason doth not oblige me to acknowledge such a *nature* as we call in question, antecedent to the origin of the world, so neither do I find that any *revelation*, contained in the *holy scriptures*, clearly teaches that there was then such a being. For in the history of the Creation it is expressly said that *in the beginning God made the heavens and the earth*, and in the whole account that Moses gives of the progress of it, there is not a word of the agency of *nature*; and at the latter end, when God is introduced as making a review of all the parts of the universe, it is said that *God saw every thing that he had made,*[c] and it is soon after added that *he blessed and sanctified the seventh day, because in it* (or rather, *just before it*, as I find the Hebrew particle elsewhere used) *he had rested from all his works which God created and made.*[d] And though there be a passage in the Book of *Job* that, probably enough, argues the *angels* (there called the *sons of God*) to have existed either at the beginning of the first day's work or some time before it,[e] yet it is not there so much as intimated that they were co-operators with their Maker in the framing of the world – of which they are represented as *spectators* and *applauders*, but not so much as *instruments*. But since *revelation*, as much as I always reverence it, is, I confess, a foreign principle in this *philosophical enquiry*, I shall waive it here, and tell you that, when I consult only the light of reason, I am inclined to apprehend the first formation of the world after some such manner as this.

I think it probable (for I would not dogmatize on so weighty, and so difficult, a subject) that the great and wise Author of things did,

---

[c] *Genesis* i. 31.
[d] *Genesis* ii. 3.
[e] *Job* xxxviii. 4–7.

when he first formed the universal and undistinguished matter into the world, put its parts into various motions, whereby they were necessarily divided into numberless portions of differing bulks, figures, and situations in respect of each other; and that by his infinite wisdom and power he did so guide and overrule the motions of these parts at the beginning of things, as that (whether in a shorter or a longer time, reason cannot well determine) they were *finally* disposed into that beautiful and orderly frame we call the *world*, among whose parts some were so curiously contrived as to be fit to become the seeds, or seminal principles, of plants and animals. And I further conceive that he settled such laws or rules of local motion among the parts of the universal matter that, by his ordinary and preserving *concourse*, the several parts of the universe, thus once completed, should be able to maintain the great construction, or system and economy, of the mundane bodies, and propagate the species of living creatures. So that, according to this hypothesis, I suppose no other efficient of the universe but *God* himself, whose almighty power, still accompanied with his infinite wisdom, did at first frame the corporeal world according to the divine *ideas* which he had, as well *most freely* as *most wisely*, determined to conform them to. For I think it is a mistake to imagine (as we are wont to do) that what is called the *nature* of this or that body is wholly comprised in its *own matter* and its (I say not *substantial*, but) *essential form*, as if from that or these only all its operations must flow. For an individual body, being but a part of the world and encompassed with other parts of the same great *automaton*, needs the assistance or concourse of other bodies (which are external agents) to perform divers of its operations and exhibit several phenomena that belong to it. This would quickly and manifestly appear if, for instance, an animal or a herb could be removed into those imaginary spaces the schoolmen tell us of, beyond the world, or into such a place as the Epicureans fancy their *intermundia*, or empty intervals, between those numerous worlds their master dreamed of. For, whatever the structures of these living engines be, they would as little, without the co-operations of external agents such as the *sun*, *aether*, *air*, &c., be able to exercise their functions, as the great mills commonly used with us would be to grind corn, without the assistance of wind or running water: which may be thought the more credible if it be considered that, by the mere exclusion of the air (though not of light, or the earth's magnetical effluvia, &c.) procured by the air-pump, bodies placed in an extraordinary large glass will presently come into so differing a state that warm animals cannot live in it, nor flame (though of pure spirit of wine) burn, nor syringes draw up water, nor bees or such winged insects fly, nor caterpillars crawl – nay, nor fire run along a train of dried gunpowder – all which I speak upon my own experience. According to the foregoing hypothesis, I consider the frame of the world, already made, as a great and, if I may so speak, pregnant *automaton*, that, like a *woman* with twins in her womb, or a *ship* furnished with pumps, ordnance, &c., is such an engine as comprises or consists of several lesser engines. And this compounded *machine*, in conjunction with the *laws of motion* freely established and still maintained by God among its parts, I look upon as a *complex principle*, whence results the settled order or course of things corporeal. And that which happens according to this course may, generally speaking, be said to come to pass *according to nature*, or to be *done by nature*, and that which thwarts this order may be said to be *preternatural* or *contrary to nature*. And indeed, though men talk of *nature* as they please, yet whatever is done among things inanimate, which make incomparably the greatest part of the universe, is really done but by particular bodies, acting on one another by *local motion*, modified by the other *mechanical affections* of the agent, of the patient, and of those other bodies that necessarily concur to the effect or the phenomenon produced.

SOME PHYSICO-THEOLOGICAL
CONSIDERATIONS ABOUT THE
POSSIBILITY OF THE RESURRECTION

The question about which my thoughts are desired being this, *whether to believe the resurrection of the dead, which the Christian religion teaches, be not to believe an impossibility*, I shall before I proceed any further crave leave to state the question somewhat more clearly and distinctly, that, being freed from ambiguities, you may the better know in what sense I understand it in my answer: in the returning whereof your friend need not desire me to insist but upon my own thoughts, unless he could do me the favour to direct me to some author, which I have not yet seen, that has expressly treated upon philosophical grounds of the question he proposes.

First, then, I take it for granted that he does not mean *whether the resurrection is a thing knowable, or directly provable, by the mere light of nature.*° For if God had not in the scripture positively revealed his purpose of raising the dead, I confess I should not have thought of any such thing; neither do I know how to prove that it will be, but by flying not only to the veracity but the power of God, who having declared that he will raise the dead, and being an almighty agent, I have reason to believe that he will not fail to perform what he has foretold.

Nor do I (secondly) understand the question to be *whether the resurrection be possible to be effected by merely physical agents and means.*° For that it is not to be brought to pass according to the common course of nature, I presume, after the universal experience of so many ages which have afforded us no instances of it. And though perhaps in speculation it seems not absolutely repugnant to reason that the scattered parts of a dead body might be reconjoined soon after the death of the man, yet I think you will easily grant it to be morally impossible that this should happen to any one person, and much more that it may – nay, that it will – happen to all the persons of mankind at the world's end: so that when I treat of the possibility of the *general resurrection*, I take it for granted that God has been pleased to promise and declare that there shall be one, and that it shall be effected not by, or according to, the ordinary course of nature, but by his own power. On which occasion, I remember that when our Saviour, treating of the resurrection, silenced the Sadducees that denied it, he conjoins as the causes of their error the two things I have pointed at in this observation, and in the first that preceded it: '*You err,*' says he, '*not knowing the scriptures, nor the power of God.*' And when an angel would assure the blessed virgin that she should bear a child without the intervention of a man (which was a case somewhat akin to ours, since it was a production of a human body out of a small portion of human substance in a supernatural way), he concludes his speech by telling her *that nothing shall prove impossible to God.*

In the third place, I suppose that the article of the resurrection taught by the Christian religion is not here meant by the proposer in such a latitude as to comprise all that any particular church or sect of Christians, much less any private doctor or other writer, hath taught about the resurrection, but only what is *plainly* taught about it in the holy scriptures themselves. And therefore if, besides what is there so delivered, the proposer hath met with anything that he judges to be impossible in its own nature, he hath my free consent to deal with the authors and abettors of such unreasonable opinions (which I declare myself to be not only unconcerned to defend, but sufficiently disposed to reject) as rashnesses unfriendly to the growth of Christianity.

Fourthly:[1] And now, that I may yet further clear the way for the discourse that is to follow, and obviate some objections and scruples which I think it is better seasonably to prevent than solemnly to answer, I shall desire your leave to lay down in this place a couple of considerations, of which I shall begin with this: that it is no such easy way as at first it seems, to determine what is absolutely necessary and but sufficient to make a portion of matter, considered at differing times or places, to be fit to be reputed the *same* body.

That the generality of men do in vulgar speech allow themselves a great latitude about this affair will be easily granted by him that observes the received forms of speaking. Thus *Rome* is said to be the *same* city, though it hath been so often taken and ruined by the barbarians and others that perhaps scarce any of the first houses have been left standing, and at least very few remain in comparison of those that have been demolished and have had others built in their stead. Thus a *university* is said to be the *same*, though some colleges fall to ruin and new ones are built, and though once in an age all the persons that composed it decease and are succeeded by others. Thus the *Thames* is said to be the *same* river that it was in the time of our forefathers, though indeed the water that now runs under London Bridge is *not the same* that ran there an hour ago, and is quite other than that which will run there an hour hence. And so the *flame* of a candle is said to be the *same*° for many hours together, though it indeed be every minute a new body, and the kindled particles that compose it at any time assigned are continually putting off the form of flame, and are repaired by a succession of like ones.

Nor is it by the vulgar only that the notion of *identity* has been uneasy to be penetrated. For it seems that even the ancient philosophers have been puzzled about it: witness their disputes whether the ship of *Theseus* were the *same* after it had (like that of Sir Francis Drake) been so patched up from time to time to preserve it as a monument that scarce any plank remained of the former ship, new timber having been substituted in the place of any part that in length of time rotted. And even in metaphysics themselves, I think it no easy task to establish a true and adequate notion of *identity*, and clearly determine what is the true principle of *individuation*. And at all this I do not much wonder; for almost every man that thinks conceives in his mind this or that quality, or relation, or aggregate of qualities, to be that which is essential to such a body and proper to give it such a denomination: whereby it comes to pass that, as one man chiefly respects this thing, and another that, in a body that bears such a name, so one man may easily look upon a body as the *same*, because it retains what he chiefly considered in it, whilst another thinks it to be changed into a new body, because it has lost that which *he* thought was the denominating quality or attribute. Thus philosophers and physicians disagree about *water* and *ice* – some taking the latter to be but the former disguised, because they are both of them cold and simple bodies, and the latter easily reducible to the former by being freed from the excessive and adventitious degree of coldness; whilst others, looking upon fluidity as essential to water, think ice upon the score of its solidity to be a distinct species of bodies. And so Peripatetics and chemists often disagree about the ashes and calces of burnt bodies, the first referring them to earth, because of their permanency and fixedness, and divers of the spagyrists taking them to be bodies *sui generis*, because common ashes usually contain a caustic salt whereas earth ought to be insipid; and the like may be said of some wood-ashes and limestone and even coral, which, when well calcined and recent, have a biting taste, besides that some of them that are insipid may be reduced into metals, as may be easily enough tried in the calces of lead and copper.

These difficulties about the notion of *identity* I have therefore taken notice of, that we may not think it strange that among the ancient Hebrews and Greeks, whose languages were so remote in several regards from ours, the familiar expressions employed about the *sameness* of a body should not be so precise as were requisite for *their* turn, who maintain the resurrection in the most rigid sense. And this leads me from the first of my two considerations to the second.

That (then) it is not repugnant or unconsonant to the holy scripture to suppose that a comparatively small quantity of the matter of a body, being increased either by assimilation or other convenient apposition of aptly disposed matter, may bear the name of the former body, I think I may reasonably gather from the three following expressions I meet with in the Old and New Testament.

For first, St Paul in the 15th chapter of his *First Epistle to the Corinthians*, where he professedly treats of the resurrection, and answers this question, 'But some man will say, How are the dead raised up? and with what body do they come?',[a] he more than once explains the matter by the similitude of *sowing*, and tells them: 'That which thou sowest, thou sowest not that body that shall be, but bare grain, it may chance of wheat, or of some other grain',[b] adding that God gives this seed 'a body as he thought fit, to each seed its own body'.[c] Now, if we consider the multitude of grains of corn that may in a good soil grow out of one, insomuch that our Saviour, speaking in the parable *de agro dominico* of a whole field, tells us that the grain may well bear a hundred for one, we cannot but think that the portion of the matter of the seed that is in each of the grains (not to reckon what may be contained in the roots, stalk, and chaff) must be very small.

I will not now consider whether this text justifies the supposition of a plastic power in some part of the matter of a deceased body, whereby, being divinely excited, it may be enabled to take to itself fresh matter, and so subdue and fashion it as thence sufficiently to

[a] *I Corinthians* xv, 35.
[b] Ver. 37.
[c] Ver. 38.

repair or augment itself, though the comparison several times employed by St Paul seems to favour such a hypothesis. Nor will I examine what may be argued from considering that *leaven*, though at first not differing from other dough, is, by a light change of qualities that it acquires by time, enabled to work upon and ferment a great proportion of other dough. Nor yet will I here debate what may be said in favour of this conjecture from those chemical experiments by which Kircherus, a Polonian physician in Quercetanus, and others, are affirmed to have by a gentle heat been able to reproduce, in well-closed vials, the perfect ideas of plants destroyed by the fire – I will not, I say, in this place enter upon a disquisition of any of these things, both because I want time to go through with it, and because, though the resuscitation – supposing the matter of fact – may give no small countenance to our cause, yet I do not either absolutely need it, or perhaps fully acquiesce in all the circumstances and inferences that seem to belong to it. But one thing there is that I must not leave unmentioned in this place, because I received it soon after the trial was made from two eminent persons of my acquaintance, men of great veracity as well as judgement, whereof one made the experiment and the other saw it made in his own garden, where the trier of the experiment (for he was so modest that he would not confess himself to be the author of it) took some ashes of a plant just like our English red poppy, and, having sowed these alkalizate ashes in my friend's garden, they did, sooner than was expected, produce certain plants larger and fairer than any of that kind that had been seen in those parts. Which seems to argue that, in the saline and earthy, i.e. the fixed, particles of a vegetable that has been dissipated and destroyed by the violence of the fire, there may remain a plastic power, enabling them to contrive disposed matter so as to reproduce such a body as was formerly destroyed. But to this plastic power, residing in any portion of the destroyed body itself, it will not perhaps be necessary to have recourse, since an external and omnipotent Agent can without it perform all that I need contend for: as I think I might gather from that other expression of holy scripture that I meet with in the second chapter of *Genesis*, where it is said that the Lord God 'caused a deep sleep to fall upon Adam, and he slept: and he took one of his ribs, and closed up the flesh instead thereof. And the rib, which the Lord God had taken from man, made he a woman, and brought her unto the man.'[d] For since it cannot be

[d] *Genesis* ii. 21, 22.

pretended that either the whole or any considerable portion of Eve's body was taken out of Adam's, which was deprived but of a rib, and since it cannot be probably affirmed that this rib had any spermatic faculty – both because the text assigns the formation of the woman to God and because the seminal principles in animals require the commixture of male and female, the latter of which the text supposes not to have been then made – why may I not conclude that, if it please God by his immediate operation to take a portion of the matter of a human body and add to it a far greater quantity either of newly created or of pre-existent matter, the new body so framed may, congruously enough to scripture-expressions, be reputed to be made of the former body? And accordingly Adam gives the reason why he called his wife *isha*, which our translation renders *woman*, because she was taken out of *ish*, which in our version is rendered *man*. [e]

The other text that I consider to my present purpose is the mystical resurrection described in Ezekiel's vision, where all that remained[2] of the dead men that were to rise up an army of living men was a valley full of dry bones, which being by the divine power approached to one another, and made to join together in a convenient manner, were afterwards, by the supernatural apposition of either newly created or extrinsically supplied matter, furnished with sinews (by which I suppose is meant not only nerves, but vessels, tendons, ligaments, &c.) and flesh covered with skins; [f] and last of all, a vivifying spirit was conveyed into them, that made them stand upon their feet alive, an exceeding great army. [g] Whence I gather that it is not unconsonant to the expressions of scripture to say that a portion of the matter of a dead body, being united with a far greater portion of matter furnished from without by God himself, and completed into a human body, may be reputed the *same* man that was dead before: which may appear both by the tenor of the vision, and particularly from the expression set down in the 10th verse, where God, calling for the enlivening spirit, names the completed but not yet revived bodies *these slain*, as if he now counted them the same that had formerly been *killed*.

These preliminary considerations being thus laid down, we may now proceed to examine more closely those difficulties which are

[e] Ver. 23.
[f] *Ezekiel* xxxvii. 7, 8.
[g] Ver. 9, 10.

said to demonstrate the *impossibility* of the resurrection, the substance of which difficulties may be comprised in this objection:

When a man is once really dead, divers of the parts of his body will, according to the course of nature, resolve themselves into multitudes of steams that wander to and fro in the air; and the remaining parts, that are either liquid or soft, undergo so great a corruption and change, that it is not possible so many scattered parts should be again brought together, and reunited after the same manner wherein they existed in a human body whilst it was yet alive. And much more impossible it is to effect this reunion, if the body have been, as it often happens, devoured by wild beasts or fishes: since in this case, though the scattered particles of the *cadaver* might be recovered as particles of matter, yet, having already passed into the substance of other animals, they are quite transmuted, as being informed by the new form of the beast or fish that devoured them and of which they now make a substantial part.| And yet far more impossible will this redintegration be, if we put the case that the dead body be devoured by *cannibals*; for then, the same flesh belonging successively to two differing persons, it is impossible that both should have it restored to them at once, or that any footsteps should remain of the relation it had to the first possessor.

In answer to this (indeed weighty) objection, I have several things to offer.

And first, I consider that a human body is not as a statue of brass or marble, that may continue, as to sense, whole ages in a permanent state; but is in a perpetual flux or changing condition, since it grows in all its parts, and all its dimensions, from a *corpusculum* no bigger than an insect to the full stature of man, which in many persons that are tall and fat may amount to a vast bulk, which could not happen but by a constant apposition and assimilation of new parts to the primitive ones of the little embryo. And since men, as other animals, grow but to a certain pitch and till a certain age (unless perhaps it be the crocodile, which some affirm to grow always till death), and therefore must discharge a great part of what they eat and drink by insensible transpiration – which Sanctorius's statical experiments, as well as mine, assure me to be scarce credibly great, as to men and some other animals, both hot and cold – it will follow that, in no very great compass of time, a great part of the substance of a human body must be changed; and yet it is considerable that the bones are of a stable and lasting texture, as I found not only by some chemical trials, but by the skulls and bones of men whom history records to have been killed an exceeding long time ago, of which note we may hereafter make use.

Secondly, I consider that there is no determinate bulk or size that is necessary to make a human body pass for the *same*,° and that a very small portion of matter will sometimes serve the turn: as an embryo, for instance, in the womb, a new-born babe, a man at his full stature, and a decrepit man of perhaps a hundred years old, notwithstanding the vast difference of their sizes, are still reputed to be the same person, as is evident by the custom of crowning kings and emperors in the mother's belly, and by putting murderers &c. to death in their old age for crimes committed in their youth; and if a very tall and unwieldy fat man should, as it sometimes happens, be reduced by a consumption to a skeleton, as they speak, yet none would deny that this wasted man were the same with him that had once so enormously big a body.

I consider also that a body may either consist of, or abound with, such corpuscles as may be variously associated with those of other bodies, and exceedingly disguised with those mixtures, and yet retain their own nature; of this we have divers instances in metalline bodies. Thus *gold*, for example, when dissolved in *aqua regis* passes for a liquor, and when dextrously coagulated it appears a salt or vitriol. By another operation, I have taken pleasure to make it part of the fuel of a flame; being dextrously conjoined to another mineral, it may be reduced to glass; being well precipitated with mercury, it makes a glorious transparent powder; being precipitated with spirit of urine, or oil of tartar *per deliquium*, it makes a fulminating calx that goes off very easily yet is far stronger than gunpowder; being precipitated with a certain other alkali, the fire turns it to a fixed and purple calx. And yet, in spite of all these and divers other disguises, the *gold* retains its nature, as may be evinced by chemical operations, especially by reductions. *Mercury* also is a greater proteus than gold, sometimes putting on the form of a vapour, sometimes appearing in that of an almost insipid water, sometimes assuming in that condition the form of a red powder, sometimes that of a white one, and of a yellow one, or of a crystalline salt, of a malleable metal – of what not? And yet all these are various dresses of the same quicksilver, which a skilful artist may easily make it put off and reappear in its native shape.

And though it be true that instances of the permanence of

corpuscles that pass under successive disguises may be much easier found among metals and minerals, than vegetables and animals, yet there are some to be met with among these. For, not to mention Hippocrates's affirmation about purging a child with the milk of an animal that had taken *elaterium* (if I misremember not the drug) – not to mention this, I say, I remember that, when I once passed a spring in Savoy, I observed that all the butter that was made in some places tasted so rank of a certain weed that at that time of the year abounds there in the fields, that it made strangers much nauseate the butter, which otherwise was very good. If it be considered how many, if I may so call them, elaborate alterations the rank corpuscles of this weed must have undergone in the various digestions of the cow's stomach, heart, breasts, &c., and that afterward two separations at least were superadded – the one of the cream from the rest of the milk, and the other of the unctuous parts of the cream from the serum or buttermilk – it will scarce be denied but that vegetable corpuscles may, by association, pass through divers disguises without losing their nature, especially considering that the essential attributes of such corpuscles may remain undestroyed, though no sensible quality survive to make proof of it, as in our newly-mentioned example the offensive taste did. And besides what we commonly observe on the sea coast, of the fishy taste of those sea birds that feed only upon sea fish, I have purposely enquired of an observing man that lived upon a part of the Irish coast, where the custom is to fatten their hogs with a shellfish which that place very much abounds with, about the taste of their pork: to which he answered me that the flesh had so strong and rank a taste of the fish that strangers could not endure to eat it. There is a certain fruit in America, very well known to our English planters, which many of them call the *prickle-pear*, whose very red juice, being eaten with the pulp of the fruit whereof it is a part, doth so well make its way through the divers strainers and digestions of the body, that it makes the urine red enough to persuade those that are unacquainted with this property that they piss blood, as I have been several times assured by unsuspected eye-witnesses. But more odd is that which is related by a learned man that spent several years upon the Dutch and English plantations in the Caribee Islands, who speaking of a fruit (which I remember I have seen, but had not the liberty to make trial of it) called *janipa* or *junipa*, growing in several of those islands, he tells us among other things that *au temps*, *&c.*, which is, at the season when this fruit falls from the tree, the hogs that feed on it have both their flesh and fat of a violet colour, as experience witnesseth (which colour is the same that the juice dyes), and the like happens to the flesh of parrots and other birds that feed upon it. I shall by and by give you an instance of a vegetable substance which, though torn in pieces by very corrosive liquors, and so disguised as to leave no suspicion of what it was, does thereby not only not lose its nature, but is in an immediate capacity of reappearing clothed even with the sensible qualities of it, as colour, taste, and smell.

Having thus shown that the particles of a body may retain their nature under various disguises, I now proceed to add that they may be stripped of those disguises, or, to speak without a metaphor, be extricated from those compositions wherein they are disguised, and that sometimes by such ways as those that are strangers to the nicer operations of nature would never have thought upon, nor will not perhaps judge probable when proposed. It is not unknown to expert chemists that, in despite of all the various shapes which that proteus, *mercury*, may be made to appear in – as of a crystalline sublimate, a red precipitate, a yellow turpeth, a vapour, a clear water, a cinnabar, &c. – a skilful method of reduction will quickly free it from all that made it impose upon our senses, and reappear in the form of plain running *mercury*. And though *vitrification* be looked upon by chemists as the ultimate action of the fire and powerfullest way of making inseparable conjunctions of bodies, yet even out of glass of lead, for instance (made of sand and the ashes of a metal), though the transmutation seems so great that the dark and flexible metal is turned into a very transparent and brittle mass, yet even from this have we recovered opacous and malleable lead. And though there be several ways, besides precipitations, of divorcing substances that seem very strictly, if not unseparably, united (which though I may, perhaps, have practised, it is not now convenient I should discourse of), yet by precipitation alone, if a man have the skill to choose proper precipitants, several separations may not only be made, but be easily and thoroughly made, that everyone would not think of. For it is not necessary that in all precipitations, as is observed in most of the vulgar ones, the precipitant body should indeed make a separation of the dissolved body from the mass or bulk of that liquor or other adjunct whereto it was before united, but should not be able to perform this without associating its own corpuscles with those of the body it should rescue, and so make in some sense a new and further composition. For that some bodies may precipitate others, without uniting themselves with them, is easily proved by the experiment of refiners separating silver from copper; for, the mixture being dissolved in *aqua fortis*, if the solution be afterward diluted by adding fifteen or twenty times as much common water, and you put into this liquor a copper plate, you shall quickly see the silver begin to adhere to the plate, not in the form of a calx, as when gold is precipitated to make *aurum fulminans*, or tin-glass to make a fine white powder for a *fucus*, but in the form of a shining metalline substance that needs no farther reduction to be employed as good silver. And by a proper precipitant, I remember, I have also in a trice (perhaps in a minute of an hour) reduced a pretty quantity of well-disguised *mercury* into running quicksilver. And if one can well appropriate the precipitants to the bodies they are to recover, very slight and unpromising agents may perform great matters in a short time, as you may guess by the experiment I lately promised you: which is this, that if you take a piece of *camphor* and let it lie awhile upon oil of *vitriol*, shaking them now and then, it will be so corroded by the oil as totally to disappear therein, without retaining so much as its smell or any manifest quality whereby one may suspect there is camphor in that mixture; and yet, that a vegetable substance thus swallowed up, and changed by one of the most fretting and destroying substances that is yet known in the world, should not only retain the essential qualities of its nature but be restorable to its obvious and sensible ones in a minute, and that by so unpromising a medium as common water, you will readily grant, if you pour the dissolved camphor into a large proportion of that liquor, to whose upper parts it will immediately emerge white, brittle, strong-scented, and inflammable *camphor*, as before.

One main consideration I must add to the foregoing ones, namely that, body and body being but a parcel and a parcel of universal matter mechanically different, either parcel may successively put on forms in a way of circulation, if I may so speak, till it return to the form whence the reckoning was begun, having only its mechanical affections altered. | That all bodies agree in one common matter, the Schools themselves teach, making what they call the *materia prima* to be the common *basis* of them all, and their specific differences to spring from their particular forms; and since the true notion of body consists either alone in its extension, or in that and impenetrability together, it will follow that the differences which make the varieties of bodies we see must not proceed from the nature of matter – of which, as such, we have but one uniform conception – but from certain attributes, such as *motion, size, position,* &c., that we are wont to call *mechanical affections.*° To this it will be congruous that, a determinate portion of matter being given, if we suppose that an intelligent and otherwise duly qualified agent do watch this portion of matter in its whole progress through the various forms it is made to put on, till it come to the end of its course or series of changes – if, I say, we suppose this, and, withal, that this intelligent agent lay hold of this portion of matter clothed in its ultimate form, and, extricating it from any other parcels of matter wherewith it may be mingled, make it exchange its last mechanical affections for those which it had when the agent first began to watch it – in such case, I say, this portion of matter, how many changes and disguises soever it may have undergone in the meantime, will return to be what it was; and if it were before part of another body to be reproduced, it will become capable of having the same relation to it that formerly it had.

To explain my meaning by a gross example, suppose a man cut a large globe or sphere of soft wax in two equal parts or hemispheres, and of the one make cones, cylinders, rings, screws, &c., and, kneading the other with dough, make an appearance of pie-crust, cakes, vermicelli (as the Italians call paste squeezed through a perforated plate into the form of little worms), wafers, biscuits, &c.: it is plain that a man may, by dissolution and other ways, separate the wax from the dough or paste, and reduce it in a mould to the selfsame hemisphere of wax it was before, and so he may destroy all that made the other part of the wax pass for several bodies, as cones, or cylinders, or rings, &c., and may reduce it in a mould to one distinct semi-globe, fit to be reconjoined to the other, and so to recompose such a sphere of wax as they constituted before the bisection was made. And to give you an example to the same purpose, in a case that seems much more difficult: if you look upon precipitate carefully made *per se*, you would think that art has made a body extremely different from the common *mercury*, this being consistent like a powder, very red in colour, and purgative and for the most part vomitive in operation, though you give but four or five grains of it; and yet, if you but press this powder with a due heat, by putting the component particles into a new and fit motion you may reunite them together, so as to re-obtain or reproduce the same running *mercury* you had before the precipitate *per se* was made of it.

Here I must beg your leave to recommend more fully to your thoughts that which, soon after the beginning of this discourse, I did (purposely) but touch upon, and invite you to consider with me that the Christian doctrine doth not ascribe the resurrection to *nature*, or any created agent, but to the peculiar and immediate operation of *God*, who has declared that, before the very last judgement, he will raise the dead. Wherefore, when I lately mentioned some chemical ways of recovering bodies from their various disguises, I was far from any desire it should be imagined that such ways were the only, or the best, that can possibly be employed to such an end. For, as the generality of men, without excepting philosophers themselves, would not have believed or thought that, by easy chemical ways, bodies that are reputed to have passed into a quite other nature should be reduced or restored to their former condition, so, till chemistry and other parts of true natural philosophy be more thoroughly understood and farther promoted, it is probable that we can scarce now imagine what expedients to reproduce bodies a further discovery of the mysteries of art and nature may lead us mortals to. And much less can our dim and narrow knowledge determine what means, even *physical* ones, the most wise Author of nature and absolute Governor of the world is able to employ to bring the resurrection to pass, since it is a part of the imperfection of inferior natures to have but an imperfect apprehension of the powers of one that is incomparably superior to them. And even among us, a *child*, though endowed with a reasonable soul, cannot conceive how a *geometrician* can measure inaccessible heights and distances, and much less how a cosmographer can determine the whole compass of the earth and sea, or an astronomer investigate how far it is from hence to the moon, and tell many years before what day and hour, and to what degree, she will be eclipsed. And indeed in the Indies, not only children, but rational illiterate men, could not perceive how it was possible for the Europeans to converse with one another by the help of a piece of paper at a hundred miles distance, and in a moment produce thunder and lightning and kill men a great way off, as they saw gunners and musketeers do, and much less foretell an eclipse of the moon, as Columbus did to his great advantage: which things made the Indians, even the chiefest of them, look upon the Spaniards as persons of a more than *human* nature. Now, among those that have a true notion of a Deity – which is a being both omnipotent and omniscient – that he can do all and more than all that is possible to be performed by any way of disposing of matter and motion, is a truth that will be readily acknowledged, since he was able at first to produce the world and contrive some part of the universal matter of it into the bodies of the first man and woman. And that his power extends to the reunion of a soul and body that have been separated by death, we may learn from the experiments God has been pleased to give of it both in the Old Testament and the New, especially in the raising again to life Lazarus and Christ: of the latter of which particularly, we have proofs cogent enough to satisfy any unprejudiced person that desires but competent arguments to convince him. And that the miraculous power of God will be, as well as his veracity is, engaged in raising up the dead, and may suffice, if it be so, we may not difficultly gather from that excellent admonition of our Saviour to the Sadducees, where he tells them (as I elsewhere noted) that the two causes of their errors are their not knowing the *scriptures*, wherein God hath declared he *will* raise the dead, nor the *power of God* by which he *is able* to effect it. But the engagement of God's omnipotence is also in that place clearly intimated by St Paul where he asks king Agrippa and his other auditors why they should think it a thing not to be believed (ἄπιστον) that God should raise the dead.[h] And the same truth is yet more fully expressed by the same apostle, where, speaking of Christ returning in the glory and power of his Father to judge all mankind, after he has said that this divine judge shall transform or transfigure (μετασχηματίζειν) 'our vile bodies' (speaking of his own and those of other saints), to subjoin the account on which this shall be done he adds that it will be 'according to the powerful working (ἐνέργειαν) whereby he is able even to subdue all things to himself'.[i]

And now it will be seasonable to apply what has been delivered in the whole past discourse to our present purpose.

Since, then, a human body is not so confined to a determinate bulk, but that the same soul being united to a portion of duly organized matter is said to constitute the same man, notwithstanding the vast differences of bigness that there may be at several times between the portions of matter whereto the human soul is united;

[h] *Acts* xxvi. 8.
[i] *Philippians* iii. 21.

Since a considerable part of the human body consists of bones, which are bodies of a very determinate nature, and not apt to be destroyed by the operation either of earth or fire;

Since, of the less stable and especially the fluid parts of a human body, there is a far greater expense made by insensible transpiration than even philosophers would imagine;

Since the small particles of a resolved body may retain their own nature under various alterations and disguises of which it is possible they may be afterwards stripped;

Since, without making a human body cease to be the same, it may be repaired and augmented by the adaptation of congruously disposed matter to that which pre-existed in it –

Since, I say, these things are so, why should it be impossible that a most intelligent agent, whose omnipotency extends to all that is not truly contradictory to the nature of things or to his own, should be able so to order and watch the particles of a human body as that, partly of those that remain in the bones, and partly of those that copiously fly away by insensible transpiration, and partly of those that are otherwise disposed of upon their resolution, a competent number may be preserved or retrieved, so that, stripping them of their disguises, or extricating them from other parts of matter to which they may happen to be conjoined, he may reunite them betwixt themselves and, if need be, with particles of matter fit to be contexed with them, and thereby restore or reproduce a body which, being united with the former soul, may, in a sense consonant to the expressions of scripture, recompose the same man whose soul and body were formerly disjoined by death?

What has been hitherto discoursed supposes the doctrine of the resurrection to be taken in a more strict and literal sense, because I would show that, even according to that, the difficulties of answering what is mentioned against the possibility of it are not insuperable; though I am not ignorant that it would much facilitate the defence and explication of so abstruse a thing, if their opinion be admitted that allow themselves a greater latitude in expounding the article of the resurrection, as if the substance of it were that, in regard the *human soul* is the form of man – so that, whatever duly organized portion of matter it is united to, it therewith constitutes the same man – the import of the *resurrection* is fulfilled in this, that after death there shall be another state, wherein the soul shall no longer persevere in its separate condition, or, as it were, widowhood, but

shall be again united, not to an etherial or the like fluid matter, but
to such a substance as may, with tolerable propriety of speech,
notwithstanding its differences from our *houses of clay* (as the
scripture speaks),*j* be called a *human body*.°

They that assent to what has been hitherto discoursed of the
possibility of the resurrection of the same bodies will, I presume, be
much more easily induced to admit the possibility of the
qualifications the Christian religion ascribes to the *glorified* bodies of
the raised saints. For, supposing the truth of the history of the
scriptures, we may observe that the power of God has already
extended itself to the performance of such things as import as much
as we need infer, sometimes by suspending the natural actings of
bodies upon one another, and sometimes by endowing human and
other bodies with preternatural qualities. And indeed lightness – or
rather agility, indifferent to gravity and levity – incorruption,
transparency and opacity, figure, colour, &c., being but mechanical
affections of matter, it cannot be incredible that the most free and
powerful Author of those laws of nature, according to which all the
phenomena of qualities are regulated, may (as he thinks fit)
introduce, establish or change them in any assigned portion of
matter, and consequently in that whereof a human body consists.
Thus though iron be a body above eight times heavier, bulk for bulk,
than water, yet in the case of Elisha's helve its native gravity was
rendered ineffectual, and it emerged from the bottom to the top of
the water; and the gravitation of St Peter's body was suspended
whilst his master commanded him, and by that command enabled
him, to come to him walking on the sea. Thus the operation of the
activest body in nature, *flame*, was suspended in Nebuchadnezzar's
fiery furnace, whilst Daniel's three companions walked unharmed in
those flames that in a trice consumed the kindlers of them. Thus did
the Israelites' *manna*, which was of so perishable a nature that it
would corrupt in little above a day when gathered in any day of the
week but that which preceded the sabbath, keep good twice as long,
and, when laid up before the ark for a memorial, would last whole
ages uncorrupted. And to add a proof that comes more directly
home to our purpose, the body of our Saviour after his resurrection,
though it retained the very impressions that the nails of the cross had
made in his hands and feet, and the wound that the spear had made

j Job iv. 19.

in his side, and was still called in the scripture *his body*° – as indeed it was, and more so than, according to our past discourse, it is necessary that every body should be that is rejoined to the soul in the resurrection – and yet this glorified body had the same qualifications that are promised to the saints in their state of glory, St Paul informing us that 'our vile bodies' shall be transformed into the likeness of '*his* glorious body', which the history of the Gospel assures us was endowed with far nobler qualities than before its death. And whereas the apostle adds, as we formerly noted, that this great change of schematism in the saints' bodies will be effected by the *irresistible power of Christ*, we shall not much scruple at the admission of such an effect from such an agent, if we consider how much the bare slight mechanical alteration of the texture of a body may change its sensible qualities for the better. For, without any visible additament, I have several times changed dark and opacous lead into finely-coloured transparent and specifically lighter glass. And there is another instance which, though because of its obviousness it is less heeded, is yet more considerable: for who will distrust what advantageous changes such an agent as God can work by changing the texture of a portion of matter, if he but observe what happens merely upon the account of such a mechanical change in the lighting of a candle that is newly blown out, by the applying another to the ascending smoke? For, in the twinkling of an eye, an opacous, dark, languid, and stinking smoke loses all its stink, and is changed into a most active, penetrant, and shining body.

A DISCOURSE OF THINGS ABOVE REASON, ENQUIRING WHETHER A PHILOSOPHER SHOULD ADMIT THERE ARE ANY SUCH

The speakers are *Sophronius, Eugenius, Pyrocles,* and *Timotheus*

Eugenius. The seriousness you yet retain in your looks, and the posture we found you in at our entrance, makes me fear these two gentlemen and I are unseasonable intruders, that are so unhappy as to disturb your meditations.

Sophronius. Instead of doing that, you will much promote them if you please to accompany me in them; for the subject that busied my thoughts is both so abstruse and so important that it needs more than one to consider it, and deserves that he should be a far better considerer than I, who therefore must think myself far less fit for that task than you.

Euge. I will punish the flattery of these last words by declining to make any return to it.

Pyrocles. And I, gentlemen, to prevent the loss of time and words between you, shall without farther ceremony ask Sophronius what his thoughts were employed about when we came in.

Sophr. I was then musing upon a subject that was newly proposed to me by our common friend Arnobius, who would needs have my opinion *whether,* and, if at all, *how far,* we may employ our reasonings about things that are above our reason, as Christians grant some mysteries of their religion to be.

Euge. If by *things above reason* be meant only those that are undiscoverable by reason without revelation, I should not hesitate to say that there may be divers things of that kind; for the free decrees of God, and his determinations concerning the government of the world and the future state of mankind (to name now no others), are things which no human reason can pry into, but must owe the fundamental discovery it makes of them to the revelation of him whose purposes they are.

But if by *things above reason* be meant such as, though delivered in words free from darkness and ambiguity, are not to be conceived and comprehended by our rational faculty, I shall freely confess that I scarce know what to say upon so unusual and sublime a subject.

Pyrocl. For my part, gentlemen, I think it were very requisite to be sure in the first place that the subject of our discourses is not chimerical, but that we can really know that there are things we cannot comprehend, though they be proposed to us in expressions no less clear than such as would suffice to make other things intelligible to us.

Sophr. Your cautiousness, Pyrocles, must not be rejected by *me* who, when, before you came in, I was putting my thoughts into some order, judged it unfit to consider either how one might know what things were to be looked on as above reason, how far we may discourse of them, or whether or no any supernaturally revealed propositions – such as divines call *articles of faith*° – ought to be reckoned among them, till I should have first seriously enquired whether in general we ought to admit any such objects of our contemplation as these and the like questions suppose.

Euge. I hope, then, that this being the first thing you purposed to enquire into, we may without too much boldness desire to know what came into your mind about it.

Sophr. If I had brought my considerations to an issue upon that subject, I should with less reluctancy acquaint you with them; but,[1] since I have yet made but an imperfect progress in my enquiry, instead of delivering any positive opinion upon so abstruse a subject I shall only tell you that, as far as I could yet discern, it seemed to me that among the objects our reason may contemplate there are *some* whose nature we cannot comprehend, *others*° whose attributes or actions are such as that we cannot understand how they should belong to the subject, or else that we cannot conceive how they should consist with some acknowledged truth.

Euge. So that, if I apprehend you right, you do not only admit some things to be above reason, but make no less than three sorts of them.

Sophr. If you will needs have two of them to be coincident, I shall not much contend, but I think the number you have named may, without any great inconvenience, be admitted. For by *things above reason*° I here understand (not false or absurd ones, but) such as, though the intellect sees sufficient cause (whether on the score of experience, authentic testimony, or mathematical demonstration) to assent to, yet it finds itself reduced, when it is conversant about them, to be so with a notable and peculiar disadvantage; and this disadvantage does usually proceed either from the nature of the thing proposed, which is such that we cannot sufficiently comprehend it, or from our not being able to conceive the manner of its existing and operating, or from this, that it involves some notion or proposition that we see not how to reconcile with some other thing that we are persuaded to be a truth. The first of these three sorts of things may, for brevity and distinction's sake, be called *incomprehensible*, the second *inexplicable*, and the third *unsociable*. But for fear lest the shortness I have used in my expressions may have kept them from being so clear, I shall somewhat more explicitly reckon up the three sorts of things that seem to me above reason.

The first consists of those whose nature is not distinctly and adequately comprehensible by us: to which sort perhaps we may refer all those intellectual beings (if it be granted that there are such) as are by nature of a higher order than human souls, to which sort some of the angels (at least of the good ones) may probably belong; but more than probably we may refer to this head the divine Author of nature and of our souls, *almighty God*, whose perfections are so boundless, and his nature so very singular, that it is no less weakness than presumption to imagine that such finite beings as our souls can frame full and adequate ideas of them. We may, indeed, know by the consideration of his works, and particularly those parts of them that we ourselves are, both *that he is*, and in a great measure *what he is not*; but to understand thoroughly *what he is* is a task too great for any but his own infinite intellect. And therefore I think we may truly call this immense object, in the newly-declared sense, *supra-intellectual*.

Euge. I suppose I may now ask, what is the second sort of things above reason?

Sophr. It consists of such as, though we cannot deny *that they are*, yet we cannot clearly and satisfactorily conceive *how they can be* such as we acknowledge they are: as how *matter* can be *infinitely* (or, which is all one in our present discourse, *indefinitely*) *divisible*, and how there should be such an *incommensurableness* betwixt the side and diagonal of a square that no measure, how small soever, can adequately measure both the one and the other.

That matter is endlessly divisible is not only the assertion of Aristotle and the Schools, but generally embraced by those rigid reasoners, geometricians themselves; and may be farther confirmed by the other instance of the side and diagonal of a square, whose incommensurableness is believed upon no less firm a proof than a demonstration of Euclid, and was so known a truth among the ancients that Plato is said to have pronounced him rather a beast than a man that was a stranger to it. And yet, if continued quantity be not divisible without stop, how can we conceive but that there may be found some determinate part of the side of a square, which, being often enough repeated, would exactly measure the diagonal too? But though mathematical demonstrations assure us that these things are so, yet those that have strained their brains have not been able clearly to conceive how it should be possible that a line (for instance) of not a quarter of an inch long should be still divisible into lesser and lesser portions, without ever coming to an end of those subdivisions; or how, among the innumerable differing partitions into aliquot parts that may be made of the side of a square, not one of those parts can be found exactly to measure so short a line as the diagonal may be.

Euge. There is yet behind, Sophronius, the third sort of those things which, according to you, surpass our reason.

Sophr. I shall name that too, Eugenius, as soon as I have premised that some of the reasons that moved me to refer some instances to this head do not so peculiarly belong to those instances, but that they may be applicable to others which it was thought convenient to refer to the second or first of the foregoing heads. And this being once intimated, I shall proceed to tell you that the *third sort* of things that seem to surpass our reason consists of those to which the rules and axioms and notions whereby we judge of the truth and falsehood of ordinary or other things seem not to agree: | this third sort being such as are encumbered with difficulties or objections that cannot directly and satisfactorily be removed by them that acquiesce in the received rules of subordinate sciences and do reason but at the common rate, such objects of contemplation as this third sort consists of having something belonging to them that seems not reconcilable with some very manifest, or at least acknowledged, truths.

This it may here suffice to make out by a couple of instances, the one of a moral, the other of a mathematical nature. And first, that man has a free will, in reference at least to civil matters, is the general confession of mankind, all the laws that forbid and punish murder, adultery, theft, and other crimes, being founded on a supposition that men have a power to forbear committing them; and the sense men have of their being possessed of this power over their own actions is great enough to make malefactors acknowledge their punishments to be just, being no·less condemned by their own consciences than by their judges.| And yet (some Socinians and some few others excepted) the generality of mankind, whether Christians, Jews, Mohammedans, or heathens, ascribe to God an infallible prescience of human actions, which is supposed by the belief of prophecies and the recourse to oracles, by one or other of which two ways the embracers of the several religions newly mentioned have endeavoured and expected to receive the informations of future things and such as depend upon the actings of men. But how a certain foreknowledge can be had of contingent things, and such as depend upon the free will of man, is that which many great wits that have solicitously tried have found themselves unable clearly to comprehend; nor is it much to be admired that they should be puzzled to conceive how an infinitely perfect being should want prescience, or that their will should want that liberty whereof they feel in themselves the almost perpetual exercise.

The other instance I promised you, Eugenius, is afforded me by geometricians; for these (you know) teach the divisibility of quantity *in infinitum*, or without stop, to be mathematically demonstrable. Give me leave, then, to propose to you a straight line of three foot long, divided into two parts, the one double to the other. I suppose, then, that according to their doctrine a line of two foot is divisible into infinite parts, or it is not. If you say it is not, you contradict the demonstrations of the geometricians; if you say that it is, then you must confess either that the line of one foot is divisible into as many parts as the line of two foot, though the one be but half the other, or else that the infinite parts into which the line of one foot is granted to be divisible is exceeded in number by the parts into which the line of two foot is divisible, and consequently that the line of two foot has a multitude of parts greater than infinite: which reasonings may let us see that we may be reduced either to reject inferences legitimately drawn from manifest or granted truths, or to admit conclusions that appear absurd, if we *will* have *all* the common rules whereby we judge of other things to be applicable to infinites.

And now, gentlemen, having acquainted you with what sorts of things seem to be above reason, I must to prevent mistakes desire you to take along with you this advertisement: that though the nobleness and difficulty of so uncultivated a subject inclined me to offer something towards the elucidating of it by sorting those things into three kinds, yet I shall not and need not in this conference insist on them severally, or lay any stress on this partition. For though I have above intimated that a proposition may speak of somewhat that is *supra-intellectual*, or else contain somewhat which we cannot conceive how it may be true, or lastly teach us somewhat for a truth that we cannot reconcile with some other thing that we are convinced is true, yet, if but any one of these have true instances belonging to it, *that* may suffice for my main purpose in this place, where I need only show in general *that there may be things that surpass our reason*, at least so far that they are not to be judged of by the same measures and rules by which men are wont to judge of ordinary things; for which reason I shall often give them one common name, calling them *privileged things*.

Euge. Methinks that, to manifest the imperfections of our reason in reference to what you call privileged things, you need not have recourse to the unfathomable abysses of the divine nature, since, for aught I know, Pyrocles as well as I may be nonplussed by an instance that came into my mind *de compositione continui*.

Timotheus. Since Sophronius has not thought fit to give us any of the arguments of the contending parties, I shall be glad to know what difficulty occurred to you.

Euge. Suppose a great circle divided into its three hundred and sixty degrees, and suppose that as great a number as you please, or can conceive, of straight lines be drawn from the several designable parts of some one of these degrees to the centre: it is manifest that, the degrees being equal, as many lines may be drawn from any, and so from every, one of the others as from that degree which was pitched upon. | Then suppose a circular arch, equal to the assumed degree, to be further bent into the circumference of a little circle, having the same centre with a great one: it follows from the nature of a circle, and has been geometrically demonstrated, that the semi-diameters of a circle, how many soever they be, can nowhere touch one another but in the centre. Whence it is evident that all the lines that are drawn from the circumference to the centre of the greater circle must pass by differing points of the circumference of the smaller (for else they would touch one another before they arrive at the centre) and, consequently, that as many lines soever as can even mentally be drawn from the several points of the circumference of the great circle to the common centre of both circles must all pass through different points of the little circle, and thereby divide it into as many parts (proportionably smaller) as the greater circle is divided into: so that here the circumference of the lesser circle presents us with a curve line, which was not possibly divisible into more parts than an arch of one degree, or the three hundred and sixtieth part of the circumference of the greater circle, and yet, without being lengthened, becomes divisible into as many parts as the whole circumference of the same greater circle. And though we should suppose the circumference of the internal circle not to exceed one inch, and that of the exterior circle to exceed the circumference of the terrestrial globe or even of the firmament itself, yet still the demonstration would hold, and all the lines drawn from this vast circle would find distinct points in the lesser, to pass through to their common centre.

Timoth. Though I will not pretend to confirm what Sophronius has been proving by adding arguments *a priori*, yet I shall venture to say that I think it very agreeable both to the nature of God and to that of man that what he has endeavoured to prove true should be so; for we men mistake and flatter human nature too much, when we think our faculties of understanding so unlimited, both in point of capacity and of extent, and so free and unprepossessed, as many philosophers seem to suppose. For, whatever our self-love may incline us to imagine, we are really but created and finite beings (and that probably of none of the highest orders of intellectual creatures), and we come into the world but such as it pleased the almighty and most free Author of our nature to make us. And from this dependency and limitedness of our natures, it follows not only that we may be (for I now dispute not whether we are) born with certain congenite notions and impressions and appetites or tendencies of mind; but also that the means or measures which are furnished us to employ in the searching or judging of truth are but such as are proportionable to God's designs in creating us, and therefore may probably be supposed not to be capable of reaching to all kinds or, if you please, degrees[2] of truths, *many* of which may be unnecessary for us to know here, and some may be reserved – partly to make us sensible of the imperfections of our natures, and partly to make us aspire to that condition wherein our faculties shall be much enlarged and heightened. It seems not, therefore, unreasonable to think both that God has made our faculties so limited that, in our present mortal condition, there should be some objects beyond the comprehension of our intellects – that is, that some of his creatures should not be able perfectly to understand some others – and yet that he has given us light enough to perceive that we cannot attain to a clear and full knowledge of them.

Pyrocl. I think, Sophronius, that I now understand what you mean by *things above reason*, or, as you (not unfitly) styled them, *privileged things*. But I presume you need not be told that to explain the sense of a proposition and to make out the truth of it (unless in common notions, or things evident by their own light) are always two things, and oftentimes two very distant ones.

Sophr. I need not scruple, Pyrocles, to grant the truth of what you say, but I must not so easily admit your application of it; for among the examples I have been proposing, there are some at least that do not only *declare* what I mean by *things above reason,*° but are instances, and consequently may be *proofs* that such things there are. And to those I could have added others, if I had thought it unlikely that in the progress of our conference there may be occasions offered of mentioning them more opportunely.

Pyrocl. I have long thought that the wit of man was able to lay a fine varnish upon anything that it would recommend, but I have not till now found reason set a-work to degrade itself, as if it were a noble exercise of its power to establish its own impotency: and indeed it is strange to me how you would have our reason comprehend and reach things that you yourself confess to be above reason, which is, methinks, as if we were told that we may see things with our eyes that are invisible.

Sophr. I do not think that it is to degrade the understanding, to refuse to idolize it; and it is not an injury to reason to think it a limited faculty, but an injury to the Author of it to think man's understanding infinite like his. And if what I proposed be well grounded, I assign reason its most noble and genuine exercise, which is to close with discovered truths, in whose embraces the perfection of the intellect too much consists to suffer that perfective action to be justly disparaging to it; and a sincere understanding is to give or refuse its assent to propositions according as they are or are not true – not according as we could or could not wish they were so – and methinks it were somewhat strange that impartiality should be made a disparagement in a judge. But, Pyrocles, leaving the reflection with which you ushered in your objection, I shall now consider the argument itself, which being the weightiest that can be framed against the opinion you oppose, I shall beg leave to offer some considerations wherein I shall endeavour to answer it, both by proving my opinion by experience and by showing that experience not to be disagreeable to reason.

Pyrocl. I shall very willingly listen to what you have to say on such a subject.

Sophr. I shall, then, in the first place allege the experience of many persons, and divers of them great wits, who have perplexed themselves to reconcile, I say not the grace of God, but even his prescience, to the liberty of man's will, even in bare moral actions. And I have found partly by their writings, and by discourse with some of them, that the most towering and subtle sort of speculators, metaphysicians and mathematicians, perchance after much racking of their brains, confess themselves quite baffled by the un-conquerable difficulties they met with, not only in such abstruse subjects as the nature of God or of the human soul, but in the nature of what belongs in common to the most obvious bodies in the world, and even to the least portions of them. You will easily guess that I have my eye on that famous controversy, whether or no a continued quantity (which every body, as having length, breadth, depth, must be allowed to have) be made up of indivisibles. Of the perplexing difficulties of this controversy I might give you divers confessions or complaints, made by a sort of men too much accustomed to bold assertions and subtle arguments to be much disposed to make acknowledgements of that kind; but I shall content myself with the testimony which one of the more famous modern schoolmen gives both of himself and other learned men, and which, if I well remember, he thus expresses: '*Aggredimur continui compositionem, cuius hucusque non superata difficultas omnium doctorum male ingenia vexavit, neque ullus fuit qui illam non pene insuperabilem agnoscat. Hanc plerique terminorum obscuritate, illorumque replicatis et implicatis distinctionibus et subdistinctionibus, obtenebrant, ne aperte capiantur desperantes rem posse alio modo tractari, neque rationis lucem sustinere, sed necessario confusionis tenebris obtegendam, ne argumentorum evidentia detegatur.*'[a]

And though he had not been thus candid in his confession, yet what he says might be easily concluded by him that shall duly weigh with how great, though not equal, force of arguments each of the contending parties imputes to the opinion it opposes great and

[a] F. de Oviedo, *Physica*, lib. VI, controv. XVII.

intolerable absurdities, as contained in it or legitimately deducible from it.

Euge. I have not the vanity to think that the weakness of my reason ought to make another diffident of the strength of his; but, as to myself, what Sophronius has been saying cannot but be confirmed by several trials wherein, having exerted the small abilities I had to clear up to myself some of the difficulties about infinites, I perceived, to my trouble, that my speculations satisfied me of nothing so much as the disproportionateness of those abstruse subjects to my reason. But, Sophronius, may it not be well objected that, though the instances you have given have not been hitherto cleared by the light of reason, yet it is probable they may be so hereafter, considering how great progress is, from time to time, made in the discoveries of nature in this learned age of ours?

Sophr. In answer to this question, Eugenius, give me leave to tell you, first, that you allow my past discourse to hold good, *for aught yet appears to the contrary*: whence it will follow that your objection is grounded upon a hope, or at most a conjecture, about which I need not therefore trouble myself till some new discoveries about the things in question engage me to a new consideration of them. But in the meanwhile, give me leave to represent to you, in the second place, that though I am very willing to believe, as well as I both desire and hope it, that this inquisitive age we live in will produce discoveries that will explicate divers of the more hidden mysteries of nature, yet I expect that these discoveries will chiefly concern those things which either we are ignorant of for want of a competent history of nature, or we mistake by reason of erroneous prepossessions or for want of freedom and attention in our speculations. But I have not the like expectations as to all metaphysical difficulties (if I may so call them), wherein neither matters of fact nor the hypotheses of subordinate parts of learning are wont much to avail. But however it be as to other abstruse objects, I am very apt to think that there are some things relating to that infinite and most monadical being (if I may so speak) that we call *God*, which will still remain incomprehensible even to philosophical understandings. And I can scarce allow myself to hope to see those obstacles surmounted, that proceed not from any personal infirmity or evitable faults, but from the limited nature of the intellect. And to these two considerations, Eugenius, I shall in answer to your question add this also: that as men's inquisitiveness may hereafter extricate some of those grand difficulties that have hitherto perplexed philosophers, so it may possibly lead them to discover new difficulties more capable than the first of baffling human understandings. For even among the things wherewith we are already conversant, there are divers which we think we know, only because we never with due attention tried whether we can frame such *ideas* of them as are clear and worthy for a rational seeker and lover of truth to acquiesce in. This the great intricacy that considering men find in the notions commonly received of space, time, motion, &c., and the difficulties of framing perspicuous and satisfactory apprehensions even of such obvious things, may render highly probable. We see also that the angle of contact, the doctrine of asymptotes, and that of surd numbers and incommensurable lines, all which trouble not common accountants and surveyors (who, though they deal so much in numbers and lines, seldom take notice of any of them), perplex the greatest mathematicians, and some of them so much that they can rather demonstrate that such affections belong to them than they can conceive how they can do so: all which may render it probable that men's growing curiosity is not more likely to find the solutions of some difficulties, than to take notice of other things that may prove more insuperable than they.

Timoth. This conjecture of yours, Sophronius, is not a little favoured by the *rota Aristotelica*; for though the motion of a cart-wheel is so obvious, and seems so plain a thing, that the carman himself never looks upon it with wonder, yet after Aristotle had taken notice of the difficulty that occurred about it, this trivial phenomenon has perplexed divers great wits, not only schoolmen but mathematicians, and continues yet to do so: there being some circumstances in the progressive motion and rotation of the circumference of a wheel and its nave, or of two points assigned the one in the former and the other in the latter, that have appeared too subtle and (even to modern writers) so hard to be conceived and reconciled to some plain and granted truths, that some of them have given over the solution of the attending difficulties as desperate – which, perchance, Pyrocles would not think strange, if I had time to insist on the intricacies that are to be met with in a speculation that seems so easy as to be despicable.

Sophr. Your instance, Timotheus, must be acknowledged a very pregnant one, if you are certain that a better account cannot be given of the *rota Aristotelica* than is wont to be in the Schools, by those

Peripatetics that either frankly confess the difficulties to be insoluble, or less ingenuously pretend to give solutions of them, that suppose things not to be proved or perhaps so much as understood (as rarefaction and condensation strictly so called), or lose the question, and perhaps themselves, by running up the dispute into that most obscure and perplexing controversy *de compositione continui*.

Euge. I am content to forbear pressing any further at present an objection, much of whose force depends on future contingents; and I shall the rather dismiss the proof drawn from experience, that I may the sooner put you in mind of your having promised us another argument to the same purpose, by manifesting the opinion to be agreeable to reason.

Sophr. I understand your pleasure, Eugenius, and shall endeavour to comply with it, but the difficulty and intricateness of the subject of our discourse obliges me to do it by steps; and for fear we should want time for more necessary things, I will not now stay to examine whether all the things, that hitherto have appeared above reason, be impenetrable to us because of an essential disability of our understandings – proceeding from the imperfection and limitedness of their nature – or only because of some other impediment, such as may be especially the condition of the soul in this life or the infirmities resulting from its state of union with a gross and mortal body.

Forbearing, then, to discourse how this came into my mind, and what thoughts I had upon it, I shall proceed in my considerations; and to clear the way for those that are to follow, I shall in the first place observe to you that, whatever be thought of the faculty *in abstracto*, yet reason operates according to certain notions or ideas, and certain axioms and propositions, by which, as by prototypes or models, and rules and measures, it conceives things and makes estimates and judgements of them. And indeed, when we say that such a thing is 'consonant' to reason, or 'repugnant' to it, we usually mean that it is either immediately or mediately deducible from, or at least consistent with, or contradictory to, one or other of those standard notions or rules.

And this being premised, I consider in the next place that, if these rules and notions be such as are abstracted only from finite things, or are congruous but to them, they may prove useless or deceitful to us, when we go about to stretch them beyond their measure and apply them to the infinite God, or to things that involve an infiniteness either in multitude, magnitude, or littleness.

To illustrate and confirm this notion, give me leave to represent, in the third place, that in my opinion all the things that we naturally do know or can know may be divided into these two sorts: the one such as we may know without a *medium*, and the other such as we cannot attain to but by the intervention of a medium or by a discursive act. To the first belong such notions as are supposed to be *connate* or, if you please, *innate*, such as that *two contradictories cannot be both together true, the whole is greater than any part of it,*° *every (entire) number is either even or odd,* &c.; and also those other truths that are assented to upon their own account without needing any medium to prove them, because that as soon as, by perspicuous terms or fit examples, they are clearly proposed to the understanding, they discover themselves to be true so manifestly by their own light, that they need not be assisted by any intervening proposition to make the intellect acquiesce in them: of which kind are some of *Euclid's axioms,* as that *if to equal things equal things be added the totals will be equal,* and that *two right lines cannot include a space.* To the second sort of things knowable by us belong all that we acquire the knowledge of by ratiocinations, wherein by the help of intervening propositions or mediums we deduce one thing from another, or conclude affirmatively or negatively one thing of another. This being supposed, and we being conscious to ourselves, if it were but upon the score of our own infirmities and imperfections, that we are not authors of our own nature, for aught we know it may be true – and all the experience we have hitherto had leads us to think it is true – that the measures suggested to us either by sensations, the results of sensible observation, or the other instruments of knowledge, are such as fully reach but to finite things or beings, and therefore are not safely applicable to others. And divers of those very principles that we think very general may be (if I may so speak) but gradual notions of truth, and but limited and respective, not absolute and universal.

And here give me leave, as a farther consideration, to take notice to you that, though perfect syllogisms be counted the best and most regular forms that our ratiocinations can assume, yet even the laws of these are grounded on the doctrine of proportions: for even between things equal there may be a proportion (namely that of equality), upon which ground I suppose it is that mathematical demonstrations have been publicly proposed of the grand syllogistical rules. And, in consequence of this, I shall add that geometricians will tell you that there is no proportion betwixt a finite line and an infinite, because the former can never be so often taken as to exceed the latter, which, according to Euclid's definition of proportion,[b] it should be capable to do. Of which premises the use I would make is to persuade you that, since the understanding operates but by the notions and truths it is furnished with, and these are its instruments by proportion to which it takes measures and makes judgements of other things, these instruments may be too disproportionate to some objects to be securely employed to determine divers particulars about them: so, the eye being an instrument which the understanding employs to estimate distances, we cannot by that safely take the breadth of the ocean, because our sight cannot reach far enough to discover how far so vast an object extends itself. And not only the common instruments of surveyors, that would serve to measure the height of a house or a steeple, or even a mountain, cannot enable them to take the distance of the moon; but when astronomers do, by supposition, take a chain that reaches to the centre of the earth (and therefore is by the moderns judged to be above four thousand miles long) – even then, I say, though by the help of this and the parallaxes they may tolerably well measure the distance of some of the nearer planets, especially the moon, yet with all their great industry they cannot by the same way (or perhaps any other yet known) with anything tolerable accurateness measure the distance of the fixed stars – the semi-diameter of the earth bearing no sensible proportion to that of so vast a sphere as the firmament, whose distance makes the parallaxes vanish, it being as to sense all one whether, at so great a remove, a star be observed from the centre or from the surface of the earth.

Euge. In a matter so abstruse, a little illustration by examples may be very proper and welcome.

Sophr. It is scarce possible to find very apposite examples to illustrate things of a kind so abstruse and heteroclite as those may well be supposed that do surpass our reason.| But yet some assistance may be borrowed from what we may observe in that other faculty of the mind which is most of kin to the intellect – I mean the *imagination.* For when, for instance, I think of a triangle or a square, I

---

[b] '*Rationem habere inter se quantitates dicuntur, quae possunt multiplicatae sese mutuo superare.*' – Euclid, *Elements* V, def. iv.

find in my fancy an intuitive *idea* (if I may so call it) of those figures: that is, a picture clear and distinct, as if a figure of three sides, or four equal sides and angles, were placed before my eyes. | But if I would fancy a *myriagon*, or a figure consisting of ten thousand equal sides, my imagination is overpowered with so great a multitude of them, and frames but a confused idea of a *polygon* with a very great many sides; for if (to speak suitably to what the excellent Descartes has well observed in the like case) a man should endeavour to frame ideas of a *myriagon* or a *chiliagon*, they would be both so confused that his imagination would not be able clearly to discriminate them, though the one has ten times as many sides as the other. So if you would imagine an atom – of which perhaps ten thousand would scarce make up the bulk of one of the light particles of dust, that seem to play in the sunbeams when they are shot into a darkened place – so extraordinary a littleness, not having fallen under any of our senses, cannot truly be represented in our imagination. So when we speak of God's primity (if I may so call it), omnipotence, and some other of his infinite attributes and perfections, we have some conceptions of the things we speak of, but may very well discern them to be but inadequate ones. And though divers propositions relating to things above reason seem clear enough to ordinary wits, yet he that shall with a competent measure of attention, curiosity, and skill, consider and examine them, shall find that either their parts are inconsistent with one another, or they involve contradictions to some acknowledged or manifest truths, or they are veiled over with darkness and encumbered with difficulties from whence we are not able to rescue them. Thus when the side and diagonal of a square are proposed, we have clear and distinct ideas of each of them apart; and when they are compared, we may have a conception of their incommensurableness. But yet this negative notion, if it be thoroughly considered and far enough pursued, clearly contains that of a straight line's being divisible *in infinitum*; and that divisibility is encumbered with so many difficulties, and is so hard to be reconciled to some confessed dictates of reason, that (as we have seen already) philosophers and geometricians that are convinced of the truth are to this day labouring to extricate themselves out of those perplexing intricacies.

I will not trouble you with the puzzling if not insuperable difficulties that encumber the doctrine of *eternity*, as it is wont to be proposed in the schools of divines and philosophers, lest you should allege that these difficulties spring rather from the bold assumptions and groundless subtleties of the schoolmen than from the nature of the thing itself; but I will propose somewhat that cannot be denied, which is that some substance or other – whether, as I believe, *God*, or, as the Peripatetics say, the *world*, or, as the Epicureans contend, *matter* – never had a beginning, that is, has been for ever. But when we speak of an eternity *a parte ante* (as they call it), we do not speak of a thing whereof we have no conception at all, as will appear to a considering person; and yet this general notion we have is such that, when we come attentively to examine it by the same ways by which we judge of almost all other things, the intellect is nonplussed: for we must conceive that the time effluxed since Adam (or any other man as remote from us as he is said to have been) began to live bears no more proportion to the duration of God, or of matter, than to those few minutes I have employed about mentioning this instance. Nay, if we would be Aristotelians, the same thing may be said as to those men that lived many thousand millions of years before the time we reckon that Adam began to live in: for each of these times, being finite and measurable by a determinate number of years, can bear no proportion to that infinite number of years (or somewhat that is equivalent) which must be allowed to a duration that never had a beginning. And as there are some things whose nature and consequences pose our faculties, so there are others whereof, though we have a notion, yet the *modus operandi* is beyond our comprehension. I do not mean only the *true* and certain *modus operandi*, but even an *intelligible* one: as, though divers learned men, especially Cartesians, and that upon a philosophical account, assert that God created the world, yet how a substance could be made out of nothing (as they and the generality of Christians confessedly hold) I fear we cannot conceive. And though all philosophers, very few excepted, believe God to be the *maker* of the world (out of pre-existent matter), yet how he could make it but by locally moving the parts of the matter it was to consist of, and how an incorporeal substance can move a body which it may pass through without resistance, is that which I fear will be found hardly explicable: for if it be said that the soul, being an immaterial substance, can nevertheless move the limbs of the human body rightly disposed, I shall answer that it does not appear that the rational soul doth give any motion to the parts of the body, but only *guide* or *regulate* that which she finds in them already.

Timoth. May it not, then, be rationally said that, by making observations of such things that are the proper objects of our faculties, and by making legitimate deductions from such observations and from our other knowledges whether innate or acquired, we may come to be certain that some things *are*, and so have general and dark *ideas* of them, when at the same time we are at a loss to conceive *how they can be* such, or how they can operate and perform what they do, supposing the truth and sufficiency of some other things we are convinced of? To be short, negative apprehensions we may have of some privileged things, and positive but indistinct apprehensions we may have of others; and that is enough to make us in some sort understand ourselves and one another when we speak of them, though yet, when we sufficiently consider what we say, we may find that our words are not accompanied with clear, distinct, and symmetrical, conceptions of those abstruse and perplexing things we speak of. And since, as hath been already shown, we find by experience that we are unable sufficiently to comprehend things that by clear and legitimate consequences may be evinced to *be*, why should not this cogently argue that some of our conceptions may be of things to which somewhat belongs that transcends our reason and surpasses our comprehension? And if I would play the logician with Pyrocles, I would tell him that his objection destroys his opinion. For since he talks to us of what is 'incomprehensible', that term must or must not be attended with some suitable *idea*: if it be not, let him consider whether, in his own phrase, he speaks sense and not like a parrot; but if it be, let him then confess that one may have some kind of idea of a thing incomprehensible. But, Pyrocles, whether or no you think I prevaricate in this, you will not, I hope, suspect me of doing it in adding that, when natural theology had taught men (as well philosophers as others) to believe God to be an infinitely perfect being, we ought not to say that they had no idea of such a being, because they had not a *clear and adequate* one. And since Aristotle discourses *ex professo* and prolixly enough *de infinito*, and cites the ancienter philosophers for having done so before him, and since (besides his commentators and followers) Democritus, Epicurus, followed by Gassendus and other late philosophers, maintain either that the world is boundless, or that space (real or imaginary) is not *finite* in *extent*, or that the world consists of atoms *infinite* in *number*, I hope you will not put such an affront upon all these great persons as to think they said they knew not what when they discoursed *de infinito*, as they must have done if they spake without ideas of the things they spake of – though it may be justly supposed that, the subject being *infinite*, the ideas they framed of it could not be *comprehensive* and accurate.

Euge. So that according to you, Sophronius, it may be said that by reason we do not properly *perceive things above reason*, but only *perceive that they are above reason*, there being a dark and peculiar kind of impression made upon the understanding while it sets itself to contemplate such confounding objects; by which peculiarity of impression, as by a distinct and unwonted kind of internal sensation, the understanding is brought to distinguish this sort of things (namely, transcendent or *privileged* ones) from others, and discern them to be disproportionate to the powers with which it uses thoroughly to penetrate subjects that are not impervious to it: as when the eye looks into a deep sea, though it may pierce a little way into it, yet when it would look deeper it discovers nothing but somewhat which is dark and indistinct, which affects the sensory so differingly from what other more genuine objects are wont to do, that by it we easily discern that our sight fails us in the way before it arrives at the bottom, and consequently that there may be many things concealed there that our sight is unable to reach.

Timoth. I guess, gentlemen, by the silence you seem to conspire in after so long a debate, that you have now said as much as at present you think fit to say for and against this proposition that there are things above our reason.

Sophr. I shall not, for my part, cross your observation, Timotheus, but instead of adding any new proofs shall only desire you to look back upon those I have presented you already, and to let me remind you that, of the two arguments by which I attempted to show that there are some things above reason, the first and chiefest was suggested by experience, and the other, which was drawn from the nature of things and of man, was brought as it were *ex abundanti*, to illustrate and confirm the former and give occasion to some hints about privileged subjects. And therefore, though I hope what has been discoursed by these gentlemen and me may be able to persuade Pyrocles that the acknowledgement that some things are above reason may fairly comply with the dictates of it, yet, whatever he thinks of the cogency of our discourse, the truth of the main conclusion may be sufficiently evinced by our first argument drawn from experience. For if we really find that there are things which our reason cannot comprehend, then, whether the account these gentlemen and I have given why our faculties are insufficient for these things be good or not, yet still some true account or other there must be of that insufficiency. And as we should very thankfully receive from Pyrocles any better account than what we have propounded, so, if he cannot assign any better, I hope he will join with us in looking upon this as very agreeable to our hypothesis: since hereby some things must appear to us so sublime and abstruse, that not only we find we are not able to comprehend them, but that we are unable to discern so much as upon what account it is that they cannot be comprehended by us.

Euge. I am not averse, Sophronius, from your paradox about *gradual* notions; and I am the more inclined to think that some of the axioms and rules that are reputed to be very general are not to be indifferently extended to all subjects and cases whatsoever, when I consider the differing apprehensions that the mind may frame of the same object, as well according to the vigour or (if I may so call it) rank of the understanding, as according to the differing information it is furnished with. For if one should propose to a child, for instance, of four or five years old, the demonstration of the one hundred and seventeenth proposition of Euclid's tenth Book, wherein he proves the side and diagonal of a square to be incommensurable, though possibly he may be able to read the words that express the *theorem*, and though he have eyes to see the scheme employed for the demonstration, yet, if you should spend a whole year about it, you would never be able to make him understand it, because it is quite above the reach of a child's capacity. And if one should stay till he be grown a man, yet supposing him to have never learned geometry, though he may easily know what you mean by two incommensurable lines, yet all the reason he has attained to in his virile age would but indispose him to attain to that demonstration; for all the experience he may have had of lines will but have suggested to him, as a manifest and general truth, that of any two straight lines we may, by measuring, find how many feet, inches, or other determinate measure, the one exceeds the other. And though one that has been orderly instructed in all that long train of propositions, that in Euclid's *Elements* precede the one hundred and seventeenth of the tenth Book, will be also able to arrive at an evidence of this truth, *that those two lines are incommensurable*, yet (as Sophronius formerly noted) how it should be possible that, two short lines being proposed, whereof each by itself is easily measurable among those innumerable multitudes of parts into which each of them may be mentally divided, there should not be any one capable of exactly measuring both, is that which even a geometrician that knows it is true is not well able to conceive. But, gentlemen, that you may not accuse my digression, I shall urge these comparisons no further, my scope in mentioning them being to observe to you that, for aught we know to the contrary, such a difference of intellectual abilities as is but gradual in children and men may be essential in differing ranks of intellectual beings. And so it may be that some of those axioms that we think general may, when we apply them to things whereof they are not the true and proper measures, lead us into error, though perhaps intellects of a higher order may unriddle those difficulties that confound us men: which conjecture I should confirm by some things that would be readily granted me by Christians, if I thought it proper to play the divine in a discourse purely philosophical.

Pyrocl. You, gentlemen, have taken the liberty to make long discourses, and I shall not much blame you for it, because it is a thing as more easily, so more speedily, done, to propose difficulties than to solve them; yet methinks, amongst you all, you have left one part of my objection unanswered, not to say untouched.

Sophr. I suppose, Pyrocles, you mean what you said about discerning invisible things with the eye; but I purposely forbore to take notice of *that*, because I foresaw it might be more seasonably done after some other points had been cleared. Wherefore give me leave *now* to represent to you, as a corollary from the foregoing discourses, that nothing hinders but that we may reasonably suppose that the great and free Author of human nature, God, so framed the nature of man as to have furnished his intellective faculty with a light, whereby it can not only make estimates of the power of a multitude of other things, but also judge of its own nature and power, and discern some at least of the limits beyond which it cannot safely exercise its act of particularly and peremptorily judging and defining. And now, that God, who (as I said) is a most free agent, may have given the mind of man such a limited nature, accompanied with such a measure of light, you will not, I presume, deny; but the question is, you will tell me, whether he *hath* done so. But I hope what has been formerly discoursed by these gentlemen and me has put that almost quite out of question. However, I shall now invite you to observe with me that the rational soul does not only pass judgements about things without her, but about herself and what passes within her: she searches out and contemplates her own spirituality and union with the body. The intellect judges wherein its own nature consists, and whether or no itself be a distinct faculty from the will: and to come yet closer to the point, be pleased to consider that logic and metaphysics are the works of the human intellect, which, by framing those disciplines, manifests that it does not only judge of ratiocinations, but of the very principles and laws of reasoning, and teaches what things are necessary to the obtaining of an evidence and certainty, and what kind of mediums they are from whence you must not expect any demonstrative arguments concerning such or such a subject. To these things it is agreeable that, if we will compare the bodily eye with the understanding, which is the eye of the mind, we must allow this difference, that the intellect is as well a looking-glass as a sensory, since it does not only see other things, but itself too, and can discern its own blemishes or bad conformation or whatever other infirmities it labours under. Upon which consideration, we may justify the boldness of our excellent Verulam, who, when he sets forth the four sorts of idols (as he calls them) that mislead the studiers of philosophy, makes one of them to be *idola tribus* – by which he means those notions that, though radicated in the very nature of mankind, are yet apt to mislead us – which may confirm what I was saying before, that the soul, when duly excited, is furnished with a light, that may enable her to judge even of divers of those original notions by which she is wont to judge of other things. To be short, the soul upon trial may find by an inward sense that some things surpass her forces, as a blind man that were set to lift up a rock would quickly find it too unwieldy to be managed by him, and the utmost exercise of his strength would but convince him of the insufficiency of it to surmount so great a weight or resistance: so that we do not pretend that the eye of the mind should see invisibles, but only that it shall discern the limits of that sphere of activity within which nature hath bounded it, and consequently that some objects are disproportionate to it. And I remember that Aristotle himself says that the eye sees both light and darkness: which expression, though somewhat odd, may be defended by saying that though, since darkness is a privation, not a being, it cannot properly be the object of sight, yet it may be perceived by means of the eye, by the very differing affection which that organ resents, when it is impressed on by luminous or enlightened objects, and when it is made useless to us by darkness.

Timoth. What you have said, Sophronius, has in great part prevented one thing that might be said to strengthen Pyrocles's objection: namely, that whereas, when we see with our bodily eyes, there is besides the outward organ an internal and rational faculty, that perceives by the help of the eye that which is not directly the object of sight, in the eye of the mind – the intellect – there is but one faculty to perceive and judge. For according to your notion, it may be well answered that, the intellect being capable by its proper light to judge of itself and its own acts as well as of other things, there is no need of two principles, the one to perceive and the other to judge, since one is sufficient for both those purposes.[3]

Pyrocl. When I have time to reflect on all that I have heard alleged amongst you, gentlemen, I shall consider how far your arguments ought to obtain my assent; but in the meanwhile I must tell you that they will scarce have all the success I presume you desire, unless you add somewhat to free me from what yet sticks with me of a scruple, that is much of the nature of that which I formerly proposed, being this: *how we can justify our presuming to discourse at all of things transcending reason.* For I cannot understand how a man that admits your opinions can intelligibly speak (and to speak otherwise misbecomes a rational creature) of what is infinite, or anything that surpasses our reason, since, when we discourse of such things, either our words are or are not accompanied with clear and distinct ideas or conceptions of the things we speak of: if *they be not,* what do we other than speak nonsense, or (as hath been already said) like parrots entertain our hearers with words that we ourselves do not understand? and if *they be,* then we do in effect *comprehend* those things which yet you would have me think to be, on some account or other, *incomprehensible.*

Sophr. I acknowledge this difficulty, Pyrocles, to be a great one, but yet I think it not so great as that it ought to interdict us all discoursing of things above reason: and this would perhaps appear probable enough, if, as your objection borrows much of what you have formerly alleged, so I may be allowed as well to repeat some things, as propose others, in making answer to it.

Timoth. I for my part shall not only give you my consent to do so, but make it my request that you would do it: for when I look back upon our conference, methinks I plainly perceive that partly the objections of Pyrocles, and partly some (I fear impertinent) interpositions of mine, have kept your discourse from being so methodical as otherwise you would have made it; and therefore to be reminded of some of the chief points of your doctrine, as well as to connect them with those you shall judge fit to strengthen or illustrate them, may much conduce to make us both understand it more clearly and remember it better.

Euge. I am much of your mind, Timotheus; but though my interpositions have been far more frequent and much less pertinent than yours, yet I am not troubled that the method of our conference has been so much disturbed: because I think such a free way of discoursing, wherein emergent thoughts, if they be considerable, are permitted to appear as they arise in the mind, is more useful than a nice method, in a debate about an uncultivated and highly important subject, in which I think we should aim at first rather to enquire than to resolve, and to procure as many hints and considerations as we can in order to our fuller information against our next meeting – without suppressing any that is true or useful, only because it agrees not so well with a regular method as it does with the design of our conference.

Sophr. Without reflecting upon either of those gentlemen that have been pleased to accuse themselves, I shall readily comply with the motion made by Timotheus, and, after having proposed some distinctions, make application of them.| And the better to clear this matter in reference to Pyrocles's objection, I shall first take the liberty to make some distinctions of the notions or conceptions of the mind, and, for brevity's sake, give names to those I have now occasion to employ.+

I consider, then, that whether the conceptions or ideas we have of things be simple or compounded, they may be distinguished into such as are particular or *distinct*, and such as are only general, dark and confused, or *indistinct*.° So, when a navigator to unknown countries first gets a sight of land, though he may be satisfied that it is land, yet he has but a very dark and confused picture of it made in his eye, and cannot descry whether or no the shore be rocky, or what creeks or harbours (if any) it have in it; much less whether the coast be well inhabited, and, if it be, what kind of buildings it has: all which he may plainly and distinctly see upon his going ashore. And this mention of the sea puts me in mind to point at another distinction, which is that of some things we have an *adequate*, of others but an *inadequate*, conception: as if we suppose the navigator I was speaking of should look towards the main sea, though he might see a good way distinctly, yet at length it would appear so darkly and confusedly to him that, at the verge of the sensible horizon, his sight would make him judge that the sea and sky come together; and yet he would conclude that the utmost part of the sea he could descry was but a part of the ocean, which may, for aught he knows, reach to a vast extent beyond the visible horizon.

To our confused, and often also to our inadequate, conceptions belong many of those that may be called *negative*,° which we are wont to employ when we speak of privations or negations, as blindness, ignorance, death, &c. We have a positive idea of things that are square and round, and black and white, and in short of other things whose shapes and colours make them the objects of our sight. But when we say, for instance, that a spirit or an atom 'is invisible', those words are attended with a negative conception which is commonly but dark and confused, because it is indefinite and removes or lays aside those marks by which we are wont clearly to perceive and distinguish visible substances; and when we say that such a thing 'is impossible', we have some kind of conception of what we speak of, but it is a very obscure and indistinct one at best, exhibiting only a general and very confused representation of some ways whereby one might think the thing likely to be effected, if it were at all performable, accompanied with a perception of the insufficiency of those ways.⁺

There is yet another difference in the notions we have of things, which, though not wont to be observed, is too important to be here pretermitted, and it is this: that of some things we have a knowledge that, for want of a fitter term, may be called *primary*° or *direct*;° and of some other things the knowledge we have is acquired but by inferring it from some more known or clearer truth, and so may be called *inferred*° or *illative*° knowledge. As when a geometrician defines to me a *hyperbola*, I quickly gain a clear and distinct idea of it; but when he proves to me that this hyperbola may have such a relation to a straight line which he calls *asymptote*, that this line being continued still comes nearer and nearer to the prolonged side of the hyperbola and yet, how far soever both be drawn, it will never come to touch it, his subtle demonstrations present me with an inferred or illative truth, at which we arrived not but by the help of a train of ratiocinations, and on which if we exercise our imagination we shall find this factitious truth, if we may so call it, accompanied but with a very dim and confused idea.+

To the foregoing distinctions give me leave to add but this one more, which belongs chiefly to the notions we have of true or false propositions, namely, that of our conceptions of things some are *symmetrical* (if I may so call them) or every way consistent, by which I mean those that have these two qualifications: the *one*, that all the parts are consistent among themselves, and the *other*, that the entire idea is consistent with all other truths; and some are *chimerical* or *asymmetrical*, by which I understand those that are *either* self-destroying by the contrariety of the parts themselves they are made up of – as if one should talk of a triangular square or a sunshiny night – *or*, being extravagant, lead to some manifest absurdity that may be legitimately inferred from them, or into inextricable difficulties, or involve a real repugnancy to some acknowledged truth or rule of reason.

To what I have hitherto said I must add these two observations: the first, that the mind of man is so framed that, when she is duly instructed and is not wanting to herself, she can perceive a want of light in herself for some purposes, or of clearness and completeness in the best ideas she is able to frame of some things, and on this account can so far take notice of the extent and imperfection of her own faculties as to discern that some objects are disproportionate to her – as, when we attentively consider the dimensions of space, or (if the Cartesians judge aright, that body is nothing but extended substance) those of the universe, we may by trial perceive that we cannot conceive them so great but that they may be yet greater, or, if you please, may exceed the bounds, how remote soever, which our former conception presumed to assign them: which may be illustrated by what happens to the eye when it looks upon the main sea, since we easily grow sensible that, how far soever we can discover it, yet our sight falls far short of the extent of that vast object. And it is by the sense which the mind has, of her own limitedness and imperfection on certain occasions, that I think we may estimate what things ought not, and what ought, to be looked upon as *things above reason*. For by that term I would not have you think I mean such things as our rational faculty cannot at all reach to, or has not any kind of perception of, for of such things we cannot in particular either speak or think like men; but my meaning is this, that whereas the rational soul is conscious to her own acts, and feels that she knows divers sorts of things truly and clearly, and thereby justly concludes them to be within the compass of her faculties, when she contemplates some few things that seem to be of another order she is convinced that, however she strain her power, she has no such ideas or perception of them as she has, or may have, of those objects that are not disproportionate to her faculties. And this is my first observation.

The other thing that I was to observe about the nature of the mind is that it is so constituted that its faculty of drawing consequences from known truths is of greater extent than its power of framing clear and distinct ideas of things: so that, by subtle or successive inferences, it may attain to a clear conviction that some things *are*, of whose nature and properties (or at least of some of them) it can frame no clear and satisfactory conceptions. And that men should be better able to infer propositions about divers things, than to penetrate their nature, needs the less be wondered at, *both* because it is oftentimes sufficient for our uses to know that such things are, though that knowledge be not accompanied with a clear and distinct idea, and because oftentimes the rules (such as, *whatever is produced must have a cause*, and *from truth nothing rightly follows but truth*) are clear and easy, that enable the mind to infer conclusions about things whose nature is very dark and abstruse.

Euge. I know, Sophronius, that you have not laid down these preliminary distinctions and remarks without designing to make use of them, which the little time that now remains to manage our conference in calls upon you to proceed to do.

Sophr. I was just going to say, Eugenius, that, after what I have premised, I hope it may now be seasonable to apply the newly-delivered notions to the three sorts of things that I formerly represented as being in some sense *above reason*. For I consider that there are some objects of so immense and peculiar a nature that (if I may so speak) by an easy view of the mind – that is, without any subtle and laborious disquisition – the soul discerns and, as it were, feels the object to be disproportionate to her powers; and accordingly, if she thinks fit to try, she quickly finds herself unable to frame conceptions of them fit to be acquiesced in, and this sort of objects I do upon that account call *inconceivable*,° or (on some occasions) *supra-intellectual*.

But when, by attentively considering the attributes and operations of things, we sometimes find that a thing hath some property belonging to it, or doth perform somewhat, which, by reflecting on the beings and ways of working that we know already, we cannot discern to be reducible to them or derivable from them, we then conclude this property or this operation to be *inexplicable* – that is, such as that it cannot so much as in a general way be intelligibly accounted for – and this makes the second sort of our things above reason. But this is not all: for the rational soul, that is already furnished with innate or at least primitive ideas and rules of true and false, when she comes to examine certain things and make successive inferences about them, she finds (sometimes to her wonder as well as trouble) that she cannot avoid admitting some consequences as true and good which she is not able to reconcile to some other manifest truth or acknowledged proposition. And whereas other truths are so harmonious that there is no disagreement between any two of them, the heteroclite truths I speak of appear not symmetrical with the rest of the body of truths, and we see not how we can at once embrace these and the rest, without admitting that grand absurdity which subverts the very foundation of our reasonings, *that contradictories may both be true*: as in the controversy about the endless divisibility of a straight line, since it is manifest that a line of three foot, for instance, is thrice as long as a line of one foot, so that the shorter line is but the third part of the longer, it would follow that a part of a line may contain as many parts as a whole, since each of them is divisible into infinite parts – which seems repugnant to common sense, and to contradict one of those common notions in Euclid whereon geometry itself is built. Upon which account I have ventured to call this third sort of things above reason *asymmetrical* or *unsociable*, of which eminent instances are afforded us by those controversies (such as that of the *compositio continui*) wherein, which side soever of the question you take, you will be unable *directly* and truly to answer the objections that may be urged to show that you contradict some primitive or some other acknowledged truth.

These, Eugenius, are some of the considerations by which I have been induced to distinguish the things, that to me seem to overmatch our reason, into three kinds. For of those things I have styled *inconceivable*,[4] our ideas are but such as a moderate attention suffices to make the mind sensible that she wants either light or extent enough to have a clear and full comprehension of them; and those things that I have called *inexplicable* are those which we cannot perceive to depend upon the ideas we are furnished with, and to resemble in their manner of working any of the agents whose nature we are acquainted with; and lastly, those things which I have named *unsociable* are such as have notions belonging to them, or have conclusions deducible from them, that are (for aught we can discern) either incongruous to our primitive ideas, or, when they are driven home, inconsistent with the manifest rules we are furnished with to judge of true and false.

Euge. I presume, Sophronius, that by sorting things above reason into three kinds, you do not intend to deny but that it is possible one object may in differing regards be referred to more than one of these sorts.

Sophr. You apprehend me very right, Eugenius, and the truth of what you say may sufficiently appear in that noblest of objects, God.

Timoth. We owe so much to God, the most perfect of beings, not only for other blessings, but for those very intellects that enable us to contemplate him, that I shall be very glad to learn anything that may increase my wonder and veneration for an object to whom I can never pay enough of either.

Sophr. You speak like yourself, Timotheus, and I wish I were as able, as I ought to be willing, to satisfy your desire; but since we are now discoursing like philosophers, not divines, I shall proceed to speak of that gloriousest of objects but as his nature, or some of his attributes, afford me instances to the purpose for which I presumed to mention him. When God, therefore, made the world out of nothing, or (if Pyrocles will not admit the Creation) when he discerns the secretest thoughts and intentions of the mind, when he unites an immaterial spirit to a human body and maintains, perhaps for very many years, that unparalleled union with all the wonderful conditions he has annexed to it – when, I say, he doth these and many other things that I must not now stay to mention, he supplies us with instances of things that are *inexplicable*. For such operations are not reducible to any of the ways of working known to us, since our own minds can but modify *themselves* by divers manners of thinking; and as for things without us, all that one body can do to another by acting on it is to communicate local motion to it, and thereby produce in it the natural consequences of such motion: in all which there is no action like any of those I just now ascribed to God. And if we consider that the prescience of those future events that we call contingent, being a perfection, is not to be denied to God, who is by all acknowledged the perfectest of beings, and that yet the greatest wits that have laboured to reconcile this infallible precognition with the liberty of man's will have been reduced to maintain something or other that thwarts some acknowledged truth or dictate of reason – if we duly consider this (I say) it will afford us an instance of truths whose consistency and whose symmetry with the body of other truths our reason cannot discern, and which, therefore, ought to be referred to that sort of things above reason that I call *unsociable*. And now I come to the third sort of these things, which is that I formerly mentioned first, under the name of *incomprehensible* or *supra*-intellectual: which title, whether or no it belongs to any other object (which I will not now enquire), doth certainly belong to *God*, whose nature, comprehending all perfections in their utmost possible degrees, is not like to be comprehensible by our minds, who altogether want *divers* of those perfections, and have but moderate measures (not to call them shadows) of *the rest*. We are indeed born with, or at least have a power and divers occasions to frame, an idea of a being infinitely perfect, and by this idea we may sufficiently discriminate the original of it, God, from all other objects whatsoever. But then, when we come to consider attentively and minutely what is contained in the notion of omnipotence, omniscience, eternity, and those other divine attributes that are all united in that great confluence and abyss of perfections, God, we may be sure to find that our faculties are exceedingly surmounted by the vastness and gloriousness of that *unlimited* and *unparalleled* object: about which, as we can discover that it *exists* and that it possesses *all the perfection* we can conceive, so we may at the same time discern that it must have *degrees of perfection* which, because of the inferiority of our nature, we are not able to conceive.

And yet this discovery of God's incomprehensibleness may be made, without subtle disquisitions and without trains of consequences, though not without due attention, by a direct view of the mind (if I may so term it), who finds herself, upon trial, as unable fully to measure the *divine perfections* as the *dimensions of space* – which we can conceive to be greater and greater, without ever being able to determine any extent beyond whose limits they cannot reach.

Pyrocl. I suspected, Sophronius, by the tenor of your discourse, that the last questions these gentlemen asked you diverted you from saying somewhat more than you did by way of application of your preceding discourse.

Sophr. I was then indeed about to make, as I now shall, this use of what I had been saying: that I readily acknowledge that it is an arrogance to talk of infinite or of privileged things with the same confidence, or to pretend to do it with the same clearness, wherewith knowing men may speak of things unquestionably within the compass of our intellect; but that this need not hinder us from speaking, nor doth disable us from speaking rationally, of privileged things themselves. For all the notions that are allowable are not of the same sort or order: and if none were to be admitted but those that enable us to comprehend the object – that is, which give us a clear and distinct knowledge of all that it contains or that belongs to it – I must confess that we have no good notions of privileged things in particular; but then I must add that I fear we have few or none even of many things that we think ourselves very knowing in. And when we speak of things as being *above reason*, though we have no clear, distinct, and adequate, notion of them, yet we may have a general, confused, and inadequate, notion of them, which may suffice to make us discriminate their respective objects from all else and from one another: as may be observed in several ideas that are negatively framed, such as those we have of invisible, incomprehensible, and in others which I formerly called *inferred* – because they accompany the remote inferences whereby one truth is concluded from another – as when geometricians infer from some propositions in Euclid that any straight line may be divided farther and farther without stop. For of this, and some other propositions about privileged things, we are not quite destitute of allowable notions: as may appear by *some* of the admirably ingenious speculations of mathematicians about the affections of *surd numbers*, and about *incommensurable magnitudes*, about some of which we have no such clear and symmetrical conceptions as we have of many other things that are of a nearer and more intelligible order. And on this occasion I shall not scruple to acknowledge that, partly by my own experience, and partly by the confessions of others and by their unsuccessful attempts, I am induced to think that God, who is a most free agent, having been pleased to make intelligent beings, may perhaps have made them of differing ranks or orders whereof men may not be of the principal; and that, whether there be such orders or no, he hath at least made us men of a limited nature (in general), and of a bounded capacity. Congruously to this, I think also that he hath furnished man either with certain innate *ideas* or models and principles, or with a faculty or power and disposition easily to frame them, as it meets with occasions (which readily occur) to excite them. But because that (as I lately noted) God intended the mind of man but of a limited capacity, his understanding is so constituted that the inbred or easily acquired ideas and primitive axioms wherewith it is furnished, and by relation or analogy whereunto it judges of all other notions and propositions, do not extend to all knowable objects whatsoever; but reach only to such as have a sufficient affinity, or bear some proportion, to those primary ideas and rules of truth which are sufficient, if duly improved, to help us to the attainment, though not of the perfect knowledge of truths of the highest orders, yet to the competent knowledge of as much truth as God thought fit to allow our minds in their present (and perchance lapsed) condition, or state of union with their mortal bodies.

Euge. Your opinion, Sophronius, if I apprehend it aright, contains two very differing assertions: one, that it is allowable to contemplate and even to discourse of things *above reason*, since we may have some conceptions of them, though they be but very dim and imperfect; and the other, that we ought not to look upon or speak of such objects as things that we *comprehend*, or have even such a measure of knowledge of as we have of things that are not privileged. For of these we are not to speak but with a peculiar wariness and modest diffidence.

Sophr. You have expressed my thoughts, Eugenius, since I intend not to enjoin silence, or dissuade curiosity, but yet forbid presumption, in reference to privileged things.

Timoth. And truly, Sophronius, I see no reason to repine at the limits which your late discourse hath, in imitation of the Author of nature himself, assigned to human knowledge. For the number of privileged things is altogether inconsiderable in comparison of the multitude of other things to which our knowledge may be improved to reach, and which it far more concerns us to know well than it doth to resolve puzzling questions about things incomprehensible: there being within the compass of those truths enough to employ and reward our curiosity, without straining and tiring our reason about objects that transcend it. And yet even about *these* some disquisitions may be allowed us; for an object that, on the account of some of its properties, may be a privileged one, may have divers other things belonging to it that do not surpass our reason, and whose knowledge may therefore be attained by the due employment of it.

Thus we usefully study the nature of bodies, which make up the object of the excellent science of natural philosophy, though the true notion of body in general be a thing so difficult to frame that the best of our modern philosophers can by no means agree about it: which I do not wonder at, because, if we pursue the notion of a body to the uttermost, it will lead us to the perplexing controversy *de compositione continui*, and there you will not deny but that the understanding will be left in the dark. Thus surveyors, carpenters, architects, and many others, know divers *affections* of the square figure that are of great use to them in their respective employments, though that *property* of the square, that *its side and diagonal are incommensurable*, be unknown to most of them and, if they were told of it and would prosecute the speculation, would involve them in exceeding great and probably insuperable difficulties.

Sophr. To confirm what you have been telling us, Timotheus, I shall venture to add that, even about privileged things, our enquiries, if modestly and discreetly managed, may not only be allowable but sometimes profitable. For, even of such subjects, a studious search may bring us to know more than we did, though not so much as we would, nor enough to be acquiesced in: so that such enquiries may probably teach us to know the objects better, and ourselves better too, by giving us such a sensible discovery of the insufficiency of our understandings to comprehend all sorts of things, as may be very useful, though not pleasing, and may richly recompense us for the pains that ended in so instructive a disappointment. And let me add, to the pertinent instances that have been mentioned, the noblest that can be given – I mean the contemplation of God himself. For he hath so ordered all things that it is scarce possible for us to be destitute of an *idea* of him, which will at least represent him as an *existent being* and more *perfect* than any other being; and yet when we come with sufficient application of mind to pry into the wonderful attributes of this most singular and adorable being, we are, as was lately observed, sure to find ourselves unable to comprehend so unbounded an object: which yet ought not to discourage us from so noble a study, since we are allowed the great contentment and honour to make further and further discoveries of the excellentest of objects, by that very *immensity* of his perfections that makes it impossible for us to reach to the bounds of his excellency – or rather, to discover that it has any bounds at all.

But, gentlemen, I perceive I have been so transported by the mention of this vast and divine subject, in whose contemplation it is so easy and so pleasant to lose oneself, that I have forgot the notice Eugenius gave me, a pretty while since, that the time allotted for our present conference was then near expiring. And therefore I shall leave you to pick out of the excursions, to which your interpositions tempted (not to say obliged) me, the applications that I intended to make more methodically of the distinctions I laid down. And I am the less troubled to be hindered from proposing to you my thoughts about the way of distinguishing privileged things from others, because we have a domestic monitor, or a kind of an internal *criterium*, always at hand to help us. For I think it may well be said that the wise Author of nature has endued the understanding with such a quick, though internal, sensation (if I may so call it) that, when due attention is not wanting, it can feelingly discern between other objects and those that are disproportionate to its ability: as, even in beasts, the eye is so framed (according to the institution of nature) that, if it be obverted to the bright noonday sun, there needs no monitor but the operation of the same sun to make it wink (and perhaps water), and thereby discover itself to be dazzled and overpowered by the disproportionate object.

Pyrocl. I confess your discourses, gentlemen, have made an unexpected impression upon me; but whether that will amount to a conviction will scarce appear till our next conference. Only thus much I shall tell you now: that it would much facilitate our agreement in opinion, if you did not contend for altogether so much, but would be pleased to leave it undetermined whether man's intellectual *faculty itself* is uncapable, by the help of any degree of light, to discover and know those things which you call *above reason*,° and would content yourselves to say that there are some things belonging to these subjects, which we must confess we have less clear and distinct notions of than we have even of the difficultest of those things that are acknowledged not to surpass our reason; and that, if we will take upon us to determine positively and particularly about these transcendent things, we must employ ways of reasoning congruous to their peculiar natures.

Sophr. I shall readily consent not to expect your final resolution before our next meeting, having no cause to fear that Time will be unfriendly to her daughter Truth.

Timoth. And in the meanwhile, Pyrocles, I am glad to find, by the last part of what you just now said, that you seem to be no longer indisposed to admit some things that (at least in our present state) do some way or other surpass our reason. For I think that, instead of *exalting* that faculty, we injure and *defraud* it, if we do not freely allow it as much enjoyment of truth as we are able to procure it; and consequently, if geometry or revelation or experience assure us of divers things of which we can know but *that they are* and *what they do*, not *what they are* and *how they act*, we must neither refuse nor neglect the study of such truths, any more than we would refuse to *look into* any other objects than those that we can *look through*. And therefore, to enrich the intellect as much as we are able, we must entertain not only those truths that we can *comprehend*, but those also, how sublime soever, that we can have any *certain*, though but a very imperfect, *knowledge* of — especially since those remote and abstruse subjects may be as much more *noble* as more *dark* than others, and thereby render an imperfect discovery of them more desirable than a far clearer one of inferior things.

TEXTUAL NOTES

These notes are intended to record, with a minimum of ceremony, the main deviations in this edition from the wording of the First Editions, and also the main divergences between First and Second Editions in two works which ran into two English editions. Where an expression is said to have been 'added', it was added immediately after the word in the text which carries the reference to the note; replacement-expressions replace the single word marked in the text unless otherwise indicated. Boyle's own First Edition *corrigenda* have normally been incorporated into the main text without comment.

THE ORIGIN OF FORMS AND QUALITIES

[1] The original full title of the work was *The Origin of Forms and Qualities (According to the Corpuscular Philosophy), Illustrated by Considerations and Experiments (Written Formerly by Way of Notes upon an Essay about Nitre)*. The sectional heading was amended in the 2nd Edition to 'The Author's Proemial Discourse to the Reader'. Both editions carry a note to distinguish this from the Preface 'addressed only to Pyrophilus'.

[2] 2nd Edition: 'metal'.

[3] 2nd Edition: 'employed'.

[4] 2nd Edition adds 'very'.

[5] In the footnote Boyle gave page references (341–2) apparently to the 1630 Mainz edition of Suarez. In that case the second quotation contains an intrusive second '*et*', and '*puro*' is an error for '*pura ratione*'.

[6] 2nd Edition adds 'a'.

[7] In this sentence Boyle italicized 'them', and added the following: 'and though there be some *other* particulars, to which the importance of the subjects and the greatness of the (almost universal) prejudices that lie against them will oblige me immediately to annex (for the seasonable clearing and justifying of them) some annotations, yet that they may as little as I can obscure the coherence of the whole discourse, as much of them as conveniently may be shall be included in [   ] paratheses.' This passage is omitted from the present text since the typographical convention referred to was never adopted.

[8] 2nd Edition omits 'if'.

[9] 1st Edition adds 'which'.

[10] 2nd Edition omits 'it'.

[11] 1st and 2nd Editions add 'and'.

[12] 1st Edition omits 'it'.

[13] 2nd Edition: 'other'.

[14] 1st and 2nd Editions add 'either'.

[15] 2nd Edition: 'although'.

[16] 2nd Edition: 'shall'.

[17] 2nd Edition: 'situate'.

[18] 1st and 2nd Editions: 'finger'.

[19] 1st and 2nd Editions add 'and'.

[20] 2nd Edition adds 'one'.

[21] 1st Edition: 'those'.

[22] 2nd Edition 'cannot'.

[23] 2nd Edition: 'operation'.

[24] 2nd Edition places 'but' after 'to be'.

[25] 1st Edition adds 'that'.

[26] 1st and 2nd Editions: 'First'.

[27] 2nd Edition omits 'both'.

[28] Re-titled in 2nd Edition: 'An Examen of the Origin (and Doctrine) of Substantial Forms, as it is Wont to be Taught by the Peripatetics'. The original title was printed for the 2nd Edition also, then cancelled, but a number of surviving copies retain both title sheets.

[29] 1st and 2nd Editions print the footnote at the base of the first page of this paper, without any index mark in the text.

[30] 2nd Edition omits 'and'.

[31] 2nd Edition adds 'it'.

[32] 2nd Edition: 'degenerated'.

[33] 1st Edition: 'acknowledge'.

[34] 2nd Edition omits 'yet'.

[35] 2nd Edition: 'questions'.

[36] 1st Edition adds 'since'.

[37] 1st and 2nd Editions add 'these'.

[38] 2nd Edition adds 'and'.

[39] 2nd Edition: 'chose'.

[40] 2nd Edition omits 'of'.

[41] Boyle's quotation from Purchas is very free, involving five changes of wording, one of which materially affects the sense, by the insertion of 'a' before 'little'.

[42] 1st and 2nd Editions: 'John'. At the start of the Boym quotation just below, '*&c.*' is omitted in the 1st Edition.

[43] 2nd Edition omits 'together'.

[44] 1st and 2nd Editions add 'not'.

[45] 2nd Edition omits 'at'.

AN INTRODUCTION TO THE HISTORY OF PARTICULAR QUALITIES

[1] This title is derived from the title-page of the volume of *Tracts* in which the paper appears, and is subsequently repeated on a half-title. The first page of text was headed, less appositely, 'The History of Particular Qualities'.

[2] 1st Edition: 'thought'. But cf. the previous paragraph but one.

[3] 1st Edition: 'ten'. But cf. the immediately previous discussion.

[4] 1st Edition omits 'a'.

⁵ 1st Edition: 'ten remaining'. But the number is contrary to sense and is omitted in the Latin version. Perhaps Boyle originally wrote 'each remaining of the ten' (i.e. *eleven* – cf. note 3 above).

MS NOTES ON A GOOD AND AN EXCELLENT HYPOTHESIS

¹ MS untitled. The first line of text takes up the title space. The marginal numbers were not part of the original copy but were pencilled in afterwards.

² MS omits 'be'.

ABOUT THE EXCELLENCY AND GROUNDS

¹ Subtitle here omitted: 'Some Considerations, Occasionally Proposed to a Friend'. Some editions carry a cancelled title: 'Some Occasional Thoughts, Written to a Friend, About the Excellency and Grounds of the Mechanical Hypothesis'. The paper is sometimes known by the internal title printed at the head of the first page of text: 'Of the Excellency and Grounds of the Corpuscular or Mechanical Philosophy'.

² 1st Edition closes parenthesis after '*explications*'. The 1674 Latin edition is followed here.

³ 1st Edition: 'principle'.

⁴ 1st Edition: 'who'.

⁵ 1st Edition: 'that'.

AN ESSAY, CONTAINING A REQUISITE DIGRESSION

¹ Original heading: 'Essay IV' (sc. of *Some Considerations Touching the Usefulness of Experimental Natural Philosophy*).

² In the footnote reference to Aristotle, a wrong reference has been amended; but Boyle's Greek has been left, though it does not correspond exactly with any seventeenth-century edition of Aristotle that has been examined.

³ For 'against ... chest' 2nd Edition has '(against the liquors and the sucker's chest)'.

⁴ 1st and 2nd Editions place 'not' after 'that'.

⁵ 2nd Edition: 'as'.

⁶ Boyle's text printed '*conciliis*' but in the repetition of the same verse at the end of the essay '*consiliis*'. Seventeenth-century editions of Lucretius that have been examined print '*consilio*' (Book V, line 419).

⁷ 1st and 2nd Editions: 'First'; and, later in the same number series, '6ly' and 'in the 7th/seventh place'.

⁸ Latin phrase was in 1st Edition *errata*, but with a wrong reference so that the correction was never incorporated. 2nd Edition (and uncorrected 1st Edition): 'centre of gravity'.

⁹ In the first quotation, Boyle introduces minor changes of wording, and a paraphrase of Linschoten's measurement, 'one hundred and two hundred mangelins'. See J. H. van Linschoten, *Discourse of Voyages into the East and West Indies* (London,

1598; repr. Amsterdam, 1974), Bk. I, ch. 85. In the footnote translation of Garcias ab Horto below, 'generated' has here been added to supply a lacuna in the sense of the first sentence.

[10] The Lactantius reference in the footnote appears to be correct (though in certain editions of Lactantius the chapter number is 12). But Boyle couples it with a Latin quotation which does not occur at that reference, and which I have not traced: '*Tanta ergo qui videat, et talia, potest existimare nullo affecta esse consilio, nulla providentia, nulla ratione divina, sed ex atomis subtilibus exiguis concreta esse tanta miracula? Nonne prodigio simile est, aut natum esse hominem qui haec diceret, ut Leucippum, aut extitisse qui crederet, ut Democritum qui auditor eius fuit, vel Epicurum in quem vanitas omnis de Leucippi fonte profluxit.*'

A FREE ENQUIRY INTO THE . . . NOTION OF NATURE

[1] 1st Edition: '*fictitious*'.
[2] 'use' here added to fill a lacuna in the sense.

SOME PHYSICO-THEOLOGICAL CONSIDERATIONS

[1] 1st Edition: '4'.
[2] 1st Edition: 'remain'.

A DISCOURSE OF THINGS ABOVE REASON

[1] 1st Edition adds 'I'.
[2] 1st Edition omits 'degrees'. The reading is conjectured from the sense of the subsequent discussion and from one of Boyle's stylistic mannerisms noted elsewhere, e.g. *The Excellency of Theology*, pt. II, sect. III: 'I will not here engage myself in a disquisition of the several kinds or, if you please, degrees of demonstration . . .' (1674 edn., pp. 139–40).
[3] This speech, and the following one of Pyrocles, survive in a slightly damaged MS draft in Volume XXXVIII of the Royal Society Boyle Papers. Boyle originally added a further passage to the end of the speech of Timotheus, then pencilled it for deletion, and in the printed version the deleted passage becomes the conclusion of Sophronius's penultimate speech in the dialogue. The speech of Pyrocles also underwent stylistic revision before publication.
[4] 1st Edition: '*unconceivable*'.

ADDITIONAL NOTE: PAGE 133

There is clearly a flaw in the current text, in the fourth line of chapter VIII of *The Imperfection of the Chemists' Doctrine*. One of the terms *bulk, size* is redundant, and Boyle must have intended either *figure* or *shape*, as the ensuing discussion confirms. The converse error occurs on page 31, line 3.

TRANSLATIONS OF QUOTATIONS

P. 8n. *And this opinion we must in any event maintain; for though it were not sufficiently demonstrable by natural reason, nevertheless it is proved conclusively from the principles of theology, particularly by virtue of the mystery of the Eucharist. . . . The primary reason in support of this opinion is that in the mystery of the Eucharist God has separated quantity from substance in the bread and wine, &c. / Now that we have thus set out this reply and contrary opinion, it cannot be easily and obviously assailed from a rigid stand in the domain of the purely natural. Nevertheless it is very adequately refuted, partly by natural reason, partly by the added evidence of the mystery.*

P. 9n. *To solve this problem, Aristotle reverts to that standard distinction of his, which he uses all through his philosophy, whenever any serious difficulty faces him – he distinguishes the 'actual' from the 'potential', &c. / This distinction is a characteristic one in Aristotle, which he applies to every matter where difficulties beset him, and using these terms like a lethal sword seems to cut through all the problem knots; for there is scarcely any difficulty which he does not think that he meets satisfactorily by distinguishing the 'actual' and 'potential'.*

P. 13n. *I tell you that no form is known to us fully and plainly, but our knowledge is as a shadow in the sunlight.* [Proverb recorded by Goclenius, *Lex. Phil.*, s.v. *umbra.*]

P. 21 line 27. *That whose being is being-in.*

P. 29n. *This explains nothing, since we question what it is to 'be of such a kind'. You say it is to 'have a quality'. A fine circle! A quality is that by which anything comes to be of such a kind, and to be of such a kind is to have a quality. / This definition admittedly seems to be essential, for this reason, that it is grounded in a relation to the formal effect with which every form is essentially associated; yet from our point of view, the proper explanation of quality remains as obscure to us as ever. / Not so much a definition as a vain trifle.*

P. 46 line 21. *The corruption of one thing is the coming into being of another, and conversely.*

P. 54n. *Our apprehension of forms is crude and confused, and can only be derived from particular circumstances* [cf. Quintilian V. x. 104]; *nor is it true that a representation of the substantial form is conveyed to the understanding, for it has not occurred anywhere in perception. / We have no apprehension of substantial forms, because they are insensible; so they are manifested by means of the qualities, which are the immediate principles of change. / In this dimness of the human mind the forms of fire and of the magnet are equally unknown.*

P. 58 lines 6–9. *Every substantial compound needs matter and substantial form, from which to be composed. Every natural body is a substantial compound. So, &c.*

P. 59n. See p. 13n.

P. 67n. *You name the form of the stone which you observe each day with your eyes, and you alone shall have the prize.* [Echo of Virgil, *Ecl.* iii. 107]

P. 69n. *He says that since everything was together and at rest for an infinite time, mind has moved and separated them.*

P. 70 line 32. *Accretions and whirling motions.*

P. 73n. *The same body, though continuous, we see sometimes as a liquid, sometimes as a solid, having undergone this change without the division or composition, revolution or contact, alleged by Democritus; for it normally passes from liquid to solid without either rearrangement or change of nature.*

P. 80 line 6. *God geometrizes.* [Plutarch, *Quaest. Conviv.* viii. 718C.]

P. 81 lines 15–17. *From these hang ropes weighted with small stones; the thick fluid, clinging to the ropes, sets into translucent shapes of shoemakers' blacking, whether as cubes or globules that give the appearance of grapes.*

P. 89n. *The truth of this is beyond doubt, since Brazil has infinitely many witnesses, &c.*

P. 121 line 37, p. 122 line 3. *Primary bearer.* [Aristotle, *Phys.* VII. iv. 248b22.]

P. 152n. *God geometrizes eternally.* [See p. 80 ref.]

P. 156n. *To the naturalist who has his mind on truth, the apprehension of last causes is not the end, but the start of a progress to the first and highest causes. / The first cause is last in order of discovery.*

P. 161 lines 26–7. *The work of nature is the work of intelligence.*

Pp. 163–83. See Boyle's translations or paraphrases in the text.

P. 217 lines 28–34. *We come to the composition of a continuum, whose hitherto unsurmounted difficulty has sorely taxed the wits of all the learned, and everyone without exception acknowledges it to be virtually insurmountable. Most of them mask it in obscure terminology with repeated and tortuous distinctions and subdistinctions, so that no-one may openly catch them despairing of other means of solution which might yield to the light of reason; but they must necessarily conceal it in the darkness of confusion, so that it may not be laid bare by perspicuous argument.*

P. 222n. *Quantities are said to be in a ratio to one another if each by multiplication can exceed the other.*

INDEX